Mary Magdalene's Dreaming

*A Comparison of Aboriginal Wisdom
and Gnostic Scripture*

Steven Strong and Evan Strong

University Press of America,® Inc.
Lanham · Boulder · New York · Toronto · Plymouth, UK

Copyright © 2008 by
University Press of America,® Inc.
4501 Forbes Boulevard
Suite 200
Lanham, Maryland 20706
UPA Acquisitions Department (301) 459-3366

Estover Road
Plymouth PL6 7PY
United Kingdom

All rights reserved
Printed in the United States of America
British Library Cataloging in Publication Information Available

Library of Congress Control Number: 2008931044
ISBN-13: 978-0-7618-4280-4 (paperback : alk. paper)
ISBN-10: 0-7618-4280-2 (paperback : alk. paper)
eISBN-13: 978-0-7618-4281-1
eISBN-10: 0-7618-4281-0

∞™ The paper used in this publication meets the minimum
requirements of American National Standard for Information
Sciences—Permanence of Paper for Printed Library Materials,
ANSI Z39.48—1984

Contents

Foreword	v
Acknowledgments	vii
Chapter 1: The First Apostle: Mary	1
Chapter 2: The Gospel Truths	13
Chapter 3: The Recurring Sentence	23
Chapter 4: The Gnostic Scriptures of Jesus	33
Chapter 5: The Gospel of Thomas	39
Chapter 6: Thomas Revisited	61
Chapter 7: The Gospel of Mary	65
Chapter 8: Dialogue of the Saviour and Associates	77
Chapter 9: The Alternate Genesis	93
Chapter 10: Mary's Legacy	101
Epilogue	113
Notes	119
Glossary	135
Bibliography	145
Index	151

Foreword

"Law never change... always stay same. Maybe it hard, but proper one for all people. Not like white European law... always changing. If you don't like it, you can change. Aboriginal law never change. Old people tell us, 'You got to keep it.' It always stays."[1] Bill Neidjie

In our previous book, *Constructing a New World Map*, we analysed a variety of myths, historical accounts, scriptures, archaeological sites and remains, all of which seem to resonate to an ancient rhythm: the *Dreaming*. However, our argument is incomplete; all we have done is to establish degrees of potential. At this juncture the very best we can claim is that the origins of *Isaic* religion, and a multitude of other esoteric philosophies, evolved out of the *Dreaming*, and the biblical records of Jesus and Mary may have been influenced by Isis and Osiris.

These two events could be coincidental and occurred independently of each other. Irrespective of whether any association is confirmed, such an acknowledgement does not mean what Mary or Jesus said or did was related to the *Dreaming*. Our next task is to examine what was actually said and done. If the bubbling spring Jesus spoke of in the *Gospel of Thomas* was identical to that first accessed in the *Dreaming*, our hypothesis takes on more substance. If so, the lines of our new world map have become considerably firmer.

Determining exactly what Mary said is a difficult task. On almost every occasion she speaks, brevity and omission blight her cameo appearances at the pulpit. The *Greater Questions of Mary Magdalene* and *The Lesser Questions of Mary Magdalene* have vanished, the four page monologue Mary offered in reply to Peter's questions in the *Gospel of Mary* have also disappeared, and in *Dialogue of the Saviour* when she decides to speak about the mystery of truth, the verses that follow have obviously been altered. The Synoptic Gospels found nothing Mary said was worthy to warrant inclusion; while in *John* all a reactive Mary is capable of offering is the inability to visually distinguish the difference between a non-descript gardener and the resurrected Saviour. Even when she is granted the right to utter a few brief syllables in the Gnostic texts, Peter is invariably lurking in the background demanding she keep quiet, stop breathing, or die.

With the exception of *Pistis Sophia*, what has slipped through the censors fingers is fragmentary, and up until recently, the accepted remnants of Mary's life presented some insurmountable problems. Fortunately there is one Nag Hammadi Gospel that resolves many of these omissions and contradicts what Christian Institutions have claimed as fact.

The *Gospel of Thomas* contains 114 verses attributed solely to Jesus, and there are no narratives, events, miracles or questions on which to respond. All that remains are pieces of advice, observations and secret teachings. The scripture was meant to be a testimonial to Jesus' life and ministry, equally the same can be said for his partner, Mary. On every occasion still remaining, she always expounded upon or agreed with Jesus. Never did she contend or dispute, and unlike Peter, there is no record of her being admonished by Jesus. In Gnostic texts she is the most favoured Apostle and the object of Jesus' admiration and constant praise.

Jesus commends Mary for being an "all-blessed fulness, thou who shalt be sung of as blessed in all generations."[2] He chose "not conceal anything from you from this hour, but I will reveal everything to you with certainty and openly. Hear now, Maria, (Mary) and give ear, all you disciples."[3] If Jesus decided to "reveal everything" to the "all-blessed" Mary, it is not illogical to propose her words are his—not simply because most of what she said has disappeared—but everything left behind is exactly the same. The reality is there are no differences between the words of Mary and Jesus.

Of all the scriptures we have examined, the *Gospel of Thomas* has the most obvious Aboriginal connections. It is our contention the document is quite literally saturated in the *Dreaming*. So much so, that the analysis of every verse we chose is accompanied by quotes from the esteemed Aboriginal Elder Big Bill Neidjie. What other option did we have? The connections were so evident and similarities between Thomas and Bill were so compelling, we felt no other approach was available or viable.

Acknowledgements

We would like to thank Jan Scherpenhuizen, Morgan Strong and Dellene Strong for their patience and editing skills. Thanks also to Samantha Kirk for her suggestions and foresight.

This book is dedicated to a culture and people who are the custodians of an ancient mystical tradition that is as relevant today as it was 50,000 years ago.

Chapter 1
The First Apostle: Mary

(Professor J.R. Porter: *Gospel of Bartholomew*) *"Mary is described in highly exalted language . . . her pre-eminence and the supreme honour owing to her are made plain."*[1]

It appears there is an increasing volume of concrete evidence, scattered throughout the globe, which substantiates our belief that ancient maritime pioneers from Australia accepted no boundaries. We believe Aboriginal people of distant times set foot in Africa, Europe, Asia and America. The evidence of their exile and influence abounds and can be found in bone, rock, cave, oral tradition, artefact and verse. After analysing a variety of sites and indicators that reflect the extent and antiquity of Aboriginal oceanic journeys, we believe there is a need to examine some of the scriptures found at Nag Hammadi and assess whether this arcane Aboriginal tradition is, as we claim, the inspiration behind the esoteric teachings of Jesus, Mary and a variety of religions.

The reputed Holy Grail that many seek and occasionally litigate over has nothing to do with bloodlines or cups. There seems little doubt Jesus and Mary were involved in a physical relationship, and more than likely had children, but the potential to have children is irrelevant. Parentage is no guarantee of wisdom or worth; nobody inherits mystical talent and compassion through any genetic process. More often than not the offspring of many kings and queens contributed nothing of value to anyone bar themselves. The concept of the son or daughter of any monarch inheriting anything blessed or special contradicts scientific fact and commonsense.

This nebulous icon many call the Grail, relates to an introspective mystical heritage that has slowly dissipated over the eons due to different resources, geography and most importantly, lifestyle. Mary's grail is open for all to access, but this rebirth or *Dreaming* is spiritual in complexion and can only be found within each soul. Of all Jesus' Apostles there was only one person who fully understood the inner nature and duality of the message he preached, and it is for this reason Mary was Jesus' chosen Apostle.

Jesus is unrestrained in his deep love and admiration for Mary, a meagre sampling of these accolades include affirmations such as; "she uttered this as a woman who had understood completely,"[2] "the Woman Who Knew All,"[3] "she would be raised above all the disciples and rule the forthcoming Kingdom of Light"[4] and "Mary the Light-bringer."[5]

Laurence Gardener claims Mary, along with Isis and Lilith, were the only women to know the "secret name of God."[6] Even the *New Testament* implicitly acknowledges her wisdom and gnosis. On each occasion when the women are detailed in any of the canonical Gospels, there is only one instance when Mary is not listed first among the women. The role-call of famous women includes the revered mother of Jesus; in those times no prostitute could realistically command such respect.

Even more revealing than the many commendations showered upon Mary is (Verse 21) of the *Gospel of Thomas*, which begins with Mary asking Jesus, "Whom are your disciples like?"[7] There is a distinct sense of separation present in this enquiry, the implication appears to be that Mary and his followers are not the same. Jesus' response has the feel of two concerned parents discussing the welfare of their somewhat wayward offspring.

Jesus' reply to Mary begins with him commenting that, "They are like children."[8] Some may have expected a correction, or even a reprimand with Jesus pointedly reminding Mary of her station and that she too, was a disciple just like them. However, nothing was said, nor was an apology sought. It would appear Jesus is indirectly accepting her implied status as being somewhere above those they are now discussing. The absence of any correction from Jesus seems to suggest that our somewhat unorthodox interpretation may have an impressive seconder.

Peter however, is far less enamoured with Mary. His dislike of her and all females is well documented, as he was renowned for his "hot-tempered"[9] disposition whenever in her presence. Mary certainly sensed the open hostility lamenting to Jesus that, "I am afraid of Peter, because he threatened me and hateth our sex."[10] Her concerns were justified, as "she hardly dares to speak to him freely."[11] Peter went to Jesus pleading with him to banish her because "Mary should leave us, for females are not worthy of life."[12]

Peter's obsession is occasionally moderated by one factor he has no control over, Mary's superior spiritual wisdom. He reluctantly acknowledges her elevated status and knowledge in matters of a deep religious nature, pleading with her to reveal more, as "we know that the Saviour loved you more . . . Tell us the words of the Saviour, which you remember—which you know but we do not, nor have we heard them."[13]

This exalted woman was the same person, according to Levi (Matthew), whom "he loved . . . more than us."[14] Philip, like Peter, is a misogynist, but has no choice other than to speak of Mary as the one Jesus, "kissed . . . often on her mouth."[15] Jesus made her superior position clear calling her the one who understood completely because she stood above, never behind or beside these men. Or, is there more, could this possibly be a partnership?

Thomas is undeniably a possessor of great gnosis. When challenged by Peter and Matthew as to what one of the three secret sayings given to him by Jesus meant, Thomas understandably baulks at the prospect of revealing it. If he did share this secret, he felt Peter and Matthew, (uninitiated in such advanced esoteric areas) would "pick up rocks and stone me, and fire will come from the rocks and consume you."[16] Stoning is mandatory; any faithful Jewish adherent of those times was obliged to reach for a handful of rocks as a response to blasphemy.

When *Bartholomew* (II.5) questioned Mary about the gnosis she and Jesus shared, she was dismayed and troubled. "Mary said unto them: Ask me not (or Do ye indeed ask me) concerning this mystery. If I should begin to tell you, fire will issue forth out of my mouth and consume all the world."[17] No Apostle or mortal made such an incredible statement. More to the point, the conversation was not recorded by Mary, but the claim is made by the male Apostle, Bartholomew. Only God can destroy humanity within an instant. If she too, can control the destiny of humanity, as alleged by Bartholomew, it would seem the woman has powers equal to Jesus.

Before such a notion of equality between Jesus and Mary is immediately discarded as an affront to all forms of Christianity and rational thought, the claim is worthy of further reflection and is not without precedent. Isis, according to Ancient Egyptian records, was "strong of tongue."[18] Graham Hancock believes Isis knew the "words of power,"[19] and because "of her voice alone, to be capable of bending reality and overriding the laws of physics."[20] If Isis is capable of altering reality and extinguishing all scientific truths, it would appear logical to assume she would also have the ability to consume the whole world. If Hancock's assertion is combined with Gardner's belief that Mary and Isis both knew the secret name of God, it seems fascinating possibilities could emerge.

Bartholomew's claim of Mary's supernatural powers, are identical to those powers attributed to Isis. This could simply be because her esoteric skills were learnt while becoming an *Isaic* Priestess. Or for those who are willing to entertain a more mystical possibility, as a natural continuation of Isis' soul reincarnating into the body of Mary. Personally we favour the idea that Mary is an Avatar of the female energy identified as Isis, though this interpretation is not central to our overall theory.

A multitude of critics could only react with indignation to such miraculous powers claimed by Mary, then chorus one predictable response, heresy! Possibly, but in a meaningful partnership between Jesus and Mary steeped in pure love there should be no secrets, everything should be shared. The qualities of equality and sharing everything are purported to be the foundations behind every traditional Christian marriage.

It would be a mistake to assume these esoteric powers were possessed by a few favoured females in the Middle East. Those adept in the more mystical aspects of the *Dreaming* possess a multitude of supernatural abilities, some are identical, while many of the skills Aboriginal Elders mastered were never accessed by Jesus and Mary. This should come as no surprise, simply because all Jesus and Mary were doing was copying an ancient precedent that began in Australia.

Furthermore, the motivation behind such a declaration about Mary, if false, is mystifying. Apart from creating ridicule and doubt, why would Bartholomew make such a startling claim, as he must have been aware of the indignation such a statement would create. It would be a huge stretch of poetic license to claim such a statement is symbolic or a metaphor, it is a literal response to a request from another. He is either lying or telling the truth, there is no other option. If Bartholomew is lying about grave matters such as these, to assume his entire Gospel was a fabrication is consistent and compulsory. However there is an alternative, consider this, if I substitute Jesus for Mary (or Isis) in *Bartholomew* (II:5), and left the rest of the passage in tact, no devout Christian would be unsettled.

Mary, as the Cathars claim, was Jesus' "concubine" or "consort." They were adamant it was never a platonic relationship. Of course many authorities vehemently dispute this belief, secure in their conviction he was above such carnal desires and neither married nor slept with any woman.

Jesus may have been celibate as some hope, but an unattached male over the age of thirty was an incredibly rare, if non-existent, commodity in those days. A sterile lifestyle was a serious offence, contravening the mores of a society where the compulsory adage, go forth and multiply, was an integral part of Jewish culture. An unwillingness to procreate was likened by some Jewish authorities to murder, it was literally a sin for a rabbi not to sleep with his consort (consort is the Hebrew word for partner) and produce many offspring.

Celibacy was a despised practice as it threatened the continuation of the tribe or family, and would have drawn unwanted attention from many detractors. The only two contemporary instances of this practise recorded in any historical writings pertained to the group known as the *Essenes*, (not one word is offered about them in either set of texts) and the first-named individual to indulge in the practice was Pin Has Pen Yair. He lived one hundred years after Jesus was crucified and his notoriety was based solely upon his celibacy. Yet amongst the many criticisms and insinuations about Jesus, there is not one contemporary critique of this abnormal sexual abstinence or alternatively, the supposedly sinful act of homosexuality.

The lack of any comment is due to one salient fact; Jesus was with the one he loved most, Mary. And that was in essence the problem, not the act of marriage or the concept of a physical union with a woman, but the character of the woman Jesus married.

Bishop John Shelby Spong is no supporter of any form of Gnosticism, and is a strong advocate of the traditional Bible, yet he feels the content within the *New*

Testament compels him to state that, "the cumulative argument is indeed in favour of Jesus and Mary being man and wife."[21]

Spong's extensive examination of many passages of the Bible, particularly *1 Corinthians* (1:5), can only be understood once the reader or student accepts their marriage as fact. His concerns were twofold; Mary is regarded as being senior to all the women assembled, and she alone had the right to both claim and anoint Jesus' body. According to all early accounts of Jewish custom, the only person permitted to perform these funerary duties or adopt this status is the wife or consort of Jesus.

If Mary is not Jesus' wife or consort, she has no reason or right to approach the crypt and would have been immediately reprimanded if she attempted to blatantly overstep her station. No-one objects; even Peter is uncharacteristically silent, as the reputed prostitute breaks a multitude of sacred Jewish prescriptions and desecrates Jesus' tomb. However if Mary was Jesus' wife, Peter would have no reason to take offence, since she was expected to behave in the manner described.

Only twice did Jesus willingly bow his head to any mortal, and on both occasions the ceremonies these people orchestrated were Egyptian in origin. The baptism and pre-funerary rites have no connection to Jewish religion. John the Baptist brought Jesus towards the light, but Mary escorted him to the level above. Mary and John stand well above all others in such esoteric wisdom. The formal act of the Saviour bowing to be consecrated gives by association, power and authority to these chosen souls.

Yet Jesus spent a lot of time defending Mary against the incessant animosity offered by the more unsophisticated members of his flock. Pleading with those less enlightened to, "Let her alone: against the day of my burying hath she kept this."[22] (*John* 12:7) Against the constant backdrop of antagonism cultured by the less aware Apostles, the Priestess Mary anointed Jesus in exactly the same manner Isis anointed Osiris before his death, and both were surely cognisant of this. Jesus knew exactly what Mary was doing, and equally, the origins of the important sacred *Isiac* ceremony. This blessed anointment took place at the residence of the priestess, Mary, and that fact alone ordains upon her a stewardship over these ceremonies. Jesus did no more than acknowledge her eminence by offering the epitaph, "that this women hath done, be told for a memorial of her."[23] (*Matthew.* 26:13)

Regrettably these affirmations were ignored by many immediately after he crossed over. Gender prejudice is as much an aspect of the times and locale, as a particular individual's personal failings. Those who denied Mary's authority were doing no more than reflecting a communal cultural prejudice. Throughout nearly the entire globe such blinkered judgements were often the expected norm.

However, there was one place where such bias was never suffered. At an archaeological site at Lake Mungo, (N.S.W.) the grave of a young Aboriginal woman (W.L.H.1) was found in 1972. One of Australia's leading archaeologists, Professor Alan Thorne, determined the site to be at least 25,000 years old. The young woman excavated was barely twenty years of age. She was most certainly not an Elder at such a tender age, and nor would her parents or bloodline have any relevance, as leadership and wisdom were earned through initiations and tests alone. Nothing except talent was ever considered relevant.

The Lake Mungo woman was cremated; her bones were then carefully broken into small pieces, covered in red ochre, and placed in a deep cylindrical pit. The time and labour involved in this process meant communal food collection must suffer while these funerary rites were enacted. The evidence supporting a belief in the afterlife existing around thirty thousand years ago is almost unchallengeable, for there could be no other justification for the use of the rare sacred red ochre on W.L.H. 1 and another male buried near this site 30.000 years earlier (W.L.H. 3). Paralleling these religious obligations and associated use of ochre, is a respect and veneration for a young woman that we claim has no global equivalent.

Within Traditional Aboriginal society there exists a common expectation that if a man witnessed a sacred secret women's ceremony, or desecrated a special woman's site, he would be physically punished, perhaps even put to death. Or worse still, the offender could be banished, resulting in his soul being separated from his birthplace and Ancestral Spirits for eternity.

The respect and gender equality of ancient Aboriginals were graphically illustrated in a series of innovative films entitled *Women of the Sun*. These four one-hour feature films were directed and scripted solely by Aboriginal people. The first episode, *Alinta the Flame*, was spoken in *Dhamarrandju* language (*Yolgnu* dialect) then subtitled in English. The story centres on the plight of two escaped convicts who were adopted by a local tribe. This was the first time they had seen a white person.

One of the convicts raped an Aboriginal woman, and was accused of "offending the women."[24] No defence was asked for, nor was it required, because making a false accusation of rape would necessitate the person who concocted these lies having to answer to their Spirits. Once accused, all that was left was to be handed a wooden shield in a forlorn attempt to deflect the outraged warrior's spears. Many Aboriginal languages had no way of expressing the concept of misleading or lying to another, simply because the Spirits, who could not be fooled, were in every blade of grass and leaf.

The overriding need to maintain tribal harmony meant sexist attitudes like those espoused by Paul, Philip and Peter could never flourish in place like this. Women were the creators, they gathered a greater proportion of the food, had their own secret sites and sacred stories, and without them, every male and infant would perish. Living day by day, relying solely on the combined talents of the group to stay alive meant everybody was judged on how they assisted the clan. Neither sex could control the means of production or monopolise massive deposits of wealth; equality of labour and respect for all was an elemental base from which their culture and lifestyle evolved. Gender meant nothing to a growling stomach, every upright soul was needed to collect food and thank their Spirits.

All Peter, Paul and Philip were doing was to remain faithful to an edict passed by Josiah, King of Judea, when he decided to reorder the priorities of the Temple cult (640-609 BCE). The *Josaic reforms* decreed the holy order of the Gods had to be amended. As it was in the *Dreaming* where Biamie had a consort of equal standing (Birrahgnooloo); so too did Yahweh have a female companion (Ashera) who was Yahweh's counter-part. Josiah saw no merit in her continued presence and decided Ashera was to be discarded and officially forgotten.

It is undeniable Josiah is still highly revered and his reign was far more benevolent than that of many of his predecessors, especially his autocratic grandfather. However the spiritual balance that should have been the essence of their society was now completely lost, as the feminine values that initially inspired their teachings were formally denounced as unworthy and second-class. From this point on, the belief in a blessing and curse interpretation of Israelite history dominated. Once a society compliantly accepts the will of their monarch (Josiah) and adopts a mentality where obedience towards a male God brings reward, while disobedience incurs punishment; the voices of the past become muted.

The Aboriginal societies of traditional times were steeped in feminine values; the land has always been their mother and all are created equal. Once this feminine tradition was abandoned, the strength and depth of whatever followed was diluted. Many early Gnostic communities attempted to redress this human error, as they knew "this divine current was perceived as the feminine, healing and nurturing energy of God's Holy Spirit."[25] Sharron Rose believes "Gnosticism places primary value on the feminine qualities of receptivity, intuitive perception, visionary experience and the art of healing."[26] Her description is a more than adequate summation of the lifestyle of a traditional Aboriginal. In a perfect world we believe the term *Dreaming* could be substituted for Gnosticism, they should be interchangeable terms. If the Gnostic texts remained steadfast to their original inspiration, the only differences between the religions should be of a superficial nature and relate more to differing cultures and times than any inherent spiritual contradictions.

Many of the early anthropologists and archaeologists who had an interest in Aboriginal society were male, and no matter how scrupulous they were, not one female secret or sacred ritual could be revealed to them. As a result, many of these academics believed this society to be a male-dominated society, and it wasn't until Dianne Bell's book *Daughter's of the Dreaming* was published it became apparent that these new truths necessitated corrections to many previous theories and observations.

This feminine counter-balance is the essential element of both the *Dreaming* and Gnosticism, and is an association that spans time and place.

Isis was not a compliant backdrop but the active feminine catalyst; she chose the timing of Osiris' death, attended to his funeral rites and used her magic to bring him back from the after-life. We believe Mary's role was no different, but many authorities have tried to cloud the issue and realign the gender balance.

In 352 A.D. the Council of Nicea was selected by the Roman Emperor Constantine, their brief was to sanctify the proper writings; thereby creating an official Christian body of scripture. Constantine claimed to believe the Christian God assisted him in winning a bloody battle. From that point on he was driven in his efforts to introduce Christianity as the official religion of Rome. As was the custom of Emperors for centuries, he was personally responsible for murdering half his immediate family to maintain the domination of all he surveyed. It could be said, with some degree of justification, Constantine's divinely endorsed dictatorship and censorship of biblical writings was motivated by self-preservation and his inflated ego; he proclaimed himself to be the thirteenth Apostle of Jesus.

The power of Mary Magdalene and her followers was far too widespread for it to continue unchecked, and something had to be done. Mary's critics in Nicea saw such a purge as essential. To justify such a measure at that time, one only had to cite passages such as, "fire will issue forth out of my mouth and consume all the world,"[27] and accuse Mary and all those who followed her of being heretical and absurd.

One of the most venerated Christian founding fathers, Tertullian, warned all followers they must believe in a bodily resurrection because, "it is absurd."[28] This is reminiscent of early biblical scholar Clements' truth steeped in faith, and on both occasions, these founding fathers seem to be demanding devotion based on "absurd" teachings, then criticise other sects for following their preference to use poetic license.

The *New Testament* tells us repeatedly the disciples were empowered to evangelise and create miracles, but it doesn't offer a specific roll call of who these advanced students were. Constantine's chosen representatives at Nicea claimed the right to decide on behalf of the congregation, adopting the role of latter day arbitrators, selecting what suited their morals and gender bias and dismissing everything else as heresy.

Of all the Gnostic texts dealing primarily with Jesus there is one scripture, *The Dialogue of the Saviour,* which may best explain why the Council of Nicea was so antagonistic towards Mary and her followers.

The text may have been penned around the time the canonical Gospels were composed (70-110 A.D.), or shortly thereafter. The real value of this account lies in examining, in some detail, what happened after the resurrected Saviour withdrew with Matthew, Thomas and Mary, and offered to share some of the mysteries he chose to withhold from the other Apostles. The content and intent of their enquiries contrasted against their interaction with Jesus reveal much more than just their individual concerns. Their words disclose a spiritual status; there is a bold delineation existing within this dialogue and carries an implication orthodox Christianity hasn't even begun to accept. A few words from Mary and Jesus may help illuminate what the mysteron is.

[53.] Mary said, "Thus with respect to the 'wickedness of each day' and the 'labourer is worthy of his food,' and 'the disciple resembles his teacher.' She uttered this as a woman who understood completely."[29]

[60.] Mary said, "Tell me Lord why have I come to this place to profit or to forfeit?"[30]

[61.] The Lord said, "You make clear the abundance of the revealer!"[31]

[69.] Mary said, "I want to understand all things, just as they are."[32]

[77.] They said to him, "What is the place to which we are going?"[33]

[78.] The Lord said, "Stand in the place you can reach!"[34]

[79.] Mary said, "Everything established thus is seen."[35]

[80.] The Lord said, "I have told you that it is the one who sees who reveals."[36]

[83.] Mary said, "There is but one saying I will speak to the Lord concerning the mystery of truth. In this we have taken our stand, and to the cosmic we are transparent."[37]

In this text, Thomas and Matthew never expound, interpret or offer any prophetic commentary or wisdom that ends in anything other than a simple question mark or a full stop. Neither received any of the personal accolades the Saviour showers upon Mary. If she does ask a question, its rhetorical nature reveals the answer within the framework of her cryptic enquiry, as one would expect nothing less from one who both sees and understands completely.

In Verse 83 Mary initiates a discussion with Jesus on an important issue she feels important in the plural form. The male Apostles would never consider speaking on behalf of the Saviour using pronouns like "we" and "our." Neither set of Gospels had any other spokesperson presuming to have the temerity or authority to be so inclusive. Mary is allowed to speak at her initiative on his behalf and is repeatedly encouraged to adopt such a privileged position. There are two Apostles and another person in this equation, two are earnestly seeking the light, while the third has already found it.

On thirteen occasions Mary offers a comment within *The Dialogue of the Saviour*; only three of her observations conclude with a rhetorical question mark.

An impartial judge may find it difficult not to accept the remotest possibility there could be some form of symbiotic inspiration within the text. Jesus is not alone in his task, there are two revealers plying their trade in this passage. When Mary asks Jesus whether our times here are an opportunity to "profit or forfeit," he adds nothing beyond a resounding endorsement of her credentials as a "revealer." No elaboration or correction was necessary when Mary speaks. A statement expounding a hidden truth needs nothing beyond wholehearted agreement.

Mary reveals many secret teachings to Matthew and Thomas; these mysteries she speaks of are matters only a revealer would be aware of. According to this text, Mary is most assuredly the only Apostle who can see these secret truths, yet all she seems to receive is resentment from some of her companions.

It is possible Jesus was indirectly responsible for some of the animosity Mary faced, before and after his ministry. If one does accept some of these Gnostic texts as being truthful, it could be proposed Jesus was throwing petrol onto fire. The times and personnel reek of testosterone. To publicly lavish praise and physical affection on this female sage may have unsettled the sensibilities of many a misogynist. Offended and unable to do anything beyond demanding death or expulsion, those who were outraged by the affront to their male sensibilities could do little more than complain, bide their time and conspire against those they saw as "unworthy of breath."

There exists a definite distinction between the numerous affirmations of Mary's wisdom and words in some Gnostic texts, to the communal reaction towards the revelations, mysteries and parables Jesus disclosed to his beloved Apostles in the *New Testament*. In the canonical Gospels, the most common response Jesus' Apostles offered to their Messiah's words of spiritual insight was an apparent lack of understanding.

The Council of Nicea and the Church authorities had to counter Mary's true status and wisdom. Their approaches varied; slander her reputation, destroy her writings and modify texts from the exoteric male parabolic writings. What was allowed to remain no longer acknowledged Mary's credentials and, most importantly, their partnership.

Propaganda, as with many vices, is an ancient curse. When the Council's task was completed, it was ordained that only Matthew and John were to be believed. Thomas, Philip, Bartholomew, James and the ilk, which obviously includes Mary, were deemed to be the purveyors of heresy, and all traces of their lies had to be purged from the planet.

Littered amongst the multitude of flaws and injustices that make up many societies of today, there is at least one healthy feature of our global community, scepticism towards those who aspire to control. Just because someone in authority claims to have a mortgage on the truth, this means very little today. As Bertrand Russell succinctly stated, "the fact that an opinion has been widely held is no evidence that it is not utterly absurd."[38]

For millennia, in Western societies, the Bible was all that was available for most who sought spiritual guidance. This book and the religion that evolved out of the teachings of Jesus were claimed to contain absolute truths. Many of the most ardent male supporters of the good book insist all other creeds are in error and must be forced to accept their light.

The irony is, every religion, including Christianity, are merely pale reflections of the first religion; the *Dreaming*. The people who became disciples of the *Dreaming* adopted a lifestyle dedicated to living in harmony with the land and God. They were the original Apostles, but they did not follow a person or worship an icon, book or financial institution; their devotion was too discriminating to mindlessly obey any mortal. Everyday and in everyway the land and everything upon it was revered as different aspects of God. Mary may well have been the first Apostle of Jesus, but well before their time of birth there was a continent where each soul spent their lives as the first Apostles of the *Dreaming*.

Elsewhere those seeking spiritual comfort and guidance turn to a book for certainty and wisdom, they rely upon the words of men, and fervently hope what is penned within their divinely endorsed scripture is perfect. Traditional Aboriginal societies sought out the wisdom of Nature and read the creations of God: for they knew no man-made book can offer anything beyond confusion, arguments over semantic interpretations and flawed perspectives.

Chapter 2
The Gospel Truths

"And I say also unto thee, That thou art Peter, and upon this rock I will build my church; and the gates of hell shall not prevail against it."[1] Matthew 16:18
"But he turned, and said unto Peter, Get thee behind me, Satan: thou art an offence unto me: for thou savourest not the things that be of God, but those that be of men."[2] Matthew 16:23

Something is seriously amiss; it is difficult to accept these two verses could possibly be describing the same person. The close proximity, spaced five verses apart, only adds to the contradiction. That Peter, the acclaimed "rock," and foundation of traditional Christianity can, within an instant, appal Jesus so greatly is a matter of deep concern. He is apparently the object of scorn and commendation, and the contrast does seem a touch inconsistent. How can Satan, be acclaimed as the revered "rock" unless he is standing on a pile of crumbling brimstone? Jesus assures us the "gates of hell" will not "prevail;" yet the gatekeeper has two Christian names, Peter and Satan.

Laurence Gardner, the author of *Bloodline of the Holy Grail*, sees the "rock" being of a less imposing dimension than many traditional advocates insist. Their interpretations are based on a semantic misunderstanding, not a resounding affirmation of Peter's infallibility. Gardner claims that, "unfortunately, the Greek word petra (rock), relating to the Rock of Israel, was mistranslated as if it had been petros (stone), referring to Peter."[3] Jesus' instruction was that their mission was to be dedicated to a community rather than become centred upon an individual. Some have erroneously nominated Peter as the sole spiritual heir-apparent to Christ's teachings, when the reality was everyone was and still is.

Peter was a simple, solid man of undoubted zeal and devotion. He was the aide and principle bodyguard of Jesus, while many of the more highly educated Apostles chose to tend to other worldly responsibilities, Peter remained steadfastly by his side. These were the undeniable talents he brought to this revolutionary ensemble. However, it should be noted, Peter was not a philosopher or the repository of all divine knowledge throughout the eons, nor was he the Saviour's infallible advocate. He was a mere mortal blessed or cursed with strengths and inadequacies, and having trouble balancing the two, just as we all do.

These contradictions are far from isolated cases of apparent anomalies, as the Gospel Truths of *Matthew, Mark, Luke* and *John* contain many incongruities, and much that is at variance with each other.

Was the Virgin Birth meant to be literal, symbolic or something else? As Philip asks, "when did a woman ever conceive by a woman?"[4] Some claim the account of divine conception a thinly veiled attempt to transpose the Isiac myth through poetic license. Rather than draw upon appropriate Gnostic scriptures to examine this narrative, there is more than enough substantive evidence within the *New Testament* to call this legend into question.

Of the four Gospels, *Luke* pushes the immaculate-wheelbarrow with the most vigour. When Jesus, unbeknown to Mother Mary, wanders off into a Jewish temple, Mary is distraught with worry. Jesus seems somewhat bemused by her troubled manner, enquiring, "How is it that ye sought me? wist ye not that I must be about my Father's business?"[5]

Jesus is correct, his mother should not be alarmed. Luke detailed an angelic manifestation, Mary's divine conception and the bearing of God's only begotten mortal child; as such, Jesus' response should be seen as stating a self-evident truth. The angel's revelations to mother Mary made it very clear her infant was special, sired by the Omnipotent Being. Her response, or rather her lack of anything, betrays something even Luke cannot manufacture or conceal, ". . . they understood not the saying which he spake unto them."[6]

As Jesus' mother, Mary's reaction is not in keeping with the knowledge she supposedly has. The assumption she is aware her child is God's unique blessing and the salvation of mankind, is not mirrored in her behaviour. It could be possible her son Jesus, was just one of seven normal children she bore.

The Blessed Mother Mary utters nothing, leaving no parables, sayings or exemplary deeds (beyond the passive Immaculate Conception) in any of the accepted Gospels. There are no primary or secondary accounts left behind in the four Gospels to reflect upon. The reverence Pope John Paul showered upon this mute shadow is mystifying, as solid evidence upon which to base this adoration is virtually non-existent.

Matthew did not see the Immaculate Conception as a point worthy of mention; he claimed Jesus was genetically linked to "the son of David."[7] Matthew agrees with Paul who stated, "he was made from the seed of David according to the flesh."[8] According to the flesh Joseph, not Mary, is the only parent who is genetically related to King David, that fact was never in dispute. However it would seem Luke and Matthew most certainly are in disagreement when addressing the issue of heritage.

The solution to Jesus' heritage may be a matter of vocabulary. When Joseph, the widely accepted *seed* of David, and Mary conceived Jesus during March, the time of their first betrothal, their shameful act broke many of the "rules of dynastic wedlock."[9] Physical consummation was expressly forbidden to occur before December, as Mary would not be recognised as being a "wife"[10] until her second marriage to Joseph. Before that date every bride was referred to as a "virgin."[11] This communal terminology refers to a stage of betrothal, not a record of sexual abstinence. It seems some may be analysing yesterday's stories using today's dictionaries, two thousand years before they are entitled to.

Many critics of those times claimed Jesus' illegitimacy left his credentials in dispute, as his birth-date was inappropriate and led some to insist his brother James, was the rightful heir to lead the House of David.

The actual authorship of these Gospel Truths is a conundrum of unfathomable proportions. The Gospels of *Mark* and *Luke* are secondary accounts, as neither of the writers had set eyes upon the Saviour. Their tutor, Paul, who was a devout follower of Peter, never met Jesus. The identity of the original author of *John* is an enigma, as strong cases can be made for Lazarus, Mary, her first male child John, Thomas, a follower of John or the first acknowledged scribe of this gospel (John). As for the origins of *Matthew*, the only fact that can be attested to with some degree of certainty is that it wasn't written by the Apostle Matthew.

Difficulties continue to arise when trying to ascertain the names of the chosen Apostles. The four Gospels, when first listing the chosen Apostles, can agree on five names; the rest, including Peter, are missing in action in at least one sanctioned account. The five Apostles acknowledged at the beginning of each Gospel are Matthew (Levi), Philip, Thomas, Bartholomew and Judas Iscariot. It may be of some interest to note three Apostles are purveyors of supposed heretical Gnostic writings, one the reviled betrayer of Christ, and the other, according to many of Jesus' Gnostic writings, is one of the favoured three male Apostles.

Ignoring these inconsistencies, and they are not infrequent, it could be asserted that *Matthew*, *Mark* and *Luke* are called the synoptic Gospels as they have much, but most assuredly not all, in common. However, *John* is never included for a variety of reasons; a brief resume of these disparities may highlight some of these contradictions.

The synoptic Gospels claim Jesus' ministry lasted one year, *John* contends it was longer than three years. Whether he died before or after Passover is also in disagreement. The timing and chronological accuracy of these texts are unreliable.

John is obsessed by the Jews, and mentions them on seventy-two occasions. The synoptic three can only amass five comments on this subject. Conversely, the synoptic Gospels have twenty-seven parables within their writings, whereas *John* has, depending on individual scholarly perspective, either one or none.

It can be confidently asserted that *John*, or as some suggest, Mary or Lazarus, is far more introspective and Gnostic in flavour than the synoptic three. Evidence suggests there are three areas of marked divergence that create a distinctly Gnostic perspective within some sections of *John*.

The Resurrection; did it occur, and, if so, what was its nature?

The whole issue of what occurred after Jesus died is not as clear-cut as some would contend. If he resurrected as an entity reanimating his mortal shell, why is it that in *John*, Mary does not recognise him, mistaking him for the gardener. After realising who this resurrected spirit is, she attempts to embrace him (a common occurrence). Jesus' response to Mary's intention was to stop her touching him. The event deserves further reflection, especially so when one considers there is no other example of any Apostle initiating close intimate contact with Jesus in either scriptures.

Nowhere within the pages of the Bible does anyone embrace Jesus whenever they feel inclined to do so. His response, "Touch me not; for I am not yet ascended to my Father,"[12] is puzzling and inconsistent if Jesus never had a physical relationship with Mary. If he had no physical contact with any female, what could inspire Mary to embrace the Saviour for the first time, and why did Jesus feel it was necessary to explain why she was not allowed to touch him? If he has never been touched, his response should reflect a degree of offence or some form of criticism of her presumptuous act. A more consistent reaction may involve an admonishment, reminding her that no-one touches me as I have always been above the world of physical contact and sexuality. Instead, on this specific occasion, he seems to be saying it is inappropriate to touch him this time, and then explains why an act that was previously an integral part of their daily life could no longer occur.

Why were Peter, Thomas and the mysterious beloved disciple also unable to recognise the risen Saviour at their first sighting on the lake? As it was implied with Mary, it appears their vision was also momentarily defective. These close and dear Apostles offer one communal reaction upon their first sighting of the Saviour since he was crucified, a lack of recognition. Either all three male Apostles are suffering from a shared defect in their eyesight or memory, or the apparition they see now is not Jesus' body, but his Spirit.

In some of the Gnostic Scriptures this apparition presents no issue of concern. Jesus' appearance could be of an old man then a young child within an instant, for the recognition of this spiritual entity relies solely within the eyes of the beholders' soul.

Other critics, including Laurence Gardener, go much further, denying Jesus died on the cross. The substitution of another disciple or the use of a soporific drug temporarily inducing a coma, are the favoured options used to explain Jesus' escape. Some claim he travelled to India, while Gardener sees a far grander existence ahead. He claims Jesus became a high priest of the Essene Priesthood, with his ascension no more than an allegorical pathway to a more prestigious career.

Even after Jesus upturned the tables, was condemned to an horrific death by religious authorities whom called him the dark prince, spoke endlessly against the rich, prayer, sexism, institutions, circumcision and stoning and all forms of extremism; he then became a bastion and spokesperson against all he preached. Not one Gospel, accepted or rejected, directly asserts this, nor are the Essenes mentioned in any account of the New Testament.

To add to the uncertainty, yet another question flows from these mysteries. Who actually saw Jesus immediately after his resurrection? Other than Mary, there is no consensus, as each Gospel presents a differing cast.

Who is the disciple most beloved *John* speaks of?

Orthodox advocates claim the apostle John was the source of inspiration. However, on every occasion the nebulous beloved entity is present, so too is Thomas. Within some Gnostic texts Mary was definitely the "one he loved more than us,"[13] these two phrases appear to be almost identical.

John (12:10) tells us that Lazarus, along with Jesus, had been sentenced to death. The Synoptic three imply, through omission, Lazarus did not rise from the dead, and nor was he a member of the elite twelve. Yet according to *John*, Lazarus was considered of such a threat to the authorities, he was sentenced to die alongside Jesus. Even the so-called solitary account of the raising of Lazarus, (his possible brother-in-law) may have been a far deeper allegory than it first seems.

Raising Lazarus could have been an elaborate symbolic ritual sourced from the *Dreaming*. When told of Lazarus' reputed demise, Jesus responded somewhat indifferently commenting, "our friend Lazarus sleepeth."[14] The recently discovered *Secret Gospel of Mark* claims Lazarus was never physically dead, but asleep. Once again we see another differing Gnostic interpretation of a well-known event. If it was indeed a ceremony, it may go some way to explain the apparently erratic response offered by Thomas in *John* (11:16) when he states, "Let us go, that we may die with him."[15] Thomas is either advocating mass suicide, or mass salvation.

Moreover, if Lazarus' death was an Isiac ritual inspired by the *Dreaming*, the women and men could have prescribed parts to play. Just as Mary and Isis greeted their consorts return in an almost identical scripted reply, such an orchestrated response may be a mandatory part of the whole ceremony.

When an initiated young Aboriginal man returns to his family after hearing the sacred *Dreaming* stories and receiving the appropriate initiation cuts, the women feign grief claiming their child has *died*. Knowing full well what has really occurred, they continue chanting and wailing in lament, feigning lack of recognition of the man who has returned. All participating know the truth of the matter, but tradition demanded this manner of formalised grieving must prevail.

Beyond and above all of these inconsistencies, is Mary Magdalene's ambivalent response upon hearing that Jesus had arrived to revive the corpse of Lazarus. Lazarus is her only brother and is supposedly dead, with Jesus deliberately waiting some considerable time before coming to Lazarus' assistance, promising to bring him back from death.

According to *John* (11: 20, 28-29):
Then Martha, as soon as she heard that Jesus was coming, went and met him: but Mary sat still in the house . . . called Mary her sister secretly, saying, The Master is come, and calleth for thee. As soon as she heard that, she arose quickly, and came unto him.[16]

Mary's only brother has supposedly been dead for over four days and has one last miraculous hope of revival, yet when Jesus arrives, she calmly "sat still" and awaited further instructions. Her quietude is puzzling. Martha has no problem welcoming and speaking to Jesus without any hesitation or caveats on behaviour. However Mary seems either unwilling or unable to move, but whatever the reason for the indifference, it is not due to apathy. Disinterest would not account for her rising "quickly," once she is given permission to emerge.

The entire account seems somewhat odd, until John's account is compared to sections of the recently discovered *Secret Gospel of Mark*. In this extensive report, Mary did come out to greet Jesus but was reprimanded by some male Apostles (including Peter). They correctly reminded her, Jewish custom demanded that the bride was not permitted to leave the house and welcome her husband of her own volition. This privilege could only occur once her husband/consort consented for her to do so. Once Martha relayed Jesus' permission, Mary was then allowed to greet her consort.

On no other occasion, in either set of texts, is Mary ever portrayed as being anything less than totally devoted when in Jesus' presence. Outside being his consort and therefore duty-bound to uphold such a custom, the only motivation that could account for Mary's inaction is an uncharacteristic disinterest in her brother's welfare.

Lazarus' possible initiation could make him a prime candidate as the beloved disciple, or, perhaps not. If one does accept it was John, as many biblical scholars insist, they may have backed themselves into an untidy moral corner.

The anonymous beloved disciple is always found resting their head on the Saviour's chest. If she is a female, particularly Mary, all is acceptable. If he is a male, or specifically John, such continuous close physical contact between two males should have set the tongue of many critics into a frenzy of insinuation and moral indignation. Not one contemporary comment on the inappropriateness of this close and affectionate male bonding can be found. This may explain why any sexist male chronicler or subsequent editor would be reluctant to provide a specific identity, especially one that has a feminine name.

The only approach left was to obscure the true identity of the chosen disciple, rearranging what was left behind so as to imply, but never implicitly state, it could be John. Alternatively if it was John, why bother manufacturing these contrived mysteries and what purpose could it possibly serve beyond causing confusion? No other disciple was subjected to such a cryptic appendage on any occasion, yet within the same Gospel there is also an Apostle who is referred to as John. The whole exercise seems rather pointless. All this obliqueness could ever do is create unnecessary confusion in a scripture that should be dedicated to illuminate, never mislead or confuse, its devotees.

Why is there such a large group of miracles that could only warrant one acknowledgement in any of the four Gospels?

Chapter 2: The Gospel Truths

Disregarding Lazarus' appearance, along with many other supernatural acts recorded exclusively in *John*, it could be of some benefit to spend a little time reflecting upon the first of Jesus' miracles. *John's* description of the transformation of water into wine at the wedding ceremony at Cana is acknowledged as Jesus' first recorded miracle, and is absent in the synoptic three Gospels.

Three contentious issues demand to be addressed; why the need for an extra six hundred litres of wine for a simple wedding, why was the Mother Mary obliged to cater for such a massive congregation of guests, when her children were supposedly not involved, and why was the expensive impost placed upon the son of an impoverished carpenter to provide liquid refreshments?

Many claim ancient Jewish lore saw the task as being the prerogative of the groom. This request could be seen as a burden and a cultural affront for any male, except the groom, to provide an extra six hundred litres of quality wine, unless he was compelled to do so. The request seems to indicate Mary and Jesus were not guests but participants. If not, it certainly puts a novel slant on the term B.Y.O.

That the three synoptic chroniclers of Jesus' history find the re-animation of a four-day old cadaver, or the manufacture of a supernatural distillery of no consequence severely challenges the credentials of the writers (which we suspect is the case), or the reality of the acts themselves. It is possible these omissions may reflect the underlying intentions of subsequent scribes and editors.

And finally: the events after the resurrection leading up to Jesus' departure. The closing sentences in each of the four Gospels are incompatible and quite possibly, later additions.

> "He was received up into heaven, and sat on the right hand of God."[17] *Mark*
> "Teaching them to observe all things . . . I am with you always *even* unto the end of the world."[18] *Matthew*
> "He was parted from them, and carried up into heaven."[19] *Luke*
> "And there are also many other things which Jesus did, the which, if they should be written every one, I suppose that even the world itself could not contain the books that should be written."[20] *John*

These are the final accounts of Jesus' ministry but, in reality, they are not. *John's* claims lead one to believe Jesus either continued on, and at a prodigious rate for an indeterminate period of time, or, nothing. But either way, there is no ascension or final destination here. *Matthew* leaves his finale a little more open ended, presenting them with one prescriptive instruction and assurances of an omnipotent presence. These two make no mention, either literally or symbolically, of an upward movement ascending towards heaven or any station in between.

Luke's narrative has the Messiah being "carried up." This is the traditionally accepted description of a third agent (angels) involved in the transportation of Jesus' body up into the divine realms. If I am carried up I am the object, not the subject, being moved by an external agent.

Yet *Mark's* account sees no other external assistance, claiming Jesus was "received up into heaven." Conversely, if you receive something it must be given to you, it is the passive acceptance of something presented by another. It appears Mark believes Jesus initiated his personal ascension through his unassisted efforts.

It is worth noting that the two who insist on the reality of some form of upward ascension were both relaying third-hand accounts, as neither they, nor their tutor, set eyes on the living Messiah. In what seems an ironic twist, the two Gospels bearing the name of an Apostle reputedly present at this miraculous ascension make no such claim, yet, in the eyes of many of the general public, the body of Jesus rose into the clouds in a material shell.

There is only one commonality within all four sentences . . . a full stop. Did Jesus leave? If he did, was it as a body or light? Did he leave himself, or was he assisted as he wandered off to other places and new faces, or are other options a possibility?

If, as *John* asserts repeatedly, the kingdom of heaven "is within," there may be some difficulty locating *Luke's* "up." Possibly it was meant to be symbolic, but surely it could not be the ancient notion of heaven, residing within a thick bank of cumulous clouds wafting through the atmosphere. If "up" is symbolic, then the rest of the statement should share the same fate.

Jesus' Apostles were not a rag-tag collection of oppressed and downtrodden peaceful individuals, but an armed regiment of fanatics, members of the general population, family, and most notably, nobility. Jesus had the lineage, means and intent to overthrow the Jewish authorities, claiming a stewardship he and many others saw as rightfully his.

These Gospels, we are led to believe, are the words and deeds of common fishermen, led by the son of an illiterate carpenter. Men of toil, not words, simple earthy folk risking their lives each day trying to eke out a meagre existence. Nothing could be further from the truth; the inner sanctum of chosen Apostles was drawn from a reservoir of at least seventy amply armed advocates of Jesus' ministry.

Jesus demanded that his followers are obligated to "sell his garmet"[21] and carry a "sword."[22] As one who came "not to send peace,"[23] some have suggested this armed group of revolutionaries were preparing to carry out a dynastic and political coup-de-tat with Jesus as the heir-apparent to the throne.

The allegation of a coup-de-tat may have some substance. If revolutionaries of today were to saunter into the outer sanctum of the Vatican, and then literally trash the place, demanding they release their untold billions to assist the oppressed, surely the authorities would immediately react. Such wanton vandalism would result in a vigorous physical response, which would see the offender firmly dealt with.

Nearly two thousand years ago a young revolutionary supposedly set such a precedent, yet not one word or act was offered as a token response. Apparently all allocated the sacred task of protecting the sanctity of the temple and its surrounds stood back mouth agape, transfixed and impotent. Many traditional Christians advocate such a stance. Other scholars, such as Ian Jones, depict a different and far more consistent scenario.

Jones saw this as the defining moment in an attempted revolution. He suggested not just the outer surrounds, but the temple itself was taken by force. Initially the revolutionary Nazarene and his troops were successful and held the temple for three days. Once the insurrection wavered, Jesus fled and his crucifixion was now set in stone. According to Jones, those in control had no other option. They had to act now or wait for Jesus to regather his followers to return once again to depose them.

The roll call of the chosen apostles only accentuates the real intent behind the burgeoning assembly of dynastic representatives. Many of these women and men were highly connected individuals who saw the Arab Herod and the dynasty that followed, as foreign pretenders who married into the throne that rightly sat with the tribe Jesus now led.

Laurence Gardner has a somewhat unusual take on the make-up of Jesus' closest disciples. He believes Thomas was also called Crown Prince Phillip, as he was Herod's son. Herod divorced Thomas' mother after she attempted to assassinate him. Judas was a warlord and leader of a *Zealot* group, and the word Iscariot means a curved dagger. Bartholomew was the chief of the *Proselytes* (a group of Gentile converts) and a leading member of the *Therapeutate* (an Egyptian healing society), while Thaddaeus was the leader of this elite group of healers and radical philosophers. Mary's father was a high priest and Mary Salome was highly educated, in fact nearly all the women that followed Jesus were from the upper levels of society.

Each Apostle seems to carry an assortment of appendages; Levi was also known as Matthew, Thomas was called Didymus, Crown Prince Phillip and the twin, Simon Magus was also Simon Zebedee, Simon the Zealot was possibly Lazarus, James and John were also referred to as sons of Zebedee and Boanerges (thunder) and so the roll call of aliases continues. Common folk were never afforded such extravagances, this is a privilege afforded to those of higher class. All but two of the inner group of Apostles were drawn from the upper echelons of society. Only two of the elite twelve were without the education and pedigree such a birthright demands, Andrew and Peter.

These are the same two protagonists in the *Gospel of Mary* who vociferously deny Mary's wisdom. The reason was patently obvious, the symbolism and the profound depth of her wisdom she revealed to the Apostles, was beyond the grasp of their collective intellect.

One must be careful not to slate all the blame on the shoulders of Andrew and Peter, as they are more a product of those times than any individual failings. Deprived of education and drawn from the general population, their response was no more than what would be expected. Andrew obviously mellows, but Peter's sexism does not and once he enlists Paul, whose misogyny surpasses his mentor's, the shortcomings and gender bias they champion became immortalised in chapter, verse and psalm.

Andrew and Peter gave the group a greater breadth and appeal and, of course, a variety of opinions. Jesus' diplomacy kept the divisions in wisdom and talents under check, yet his death was both a portent and precursor. Jesus' oft stated intention to divide every family was an integral component of his own household. Upon his death, disunity was almost immediate, as the Apostles splintered into two philosophical camps.

The *Book of Kells* is an eighth century Christian manuscript and also an ornate piece of intricate artistry of the highest order, which is divided into four equal sections. The first quarter contains events, parables, narratives etc. drawn from the four Gospels that are in complete accord with each other, the second section details events that are sourced from three Gospels, the third segment contains versions found in two Gospels, and the last quarter supplies uncorroborated information supplied in only one Gospel.

Strangely enough, the final quarter appears to contain a high proportion of the most commonly known areas of the scriptures. It would seem one person's absolute truth is another person's one quarter of a question mark. Combined, these gospels ask as many questions as they answer.

If we cannot get any consensus on one of the most basic truths of Traditional Christianity relating to how Jesus left, or, if indeed he did leave, what then can we assert is the Gospel Truth?

The appropriate texts found within Jesus' Gnostic teachings can resolve all of these conundrums so simply, he is already a spirit, as we all are when we cross over after each earthly existence. With that simple truth as a foundation, all of these accounts relating to death, no longer become inconsistent and implausible. All that is really needed is a clear and concise understanding of what occurs after we die, everything else is of secondary importance.

Chapter 3
The Recurring Sentence

I look at moon. It tell me story, like stars. Moon . . . moon is man. He said 'These people will die, but they'll come back . . . like I do. They'll come back to the earth again.' Native Cat said 'No, they will be dead and never come back.' Everyone jump on him and kill him. They burn him so he got plenty spots. Spots from hot coals.
So Moon say again, 'Man will come back, like I come back each time. He'll come back to earth.'"[1] (Bill Neidjie)

Rebirth occurs within heaven and earth; it is a process and an evolution. The task can not be accomplished in a hurry. As the "Moon" reminds Bill, his souls' evolution is dependent upon coming "back, like I come back each time." We "come back to earth," cast into flesh and bone on a revolving journey of discovery. Our only choice is simple; we are given choices, while everything else is in God's hands.

The popular Christian view seems to place all aspirants here for one relatively brief appearance, regardless of caste, status or plight, followed by eternal judgement of our worth made by Peter. We then exist in an everlasting abode of either heaven or hell. To do what?

The *New Testament* offers numerous passages, which challenge this widely accepted oversimplification. A synoptic text such as *Matthew* relates a fairly literal discourse by the Saviour, appearing to openly contest this belief in one earthly appearance.

> But I say unto you, That Elias is come already, and they knew him not, but have done unto him whatsoever they listed. Likewise shall also the Son of man suffer of them.
> Then the disciples understood that he spake unto them of John the Baptist.[2]

This esoteric revelation is not an isolated event; perhaps Matthew's talents extend into the field of clairvoyance. He may have foreseen the one mention in each Gospel approach, would not appease the appetite of future apologists of orthodoxy like Edwin Yamauchi. Perhaps Matthew's desire to make this so literal, explains why the same issues are raised in (*Matthew*: 11:12-11:15), where John and Elias are portrayed as one homogenous entity. He completes this revelation by asking for those with "ears" to understand, a trademark appendage the Saviour used to emphasise the more important sayings.

Both sets of verses appear to be saying the same thing. Whether it is Elias and John or John and Elias, it is, and they are, all the same. As their souls move through lifetimes they select new bodies, but their Spirit never changes. Despite their greatness, they were not immaculately conceived, and nor are they incarnate angels. They are and were made of common flesh and bone, just as we are. Whatever Elias and John can do so too can we, and returning into a newly designed body over numerous lifetimes is apparently an integral part of life. The same rules apply here, this was the secret teaching the "disciples understood."

Regardless, many traditional Christian scholars would object, insisting the verse is symbolic. Yet Matthew's account seems so literal, as the author chose to use specific names. If the segment is symbolic, then determining what is literal throughout the rest of the Gospel could become an exercise in personal preferences.

An esoteric interpretation of this scripture leaves no such quandary. It has no need to be pondered over. We are all stuck here until we get it right. We have been cast down onto this prison until we turn again. This truth is, in essence, one of the complementary secrets alluded to in the *New Testament*, and expanded upon in some of Jesus' Gnostic scriptures. Both speak of the same mystery; the role of the appropriate esoteric scriptures is to develop these truths.

Aboriginal *Dreaming* also acknowledges this casting down as an integral part of daily living. In many Aboriginal tribes of the past, there was a belief that men had no input into the actual moment of conception. The timing was the exclusive domain of the Ancestral Spirits and women. The male was denied the role of creator and became more a secondary facilitator than an active agent; his concern was focussed upon keeping the tribe safe and healthy. Their Creators decided when the time was ripe for another soul to be cast down yet again.

The *Dreaming* story about the Moon and Native Cat Bill shared with his tribe was a lesson and his epitaph. Every time the "Native Cat" is seen, the spots it has been cursed with serve as a warning for all to never question ancestral truths. The "Moon," as Bill pointed out, "is man" and share a common fate; both come for a period of time and appear to vanish. The moon (man) rises (lives), then vanishes (dies) but reappears again (reincarnates) and so the cycle repeats itself.

This cycle of birth and rebirth is not limited to one particular species of primate, but includes the animate and inanimate. Bill was aware how important it was to understand death, and life, and how it continues "each time."

Bill knew of his soul's revolving destination, the truth, in his eyes, is set in rock, root and star.

Stone e never move. Rock e don't move round, e got to stay for ever and ever. E'll be there million million . . . star. Because e stay e never move. Tree e follow you and me, he'll be dead behind us but next one he'll come. Same people. Aborigine the same. We'll be dead but next one, kid, he'll be born. Same this tree. Star he'll stay for ever and ever.[3]

The following selection of ten Gnostic writings found within the *Nag Hammadi* jar are concerned with the same theme, but approach it from a variety of differing perspectives. The Gnostic scriptures contradict each other in many respects, especially so when dealing with matters of the flesh, but this seems to be the one area were there is a commonality existing throughout all the divergent forms of Gnostic philosophy. The passages selected are merely an indicative sampling, there are many more to chose from.

Apocalypse of Paul (V,2) "Bring witnesses! Let them show you in what body I committed lawless deeds . . . the soul had been cast down went to a body which had been prepared for it."[4]

Dialogue of the Saviour (III,5) "Matthew said, "Why do we not rest at once?" Jesus said, "When you lay down these burdens . . . when you abandon the works which will not be able to follow you!"[5]

The *Exegesis of the Soul* (II,6) "If you return and sigh, then you will be saved and will know where you were when you trusted in what is empty."[6]

The *Book of Thomas the Contender* (II,7) "Watch and pray that you not come to be in the flesh, but rather that you come forth from the bondage of the bitterness of this life. And as you pray, you will find rest, for you have left behind the suffering and the disgrace."[7]

Apocrophyon of John (II,*1*, III,*1*, IV,*1* and BG 8502,2) "And after it comes out of the body . . . they bind it with chains and cast it into prison and consort with it until it is liberated from the forgetfulness and acquires knowledge. . .It is not again cast into another flesh."[8]

The *Book of Thomas the Contender* (II,7) "Thomas spoke, saying, "Lord, why does this visible light that shines on behalf of men rise and set? The saviour said, "O blessed Thomas, of course this visible light shines on your behalf-not in order that you remain here, but rather that you might come forth."[9]

Zostrionios (VIII,*1*) "Release yourselves and that which has bound you will be dissolved."[10]

Interpretation of Knowledge (XI,*1*) "That we might escape the disgrace of the carcass and be regenerated."[11]

Authoritative Teaching (VI,3) "But these— the ones who are ignorant . . . nor do they inquire about their dwelling—place which exists in rest."[12]

Tripartate Tractate (1,5) "It was only for certain periods and times which they were entrusted with power . . . continuing on their behalf until all come into life and leave life, while their bodies remain on Earth, serving all their sins sharing with their sufferings."[13]

Collectively, these verses must give some credence to the miniscule possibility that *Matthew* (17:12) was being intentionally literal. The Saviour used proper nouns in an attempt to add more clarity to what does seem a fairly unambiguous message. However, many church authorities and biblical scholars have contrary viewpoints; it just has to be symbolic. There is no other alternative, and since the chosen authorities believe they speak on behalf of God they must be right, as such clarity of vision and perfection has existed within church-walls since the time of Clement of Alexandria.

Infallibility and an everlasting understanding of God's master plan . . . these are the certainties the Vatican and many churches offer their congregations. Pristine absolutes encased within an ecclesiastical structure of moral certitude can lead no-one astray. Here seekers will find the endorsed scriptures sanctified by proxy, led by an approved translator where the erratic Gnostic might becomes an unchallengeable orthodox will.

Critics of Gnostic thinkers claim their might, if, and gnosis, is predicated around so many equivocations, qualifications and contradictory texts, whereas the ordained Catholic Church knows all. These secret teachings, they say, offer nothing that can be set in concrete. All Gnosticism seems to offer are possibilities; their offerings include "when, might, maybe, if, watch, might, what, until and while" [these modifiers came from the earlier ten quotes]. Equivocations are rife, but they seem unable to create any certainty.

The Catholic Church has one primary function: to provide life's answers. Questions are an irrelevance and are no longer required, simply because all truths reside within their hallowed walls. All other sects and creeds are, by comparison, in error and must be turned away from sin so that all who have fallen can see their light.

These critiques relating to Gnosticism's lack of structure and knowledge of absolute truths are not unfounded. This nebulous mystical gnosis has its customised metamorphosis moderated by choice and potential. This rest, this rebirth or reincarnation, has one major qualification; rebirth is both the process and consequence. The process ties us again and again to the prison, the flesh where the individual consequences of our plight or potential liberation are purely matters of personal choice.

Where can these lessons of death and life be earned and learnt? Many would insist after one mortal life on this planet, the learning and metamorphosis of the imperfect continues while in Heaven. Yet isn't this the only place in the cosmos where the meaning of life is revealed and every question vanishes into an ethereal haze? Such a proposal would be analogous to sitting for a University Entrance Exam in a hall where every answer is highlighted and underlined in advance, and will illuminate nothing of merit. Under these provisos each candidate is compelled to score a perfect grade. As a passive participant, all is given and laid out in front of you. There is no other way the soul could assess its worth and merit, unless there is a divine standard to exist in then contrast your karma against. The infallible norm, the place of the father, resides within absolute truth. There is nothing to be learnt in paradise but bliss. There is no avenue to make personal progress when every road is signposted in advance. It would appear that after one brief material apparition on Earth, our time to make personal discoveries and all forms of self-development come to a cessation for eternity.

Purely for the sake of being balanced and even handed, if one accepts the Orthodox version of one life on the planet, then, off to the after-life forever as a valid theory, it seems to be blighted with an inherent inconsistency. These irregularities challenge the credentials and omnipotent wisdom of any Creator. To accept this concept as an incontestable truth, one also has to admit our Creator is illogical and uncaring. If the concept of time is linear, not circular, then whether it is one minute, one year or one decade, life and death is an outrage of the highest order.

One minute . . . a child is born riddled with a variety of complications. The medical staff are powerless to do anymore other than observe, as the doomed infant valiantly struggles to draw breath. Within sixty seconds of the baby beginning its life, it is lost.

This child departs then moves onwards to be judged by Peter at the Gates of Heaven. Awarding worth and assessment will be a demanding task. Not one independent word or deed was initiated by this soul. It contributed nothing, and its only achievement was to draw half a dozen desperate gasps, cause distress for others and then expire. Many claim such innocent souls receive God's grace, moving directly into the high celestial abode. If so, some may query the motives behind this special blessing, unsure of what such immature souls did to earn a divinely assisted passage. With absolutely nothing as a yardstick to measure by, and with one innings where the batsman was cleaned bowled first ball without even offering a shot to the sum total of the soul's endeavour, assessing the worth of the soul is fraught with difficulty. We believe grace has to be earned, never expected or requested. Moreover there was no point in that individual soul turning up, since the infant's debut on the planet entitles it to nothing of consequence except a rapid departure.

Many question whether there was any value or purpose in this infant's one fleeting appearance. The individual has gained nothing from its sixty seconds of mortal life. Our deeds and words must create the legacy we are judged upon. Some may say, and often do, that God isn't fair, as it is the only logical explanation they can conceive. Many despair, asking why the infant was never given a chance, an opportunity to develop their innate talents.

Relax, respond some of the traditional spokesmen; God's grace will receive all infants in heaven. If so, they passed this test without even bothering to place their name on the examination papers. That just isn't fair! The rest of us have to struggle to survive; dealing with mortgages, lack of food and water, poverty, racism, jealousy, anger, greed, utter stupidity, temptation, environmental degradation and a multitude of injustices which plague the planet. These fallen infants came, had an extremely brief look around and strolled through the front doors of Heaven.

A lot of us aren't even sure there is a door to heaven or any other celestial destination. Perfection gained through non-participation and ignorance seems an unfair way to progress. Two rules exist here, for some all you have to do is nothing beyond dying to reach heaven, while others are compelled to experience a lifetime of angst. Yet when their judgments are meted out, with all the good and bad deeds, thoughts and words of an individual's last lifetime are scrupulously assessed, another soul can be automatically admitted after doing nothing except crossing over within seconds of coming into mortal existence.

One year . . . a baby in Dafur is born in the middle of a severe famine. Every minute of the infant's wretched life is predicated around a solitary thought, food. Nothing else counts, it never could, as no-one can seek out spiritual truths with an empty growling belly. If your body is constantly craving sustenance, the soul is mute. A meal a day is a blessing and most days are a curse. Everything past that is, at best, a blur.

Slowly, as the months drag on, the infant's eyes begin to glaze over, the stomach gradually swells and distends, and, as every day passes the zest for life dulls. Barely able to talk or crawl, this emaciated babe can take no more. One year after birth the infant is gone, apparently never to grace the material world again.

What noble deeds and worthy independent thoughts did the child concoct? None of any substance, every agonising day was a variation on the same serving of starvation and dread. With no intelligent acts or words to pass judgment upon, it would seem this child also automatically passes through the Gates of Heaven. If not, then it is grossly unfair on the individual. If the child is admitted with nothing to offer, then it is manifestly unjust for those who are stuck here and face a much longer struggle.

One decade . . . Mum and Dad are addicted to heroin and the child was born with a tailor-made habitual craving. This young soul was raised in a household where the parents, the principal role models, had a lifestyle exclusively revolving around doing anything that could facilitate the acquisition of their next hit. Everything else, including the welfare of their child, was of secondary importance.

The child's formative years were surrounded by crime and desperation. Wherever the infant looked there was nothing but a desperate struggle, where money and drugs rule every roost. By the age of nine the young juvenile was dealing, in reality, there never was anything else on offer. The child's attendance at school dramatically suffered and grades and marks plummeted. With no hint of succour or support to lean upon, this waif inevitably follows in the footsteps of the parents whose role was to supposedly nurture and educate. At the age of ten the young soul was shot dead in a gang dispute over turf and the guardianship of dealing outlets.

Within these ten years we have words, deeds and most certainly, action. The young candidate did sit for the test, and as abridged as it was, surely enough was done to warrant a grade. Peter is obliged to award the wayward sinner an F, with an eternity of damnation the everlasting grade.

It is a repeat episode; the despair that overwhelmed the child on earth is to be repeated ad-nauseam in the afterlife. However in reality what chance did the infant ever have? It seems this child was deprived the luxury of a deathbed confession, where many can recant and turn again. Many of us mature as we age, learning the error of our errant ways. This young person was apparently denied all of these opportunities to develop and slowly mature, as many slowly see the error of her or his past and then lead an exemplary life.

Inequities of this type are not isolated events, but are the norm. There are far more people living in poverty than those who have the privilege to experience a life of luxury. It appears the entire population is involved in a compulsory global one hundred-metre sprint. A few of us are permitted by the officials to begin their race fifty metres ahead of the starting blocks, while others do not have enough money to pay the price of admission to watch the race.

Three miserable lives, and in each case the judgment appears to be fatally flawed. Two did less than nothing yet gained automatic entry. The third child did plenty, yet the culprits in the young sinner's case who are the major cause of the anguish this young sinner experienced, should bear most of the responsibility. Society and the parents abandoned their duties and left the young soul totally to his or her devices. Yet it appears the person least responsible is bearing all the grief and blame forever, when others who shamefully neglected the child from the moment of birth are the real offenders.

If we are re-born time after time, then there will be plenty of time after time to redress the discrepancy. If we only granted one mortal life, there exists an inherent inconsistency, because until all get an invitation to compete in this race on equal terms, the race marshal is being grossly unjust.

Gnosticism recognises and addresses this hypocrisy, a soul must earn its right of passage, as no-one here gets an "award for being alive."[14] Until then, we are all bound by the same stringent tenancy and occupancy by-laws, in that all keep returning to the same abode until their spiritual rent and bond is fully paid up.

This acceptance of the recurring sentence is the pivotal element that binds all the diverse forms of Gnosticism and many other esoteric religions (and non-esoteric religions like Buddhism and Hinduism), yet paradoxically, is never overtly stated in specific terms in any scripture. It is possible any sceptic or defender of orthodoxy could comfortably reinterpret all ten quotes given earlier and claim alternate symbolic meanings. The reality is and was, reincarnation was such a self-evident truth, and was as much a part of daily life and death as breathing and sleeping. To implicitly assert and record the obvious would a pointless gesture, as all knew there was only one path. It was for this reason, "Gnosticism does not emphasise the doctrine of reincarnation prominently, but it is implicitly understood in most Gnostic teachings that those who have not made effective contact with their transcendental origins while they were in embodiment would have to return into the sorrowful condition of earthly life."[15]

Every Gnostic disciple knew rebirth is being cast down into the flesh for what may seem an eternity with one carrot dangling at the end of an abyss, rebirth. This path necessitates being *borne* to a new parent, one that never dies; God. For this to occur we must abandon any parent who is also cast into the material plane and this, almost invariably, requires many incarnations.

If any student needs affirmation of this ancient secret truth, the Aboriginal Dreaming provides an identical view of the afterlife. Some may claim the similarity is purely co-incidental, and perhaps they are right, but the continuous repetition of shared beliefs and approaches do create a strong circumstantial case.

Throughout the continent nearly every tribe felt the koala was a sacred animal and should not be eaten or harmed (an exception existed with one clan within the *Gumilaroi* nation). Many *Dreaming* stories tell of the koalas carrying the returning souls of infants placed there by their Ancestral Spirits. The unborn souls wait for the correct time to enter the mother's womb. If a clan member was to harm or kill the marsupial, their tribal kin are denied access to be reborn back into their tribal estate for some considerable time. To even annoy a koala (unborn clan member) is a very serious matter and the punishment would be very severe, as one should never meddle in the affairs of the Spirits or offend your returning kin.

Regardless of what Gnosticism and *Dreaming* stories allege, many orthodox Christians deny their authenticity, in their eyes one life on Earth is all we get. The supposed inconsistencies the unfaithful point to can be refashioned into an allegory, or perhaps a metaphor. If they deftly insert some symbolism, a simile or two, and all of these words become a familiar and reassuring sea of semantics that only the officially sanctified guide can navigate. All the while their truth "lays curled up on the floor."[16]

The contradictions lead to one conclusion, someone has got it wrong. There are two paths available in the after-life, but one has officially been condemned as an affront to God. If the notion of complementary scriptures is sacrilegious as the Vatican ordains, one is forced to compare and contrast, choose one option and deny the other.

All Popes are subject to many afflictions and one, apparently, is the most enigmatic of all maladies, papal infallibility. Therefore all of these differing forms of Gnosticism are blasphemies, an affront to God's dearest earth-bound representative and must be wrong. Apparently everything hidden inside the jar is inspired by evil intent, intended to subvert and lead the good astray. Orthodoxy seems hell-bent on forcing a divide that should never be. Denying the validity of the Gnostic belief in reincarnation, forces the seeker to choose between two books which essentially tell the same story.

The misunderstandings over the true nature of rebirth crystallises the diverging interpretations of the esoteric and exoteric scriptures and the need to finally address the realities as they are, not as some would prefer.

NB: Rebirth / Reincarnation. In many Western eyes these terms are synonymous and, as such, they are presented as being the same thing. However, there is a marked difference and was one of the major areas of philosophical dispute between Buddhism and Hinduism; but for the sake of convenience they are presented as being similar.

Chapter 4
The Gnostic Scriptures of Jesus

(The Gospel of Thomas VERSE 62): Jesus said, *"I disclose my mysteries to those who are worthy of my mysteries. Do not let your left hand know what your right hand is doing."*[1]

Some commentators find fault with Gnosticism's apparent austerity, suggesting it is characterised by a philosophy that is "too life defying and, seeing the world as the creation of the demi-urge, naturally devalues it."[2] Many suggest this esoteric approach demands a life of abstinence and the denial of any of life's pleasures or indulgences. There are texts found within the jar at Nag Hammadi that most assuredly fall into this category, but other Gnostic scriptures do not contain any reference to a demi-urge or living the life of a fanatic or recluse.

Many critics and supposed adherents of Gnosticism confuse the casting down into the flesh and the place where this occurs, as deserving of equal contempt. Though many critics of Gnosticism consider this an integral part of that system of belief, they are mistaken. Where we are cast (Earth) is God's creation and kingdom. Incarnation was never intended to be a penance or penalty but merely an opportunity to be grasped or wasted, nor was material life to be ignored or the earth mistreated. To admire a cascading waterfall is an acknowledgement of God's omnipotence; the rocks and water should never be regarded as a materialisation of random molecules to be dismissed as a transitory event of no spiritual significance. The truth is that everyone and everything is an integral part of God's design and can only be beneficial if interaction and assessment of its worth occurs. Monasticism and pious vows of denial have no role in any Creator's plan, and have much more to do with an individual's inability to cope with life.

The body a soul is allotted each life is an entirely different matter. It is undeniable there exists a shadow that can deceive the soul, but to treat this physical carriage as a burden and life as an imposition was never God's initiative or an element of the *Dreaming*. If Jesus repeatedly advises any seeker able to understand that the kingdom is within and before us, then both the location and the vehicle we are given to seek out this kingdom (the body) should neither be shunned nor abused, but treasured.

Perhaps some insight can be gained through examining three of Jesus' Gnostic scriptures, which we believe accurately reflect the ancient Aboriginal inspiration that lay behind all mystical philosophies, in finer detail.

Commentaries and critiques of the endorsed four Gospels abound, very few people in the west are unaware of the *Bible*, and most know of a smidgen of its contents. As for the Gnostic codices, almost all of the general public are only vaguely, if at all, aware of their existence, let alone what lay within. The obvious inconsistencies within the texts found at Nag Hammadi, particularly so when dealing with issues relating to the material world, only add to the confusion. Then to compound the difficulties many have, the meagre reservoir of reliable information is spread amongst the Internet, popular songs, books, films, *New Age* media and celebrities. But rarely, if ever, does any orthodox religious authority or spokesperson offer anything beyond a blanket denial of every Gnostic scripture's legitimacy.

The three Gnostic Gospels we feel are appropriate and in keeping with the sentiments expressed in the *Dreaming* are the *Gospel of Thomas*, the *Gospel of Mary* and *Dialogue of the Saviour* (and some complementary sources). For each of the Gospels we have selected a different form of analysis, the method of enquiry was chosen in deference to the form and condition of each text.

The *Gospel of Thomas* presents a verbatim account of Jesus' sayings, introducing the seeker to the unfathomable uncertainties of purpose and existence. We shall attempt to offer personal interpretations of what each individual saying could mean. When appropriate, as is nearly always the case, we will contrast these words against the wisdom of the great Aboriginal philosopher, *Gagadu* Elder, and one of the custodians of Kakadu National Park, Big Bill Neidjie.

The *Gospel of Mary* must be investigated as a homogenous entity and contrasted against some myths. It highlights the genesis of a philosophical and gender divide that has damaged Christianity.

The *Dialogue of the Saviour*, due to a variety of settings and the decaying physical condition of the text, has about forty verses that can be examined in detail. The balance is too fragmentary to assert anything more than possibilities. These accounts seem to establish Mary's superior status and place her well above the station of the male followers. Other esoteric scriptures and legends will be used to establish the validity of such a claim.

The *Gospel of Thomas* is the most widely known, researched and disputed of all of the Gnostic scriptures found in the Nag Hammadi jar. It was dated at around 50-70 A.D. by both Robinson and Koester, who feel it is younger than the four accepted Gospels. Koester was insistent that "if one considers the form and wording of the individual sayings in comparison with the form in which they are preserved in the New Testament. The Gospel of Thomas almost always appears to have preserved a more original form of the traditional saying . . . or presents versions which are independently based on more original forms."[3]

Chapter 4: The Gnostic Scriptures of Jesus

Professor J.R. Porter, a traditional biblical scholar, is not an advocate of Gnostic philosophies and advised any who believe the *Gospel of Thomas* deserving of special consideration, "caution is necessary before such examples in Thomas are accepted as the 'authentic' teaching of Jesus."[4] The problem Porter faced when reviewing the *Gospel of Thomas*, is that his interpretation of the text actually reinforces Koester's analysis. By also proposing the *Gospel of Thomas* text is more authentic, and presenting quite a deal of convincing evidence to support his suggestion, Porter immediately calls into question the reasons why he is so cautious and dismissive of this text. The contradictory nature of Porter's response is highlighted by the admission the *Gospel of Thomas* exhibits all the characteristics of "Jesus' original teaching."[5] His review of this gospel compelled him to conclude that it "contains genuine sayings of Jesus not found elsewhere but also preserves some of his words in a simpler and more authentic form than that found in the canonical gospels."[6] In what could only add to Porter's unease and atmosphere of confusion, he had to agree "Thomas includes several of Jesus' parables, but they almost always lack any of the interpretative elements found in the canonical gospels."[7]

As would be expected, some traditional academics have proposed dates of up to AD 150. are far more acceptable. However, Harvard biblical scholar G.W. McCrae, claims the majority of academics are in accord with Koester and Robinson's belief in an earlier date for the creation of *The Gospel of Thomas*.

The trials and tribulations of the disciples are subject to the decay of time, amendments and fallibility of human memory. The truth becomes even more difficult when attempting to keep track of Jesus' Gnostic devotees. Much has been destroyed and even more has been remodelled, but there is enough that managed to slip through the censor's fingers to be able to reconstruct the broadest of images.

In Syria some Christians insist Thomas is the actual twin brother of Jesus. Within India, the *Thomasian* nuns still perform dances made in honour of the Apostle and their founding father, Didymus Judas Thomas.

When the Portuguese attacked and pillaged the Thomasian churches on the lower west coast of India, they thought they had destroyed every remnant of this heretical outrage. However, palm scriptures recording Thomas' words were retained, as were some songs and dances. He is supposed to have died between 52-54 A.D. in India, and may have been there for about twelve years after his stay in Syria. Anything past these truths may have a germ of truth within. There are a few commentators who dismiss all of these claims as fiction, denying he left Syria.

Thomas is unlike any scripture in either set of books. It claims to exclusively contain the words of Christ. There is no narrative, miracle or parable to consider; just one hundred and fourteen sayings directly attributed to Jesus. Some have parallels to the *New Testament* Gospels, but many more do not. It is the flagship of Jesus' Gnosticism and, unlike many of the other reclaimed texts, is almost intact. Its character is extremely challenging and certainly without precedent.

There are some central themes that recur throughout the Sayings.
- Of all the Gnostic texts, it is one of the most mystical and introspective, and parallels the sentiments expressed in many Pantheist religions, in particular the *Dreaming*. This similarity is unusual as this type of primal Earth worship is almost exclusively associated with hunter-gatherer societies. It emphasises the divide between the esoteric and exoteric, particularly so when dealing with the ownership of gnosis. This approach through personal endeavour appealed to John Lennon, who said "it seems to me that the only true Christians were the Gnostics, who believe in self knowledge, becoming Christ themselves."[8]
- The *non-customs*; no prayer, no fasting, not giving alms, abandoning all marginal excess cash, the non-admission of buyers and merchants entering the places of my father, and jettisoning the ritual of circumcision, had all orthodox religious sects deeply concerned.
- As discussed earlier, Thomas has much to say when it comes to finding the Kingdom of Heaven.
- Mary and sexuality; these sayings should be analysed with Verse 106 as a measuring stick. Jesus said, "When you make the two one, you will become the sons of man, and when you say, 'Mountain move away,' it will move away."[9]
- In summation, when reading these scriptures read it as Jesus suggests, as would a traditional Aboriginal person, and become "passers-by."[10]

Gospel of Mary has large sections of the text either missing or damaged, this occurred through circumstance or design. The scripture highlights the esoteric nature of Mary's wisdom and knowledge, and the diversity of expertise and understanding amongst the male Apostles. There is a general degree of uncertainty throughout much of the text; not only are there numerous gaps, but it also has two endings.

An alternative scenario details Matthew storming off in utter disgust refusing to even speak again to any of the revered male Apostles until death. This is, most assuredly, a disturbing turn of events Christianity would have great difficulty explaining. Perhaps this concern may have inspired future editors to claim some poetic licence and revise her words and Matthew's actions into something far more accommodating to male sensibilities.

The text accentuates the major issue that lead to the splintering of the Christian movement. Peter's hatred of Mary appears in a variety of Gnostic accounts and is certainly present in this text.

The *Dialogue of the Saviour* is either a fabrication or testimony to Mary's esteem and regard. She is instigating and expanding upon all manner of esoteric topics, mainly for the benefit of Thomas and Matthew. Time after time Jesus encourages and commends her complete understanding. As one who knows all, it would appear Mary's allocated role was ordained by Jesus to be the "woman who understood completely." These assertions will be substantiated with comparisons to a variety of other introspective scriptures and accounts, including *Pistis Sophia, Greater Questions of Mary Magdalene* and *The Golden Legend.*

Chapter 5
The Gospel of Thomas

(Gospel of Thomas, Verse 114.) *Simon Peter said to them, "Let Mary leave us, for women are not worthy of life."*[1]

(VERSE 3)
Jesus said, "If your leaders you say to you, 'Look, the kingdom is in heaven,' then the birds of heaven will precede you. If they say to you, 'It is in the sea,' then the fish will precede you. Rather, the kingdom is inside you and it is outside you."
"When you know yourselves, then you will be known, and you will understand that you are children of the living father. But if you do not know yourselves, then you dwell in poverty, and you are poverty."[2]

If "the kingdom is inside you, and it is outside you," how does this location differ from "split a piece of wood . . ."[3] or finding Spirits alive within the land? The "kingdom" is all around us, we interpret the saying to refer to the pristine creations of God we call Nature. According to Jesus, heaven is not in the sky, the sea nor even the ethereal paradise. The kingdom they seek can be found in all places equally.

Jesus injects an introspective element into the equation by reminding us the "heaven" we seek is here. It doesn't exist in some obscure destination, but sits literally all around us. No blessed building or any human construction is touted as the sole residence of God's authority, if anything the opposite is indicated.

Our "leaders" are not to be listened to; it appears whatever predictions those in power or authority offer will be preceded "by the fish" or "the birds of heaven." The question that arises, relates to where the kingdom can be found. The answer is everywhere rather than any specific place; Jesus made that very clear.

Jesus asks us to approach the task of locating heaven as would every traditional Aboriginal person. Every step you take is with God's grace, and everywhere your foot is placed has God's face.

If no authority or leader is to be trusted, where does one look? The problem is many who control are afflicted with tunnel vision, which ultimately leads to a loss of peripheral vision. A book can assist marginally, but the responsibility sits squarely on the shoulders of the seeker. Jesus was adamant; each life is ultimately a personal quest and advised all, "if you do not know yourselves, then you will dwell in poverty."

Big Bill Neidjie, the revered Aboriginal Elder of the *Gagadu* tribe, agrees, but warns us the eyes will provide no assistance when involved in such an esoteric pursuit. Finding the Spirits is as easy as feeling it "with my body, with my blood. Feeling all these trees . . . You can look, but feeling . . . that make you . . . Out there in open space."[4] In Bill Neidjie's eyes empathy and intuition is all that is required, and is available for any prepared to allow the soul to accept its' anointed role. Our quest is to understand what this "feeling" is, then realise that once this link is established, it is this interconnectedness "that make you."[5] Once this mystical union is formed, "while you sleeping you dream something. Tree and grass same thing. They grow with your body, with your feeling."[6]

(VERSE 6)
His followers asked him and said to him, "Do you want us to fast? How should we pray? Should we give to charity? What diet should we observe?"
Jesus said, "Do not lie, and do not do what you hate, because all things are disclosed before heaven. For there is nothing hidden that will not be revealed, and there is nothing covered that will remain undisclosed."[7]

The Apostles inquire about the validity of fasting, diet, alms and prayer. These concerns relating to doctrines and ritual are understandable, but only a necessity if creating an institution that formalises his teachings. Further on, Jesus condemns such acts of faith as sinful, so it is patently obvious he has no interest in institutionalising his teachings.

Traditional Aboriginal spirituality was entirely oral, as there was never a sacred book or human construction to revere. Therefore every word uttered must be given due consideration. Every clan member was asked to accept the Law and respect the Spirit's gifts. In most societies there was no word for lying, and if you didn't share and help, all would surely perish. Perhaps the traditional Aboriginal lifestyle enforced this sharing, some may have resented it, but that was all that was available. The lifestyle was centred around accepting the communal good as being sacrosanct, under such conditions concocting a "lie" or wilfully harming others by doing something you "hate" was against their Ancestral Law, and is also what Jesus asked his Apostles to abstain from.

The Aboriginal people knew a malicious deed could never be concealed; the Spirits reside everywhere and would immediately know. Signs will immediately appear, a Wag Tail or totem animal would alert an Elder or even worse, the offended Spirit may take matters into their hands. Each person knew there was "nothing hidden that will not be revealed."

Big Bill Neidjie when teaching tribal kids, was concerned when they dug a hole to find yams, it was left uncovered. "'Who leave that hole? Cover him up.' They say 'We forget.' I tell them 'You leaving that hole . . . you killing yam.

You killing yourself."[8] Bill is fully aware nothing they do is hidden from the Spirits, and unless such selfish behaviour is remedied, the individual and clan will certainly suffer. He knows while the "tree same as me,"[9] there can be no secrets or lies hidden from the scrutiny of the Creation Spirits.

Jesus asks them to be truthful and act with the good of others in their heart; this is all he seeks. There is no structure or form outside personal integrity, when acts of abstinence or charity count for nothing. Esoteric sentiments like these upset many religious authorities and doctrines.

> (VERSE 13)
> Jesus said to his followers, "Compare me to something and tell me what I am like."
> Simon Peter said to him, "You are like a just messenger."
> Matthew said to him, "You are like a wise philosopher."
> Thomas said to him, "Teacher, my mouth is utterly unable to say what you are like."
> Jesus said, "I am not your teacher. Because you have drunk, you have become intoxicated from the bubbling spring that I have tended."
> And he took him, and withdrew, and spoke three sayings to him.
> When Thomas came back to his friends, they asked him, "What did Jesus say to you?"
> Thomas said to them, "If I tell you one of the sayings he spoke to me, you will pick up rocks and stone me, and fire will come from the rocks and consume you."[10]

Verse 13 seems very similar to the Synoptic accounts (*Matthew* 16:13-23, *Mark* 8:27-33 and *Luke* 9:18-22) of the journey on the road to Caesarea, Philippi, where Peter was commended as the de-facto leader of the Apostles. After comparing descriptions, noting John's non-corroborative silence on this issue and the real possibility of semantic misinterpretation, it does become difficult when assessing which male Apostle received the Lord's special blessing.

If whatever Thomas may have learnt was of such magnitude it could cause Matthew and Peter's death, this seems to separate these disciples in relation to esoteric matters. It would appear there are two types of teachings (esoteric and exoteric), and some are being denied access to one of these deeper mysteries.

Jesus tells Thomas he has become "intoxicated" from the spring "I have tended." To tend something, implicitly refutes ownership and creation. It suggests the speaker is acting as a caretaker, tending something already in existence. Jesus is not claiming ownership, but more a custodianship of God's property, an extremely Aboriginal sentiment. The spring, the "secret place is not small. Secret place is biggest one, everywhere . . . powerful,"[11] such a place took Bill Neidjie many lifetimes to locate.

Though Peter and Matthew accept Jesus as a messenger and a philosopher, it would seem Jesus denies he is either. Thomas is wrong to acknowledge him a teacher, Jesus sees himself as a caretaker. The "spring" Thomas tends and reveals from is open for all to drink from. All Jesus is doing is pointing out one way to reach an eternal constant.

That they would be outraged enough to stone Thomas, indicates whatever was heard would be beyond Peter and Matthew's wisdom and sensibilities. Stoning was the traditional Jewish punishment for blasphemy, and it could be assumed that their ears would interpret this mystical revelation as heretical. Something unusual or offensive must have been thrown into the equation, and we suspect the catalyst underpinning this offence is steeped in two cultures, *Isiac* and its primal source, the Aboriginal *Dreaming*.

As previously discussed, to acquire supernatural powers (miracles) an Aboriginal initiate must climb many rungs up the ladder of spiritual ascension. Knowledge and wisdom was given orally in the form of sayings, secrets or stories. Neither Jesus nor the *Dreaming* read from any book, or referred to the rote knowledge of some sacred written records as an essential pre-requisite for any soul's ascension. Their knowledge of these secrets can never be written in words, the moment it is transcribed the secret is lost.

Bill Neidjie can find deep wisdom within sacred places. The paintings, songs and the earth are all part of the same story, once given the skill to read the wall and land. It seems the white man can also read, but it is from the wrong book. "Now white man got learning. He got university school. He can read. But me only read a little bit. White people got computer, but Aboriginal, me . . . I just write in cave."[12]

> (VERSE 14)
> Jesus said to them, "If you fast, you will bring sin upon yourselves, and if you pray you will be condemned, and if you give to charity, you will harm your spirits.
> When you go into any region and walk through the countryside, when people receive you, eat what they serve you and heal the sick among them.
> For what goes inside your mouth will not defile you, rather, it is what comes out of your mouth that will defile you."[13]

The saying has been discussed in some detail in our first book, *Constructing a New World Map*, and needs no further commentary beyond one generalised observation.

There are ten verses that discuss rituals, the misuse of money and pragmatic codes of behaviour (Verses 6, 12, 14, 53, 63, 64, 86, 95, 100, and 114). In each case this revolutionary caretaker and introspective philosopher speaks strongly against the accepted standards of the day. There is no church here.

The sacred places that constitute Bill's church come from Nature, and are gifts from the Spirits. It seems many of the recent arrivals do not appreciate the importance of keeping such gifts in a pristine state and under the care of the original custodians. This is the gift the Spirits bequeathed to humanity, as they "walk through the countryside," however there is a new less benevolent factor that has intruded into this harmonious balance. Bill's concern was understandable as these people have no intentions of healing "the sick," they do not "receive" but take everything. He was worried because "these very important places, but we frightened that European might touch him . . . he slow to listen . . . Him got to always ask question. He want that place. That's why we frightened."[14] Bill was scared, as "him always got to ask question," but "him" is incapable of understanding the answers on the rare occasions "him" bothers to listen. It appears that when Jesus advised all to be wary about "what comes out of your mouth," the task is beyond the abilities of many of the hims now intruding into Bill's land and life.

(VERSE 16)
Jesus said, "Perhaps people think I have come to impose peace upon the world. They do not know I have come to impose conflicts upon the earth: fire, sword, war. For there will be five in a house: There will be three against two and two against three, father against son and son against father, and they will stand alone."[15]

Jesus believes the teachings of peace and harmony he wished to share were unsettling enough to undermine the foundations of the pivotal element that binds most societies; the family. The wisdom he offers is patently incapable of blending into the framework his followers, and enemies, exist within.

In Bill's world, serious internal conflicts of this nature are against the Law and the *Dreaming*. His family, and all tribes, lived with the rhythm of the land and their Ancestral Spirits; there was no other way. Everyday and in every way they were trying to live every moment in unison with the land and in accord with the wishes of their Creator. This was the same message Jesus was delivering, the problem was those who were his audience had strayed so far and lost the ability to hear anything of real value.

Bill's family could still hear the voices of the first day repeating the same story since the beginning of time, the *Dreaming*. Throughout Bill's childhood, his family lived within the Law of the land, as such, he could "never do little bit wrong . . . I frightened when young."[16] Respect towards his Elders and culture was paramount, because of this whenever his tribe ate "that fish for old people"[17] and "older people must have goose first."[18]

In Bill's world it is the "Same story for everyone,"[19] simply because it was the only script available. The need for conflict or separation does not exist, as Bill's people constantly encouraged the acquisition of esoteric wisdom and acknowledgement of the laws of the *Dreaming*.

(VERSE 18)
The followers said to Jesus, "Tell us how our end will be."
Jesus said, "Have you discovered the beginning, then, so that you are seeking the end? For where the beginning is, the end will be. Fortunate is the one who stands at the beginning: That one will know the end and will not taste death."[20]

The *Old Testament* specifies the actual ages of Noah and his descendants, and then details a series of events leading up to the birth of Christ. Many brave Christian theologians, including King Alfonso X, took the mathematics literally and claimed to be able to calculate the precise time when humanity began. They mistakenly assumed the *Bible* as a faultless historical account without contradictions.

Our historical accounts are placed on a time line, beginning at a specified point in the past and ending today. After all, stating James Cook sailed up the east coast of Australia in 1770 would appear to be the only effective way to chronicle such an event.

As our societies move through time, the Aboriginal *Dreaming* moves through space and place. As Robert Lawlor noted, "the Dreamtime, focus on place description and spatial directions rather than time designations such as when, before, or after."[21]

The power behind the *Dreaming* never finished, as there is no pause, because it is eternal. The force or significance of a site or place is proportional to the amount of spiritual energy it exudes. It does not falter, but remains constant throughout the eons. A place that abounds in spiritual power will always remain so.

Bernard Simon is adamant that Verse 18 (along with Verse 19) has a "certain flavour of the Eastern religions about them in their knowledge of totality. Only those initiated into the mysteries would necessarily have a full understanding of these passages."[22] Simon is partially correct, most assuredly many verses, including this passage have the flavour of distant shores, and as a transmission point he was looking in the right area. However the original inspiration behind these verses began in a continent to the south of Asia.

Each clan member returns lifetime after lifetime to a place, but never a time. In *Papunya Tula Art* (Central Desert, Australia), the circle is the most potent icon, and it can represent a waterhole or campsite. People and water, for these people this icon represents life, for without water there is no life. If water is plentiful, game, vegetable and fruit will be bountiful. Life and water are eternal constants, which began in the Dreaming and never end, and they have to be represented by an icon that has neither a beginning nor end.

Jesus and the *Dreaming* see the concept of time and finality as a human construct. Big Bill Neidjie saw the perpetual, circular link between the beginning and end as a natural part of the landscape. "I know I come back to my country. . .When I die, I become skeleton. I'll be in cave. That way my spirit stay there."[23]

The *Dreaming* is timeless in Bill's eyes it is eternal. He knows "Aboriginal Law never change. Old people tell us, 'You gotta keep it'. It always stays."[24] There is a repository, a place where he can find the Law. These sacred places must be creations of Nature and God. A building or monument is no more than a testimony to human ingenuity, for Bill, "Law written in cave. That painting is Law."[25]

Chapter 5: The Gospel of Thomas

(VERSE 21)
Mary said to Jesus, "What are your followers like?"
He said, "They are like little children living in a field that is not theirs. When the owners of the field come, they will say, 'Give our field back to us.' They take off their clothes in front of them in order to give it back to them, and they return the field to them.
For this reason I say, if the owner of a house knows that a thief is coming, he will be on guard before the thief arrives and will not let the thief break into the house of his estate and steal his possessions. As for you, then, be on guard against the world. Arm yourselves with great strength, or the robbers might find a way to get to you, for the trouble you will expect to come. Let there be among you a person who understands.
When the crop ripened, the person came quickly with sickle in hand and harvested it. Whoever has ears should hear."[26]

It would appear more prudent for Mary to begin her question with something along the lines of, "What are we followers like," or "Tell me about our role as followers." The common expectation would be for her to see herself as part of the flock. The fact Thomas records the enquiry in such an expansive manner, suggests he was prepared to acknowledge there was a divide in standing between Mary and the other Apostles.

Why didn't the Saviour immediately correct Mary, reprimanding and reminding her that she is not separate but a part of the group? Furthermore, Mary's gender should deny her the privilege of placing herself above any male, and her subservience should be even greater when the men referred to, are the Messiah's Apostles. Jesus certainly isn't reticent in reprimanding others when they step above their station. The content does seem to create a sense of separation between Mary and the group she refers to as "your followers."

(VERSE 25)
Jesus said, "Love your brother like your soul, guard him like the pupil of your eye."[27]

In traditional times the term "brother" meant many things, regardless of the scope, the same obligatory act of deep affection was required to be offered to various types of families. Family roles and titles are somewhat different in traditional Aboriginal societies; all the father's brothers are fathers and the mother's sisters are not aunties, but mothers. Most of the discipline is the responsibility of what we would refer to as uncles and aunts.

Within a clan, unmarried children were brothers and sisters to all other children. The family network is extremely extensive and powerful, even today third cousins would expect to be treated as a brother or sister when visiting relations. The life-long linkage through blood or moiety is a dominant factor within every clan and serves the function of binding the group by providing rules and protocol.

Beyond the clan, and then the tribe, this extended kinship continues in its spread until it encompasses all creations of the spirits. "Earth . . . exactly like your father or brother or mother."[28] Not just the soil, but everything and everyone upon it, resonates to the same ancient rhythm; the *Dreaming*. Bill sensed the presence of the secret place whenever he looked at "tree but I say . . . Just like mother, father or brother, grandma."[29]

The interrelationship between the clan and their Ancestral Estate is almost complete, but one member of the human family is missing. Fortunately, Bill is aware we all the same, and would never forget any member of this family. During these ancient times gender was never an issue when determining who deserves "love." Brother or sister, there is no difference, therefore "This earth for us. Just like mother, father, sister."[30]

(VERSE 26)
Jesus said, "You see the speck that is in your brother's eye, but you do not see the beam that is in your own eye. When you take the beam out of your own eye, then you will see clearly to take the speck out of your brother's eye."[31]

It would seem more and more of us spend a lot of time and energy finding fault and blame in others. This negative obsession is the underlying motivation behind the escalating popularity of many reality shows, like *Big Brother*, *Survivor* etc, where the result is dependent upon who is evicted, disappoints or fails. Some people gain a great deal of satisfaction in attacking and denigrating an individual, group or country during times of duress. Often, when people highlight the flaws of others, their own faults seem diminished by comparison.

Some psychologists (Hakmiller 1966, Wills 1981 and Wood 1989) refer to this process as *Downward Social Comparison*. This defensive mechanism is used when self-esteem is threatened, and has an uplifting effect on the mood and future outlook of the individual who is comparing. This comparison and denigration highlights the defects of others in a less fortunate position.

We believe that focusing on the perceived weaknesses of others can lead on to what is often referred as the *Bystander Effect* (Professors John Darley and Bibb Latane), where the more bystanders or spectators there are, the less likely help will be offered. This sanitised inertia becomes more apparent as the size of the group increases. Both distance and anonymity desensitises the onlooker, relegating them to the status of a spectator. This cultural indifference distances the onlooker from the emotion and suffering no matter how dire the situation, and replaces compassion with clinical judgements and critiques.

Backbiting and rumours will destabilise and could do nothing to maintain harmony within a small tribal unit. People will undeniably offend others regardless of upbringing or culture, but the remedies can vary. Traditional Aboriginal society would attempt to remedy the flaws of others by using communally agreed devices. A stern word or serious look would often suffice, if not, parody then shunning was used. Beyond that, for certain periods of time, the entire clan will refuse to speak to or acknowledge the presence of an offender.

Big Bill Neidjie sees finding of fault in others, be it in terms of their character or origin, is pointless because, "man can't split himself . . . Aboriginal can't growl at white European . . . Because both ways. Might be both good men, might be both no good . . . you never know."[32] Until any critic has attained perfection the nagging tongue should be kept still, and unless you are able to "get understand yourself,"[33] it should remain at rest.

Of course, there are some who will never be able to follow such a demanding personal restriction and are unwilling to look into any Aboriginal eyes. In Bill's eyes everyone is the same.

Yet on this rare occasion Bill is mistaken, as some people do see things differently. Doctor Karl Kruszelnicki, (Triple J—Thursday Science Radio Segment 11:00 - 12:00, 9th June 2005) gave a graphic account of how different that vision is. He spoke of standing beside an Aboriginal Elder from the Western Desert Region, as they both peered out onto the vast expanse of flat, almost featureless countryside. Dr. Kruszelnicki's companion drew his attention to a solitary tree some considerable distance from them, in particular the grey kangaroo standing motionless in the shade. Kruszelnicki recognised the vague shape of a tree, but saw nothing else.

The despairing sigh and body language was not hidden, as he succinctly reinterpreted the Elders' gestures as, *stupid white-man can't see past his nose*. Undeterred, and armed with a modern panacea, Kruszelnicki focussed his high-powered binoculars on the tree and the object below.

"Yes!"[34] He noticed a stationary upright blur that resembled the indistinct shape of something resembling a kangaroo. He felt a slight sense of parity and pride, which evaporated within an instant as his companion offered one final comment.

"What about the joey sitting in her pouch?"[35]

The highest magnification and futile attempts at refocussing were to no avail, in Kruszelnicki's eyes no matter what the technological assistance, there was barely a kangaroo visible and most definitely no joey.

Normal vision is expressed in terms of 6:6. The people he had the privilege to stand beside are acknowledged as having the best eyesight of any group on the planet. The experts claim their vision is measured at 6:1.5. To elaborate, what a normally sighted individual could see clearly at 1.5 metres away, a person with these abilities could see with the same clarity and detail standing another 4.5 metres behind this person.

It seems the vision of many Traditional Aboriginal people, be it through their eyes or soul, has a depth and perception all could learn from.

(VERSE 36)
Jesus said, "Do not be concerned from morning until evening and from evening to morning about what you will wear."[36]

When Bill was a child, during a time when there were no clothes, nobody was ever "concerned" about what they were about to "wear." Whether "morning" or "evening" they used what they needed, never what was desired. His childhood was full of culture and the *Dreaming,* today many are not so blessed. "Tree, grass, star . . . If you in city well I suppose lot of houses, you can't hardly look this star but might be one night you look. Have a look star because that's the feeling."[37]

For Bill, this loss of vision is a pressing issue. The noise, concrete and "lots of houses" distract many to become obsessed with every aspect of the material life. If unable to look up at a star, those existing in the city have nothing left but lower their vision and cheapen their expectations. The insatiable need to acquire fashionable clothes, cosmetics, shoes and sundry apparel are symptomatic of a loss of purpose and vision.

A change in perspective is vital, that is why Bill "like im camp outside because of course you got to sleep outside, you got to feel im that wind and look star!"[38] Outside, at the camp, away from the city and closer to nature, it is possible to see that "star" and hear the wind carrying voices of the first day. Elsewhere, away from Bill's camp, it is difficult to hear or see anything of intrinsic worth.

(VERSE 37)
His followers said, "When will you appear to us and when will we see you?"
Jesus said, "When you strip without being ashamed and you take your clothes and put them under your feet like little children and trample them, then [you] will see the child of the living one and you will not be afraid."[39]

This verse, combined with the saying that preceded it, does highlight the unimportance of clothing and, by association, the desirability of being naked. Once this occurs, the seeker will no longer experience the self-induced guilt of feeling "ashamed" or be constantly "concerned from morning to evening" over the many trivial matters involved in buying clothing. The scene depicted in this verse is somewhat synonymous with the setting of the fabled account of Adam and Eve as described in *Genesis.* A time when humanity knew no shame, standing naked and in harmony with all of God's creations.

Bill Neidjie fondly recalls a time when "my father, my mother, my grandfather all used to hunt there, use ironwood spear. No clothes then."[40] The lifestyle of his youth was steeped in the *Dreaming.* There were no personal possessions or clothes. As it was in Eden until the supposed *fall,* all were naked without being "ashamed" or "afraid" and lived in a co-operative and caring environment where every member of the tribe could do no more or less, than obey the wishes of their Gods ("the living one"). Bill recalled those he lived with were "a good mob of people all around,"[41] he, like all of the children of the *Dreaming,* "never do little bit wrong."[42]

(VERSE 39)

Jesus said, "The Pharisees and the scribes have taken the keys of knowledge (gnosis) and hidden them. They themselves have not entered, nor have they allowed to enter those who wish to. You, however, be as wise as serpents and as innocent as doves."[43]

Surely Jesus was aware of the biblical events involved in the beginning of humanity, where it was alleged the despised snake was responsible for all manner of evil deeds and advice. According to the Old Testament, the snake was directly accountable for our collective fall from grace. It was claimed this duplicitous reptile had one evil function; to deceive. Where is the wisdom gained in being banished from paradise and immortality, then given the privilege of experiencing death? Apparently, these are the curses the serpent bequeathed upon humanity.

Of course, Christian Gnostics view the serpent in a somewhat more affirming light. Our previous book, *Constructing a New World Map*, highlighted how intrinsically interwoven the serpent is within Gnosticism and the *Dreaming*. Neither could exist without the serpent as its inner core. In essence, this is the secret Jesus was alluding to in this metaphor.

Unlike nearly all recently made religions, the *Dreaming* never made a distinction between human, beast or any other object made by the spirits. However, there is one animal that has been, and still is, placed on a higher pedestal, revered above all other creations; the Serpent.

This parity between species is limitless, as Bill Neidjie pointed out "Eagle our brother, like dingo our brother."[44] If only humanity could learn to acknowledge, we are all the same, then we could then learn to be as "wise as snakes and innocent as doves."[45]

(VERSE 42)
Jesus said, "Become passers-by."[46]

Until the white invasion of Australia, this was the only habitable continent where all people lived a non-agricultural lifestyle, where any activity that necessitates ploughing the land was deemed unacceptable and worthy of banishment. Hunters, gatherers, and collectors passed from place to place seeking out food from within their tribal estate. From the moment a person could stand, they were taught how to carefully observe the signs of nature and their Creator. As they passed by from campsite to campsite, each person was constantly seeking out new resources.

However, as Bill Neidjie reminded any who cared to listen, each step had to be taken respectfully. He was always aware that he, and all of his people, had an eternal obligation to "walk on earth, we look after . . . like rainbow sitting on top."[47]

Stand back and observe, don't commit your soul to a lifestyle that idolises greed and inequity as the status quo. Any society that doesn't revere sharing as a virtue, and squandering billions on personal gratification as a mortal sin, is doomed. Many advocates of religion and profit insist meaning and purpose to life can only be found after relying upon their wisdom or books. Adherents of Gnostic thought dispute this absolutism, they place all of the responsibility on the individual to create their karma, construct their path and "become passers-by."

We need to pause and reflect, discard our obsession with technology and materialism then take the time to survey the "damage" inflicted upon both "this earth" and each soul. Jamake Highwater felt "the West has grown positively sick of looking at itself, and it is trying to catch a glimpse of some vague 'otherness', some potential alternative, some different reality previously hidden beyond the self-congratulatory mirror of a stifled windowless civilization."[48]

The irony is the "otherness" many yearn, comes from a place and time that begun in the *Dreaming*, all that is needed is to make the effort and take the time to ask. From the time that first contact between his culture and whites first took place, Bill's people sensed an acquired blindness many white-men are afflicted with. He lamented that when the whites "come to us, they started and run our life . . . quick. They bring drink. First they should ask about fish, cave, dreaming but . . . they rush in . . . Now Aborigine losing it, losing everything."[49] Until the mindless, unquestioning "rush" ceases, Bill, and all who are blessed to possess such wisdom, will never be asked anything.

(VERSE 50)
Jesus said, "If they say to you, "Where have you come from?" say to them, "We have come from the light, from the place where light came into being by itself, established [itself] and appeared in their image." If they say to you, "Is it you?" say, "We are its children, and we are the chosen of the living father." If they ask you, "What is the evidence of the father in you?" say to them, "It is motion and rest."[50]

What is "motion" and what is "rest"? This, according to Jesus, is our divinity, and the outcome of each soul's deeds and words. Movement or "motion" is our material existence on this planet, while "rest" is our existence elsewhere. The question that arises is whether life is a continuing event, or a one-off occurrence. The source is unambiguous, Bill Neidjie had no doubt, "these people will die, but they'll come back . . . like I do."[51] This is no more than an alternative way of explaining the intricacies of rebirth.

The interrelationship between the land, the Gods and the individual soul is complete. Death is a minor distraction and an opportunity to discover, yet again, an eternal connection. This is why Bill requested the link remains unbroken, insisting "I don't want coffin . . . just cave."[52]

"We have come from the light . . . where light came into being by itself," apart from God no other entity can create itself and initiate all forms of life. The creative capacity to build from nothing is the attribute that distinguishes God from all other creations. Many of the Gnostic texts that dealt with this issue

Chapter 5: The Gospel of Thomas 51

firmly believed they were at least the equal of the fallen Creator, (*Yaltaboath*) and had the innate potential to be better than the Apostles, and even Adam.

> (VERSE 51)
> His followers said to him, "When will the rest for the dead take place, and when will the new world come?"
> He said to them, "What you look for has come, but you do not know it."[53]

His followers may be looking, but perhaps they are using the wrong senses, Bill Neidjie has learnt to look at things differently. "Feeling make you, Out there in open space. He coming through your body. Look while he blow and feel with your body . . . because tree just about your brother or father . . . and tree is watching you."[54] Bill Neidjie's God resides within a tree and everywhere else, watching and judging every thought and act. Objects made by man, book or building, could never possess the Spirit of that "tree."

His Apostles ask Jesus for "when," seeking reference points they are familiar with. The Saviour replies with where, his time line is circular and, as it is with the *Dreamtime*, is of no relevance to what they seek. Until Jesus' Apostles stop using these time references to seek out redemption, their task is lost.

Bill Neidjie could see no purpose in peering inside books or keeping calendars, the "tree" was sufficient. The Ancestral Spirits shared their life force with all creations, this is why, "when you cut tree, it pump life away, all the same as blood in my arm."[55]

If "you cut tree" there is a price to be paid, but if you stop and listen there is a gift to be gained. The interrelationship between the creations of the spirits and humanity is not restricted to one location, or for that matter one continent, it encompasses the planet. Tatanga Mani (Walking Buffalo) who is the Chief of the Stony Tribe (Canada) may be separated from Bill by thousands of kilometres, but in some respects he lives next door, the words may differ slightly but the inspiration is identical.

> Did you know trees talk? Well, they do. They talk to each other, and they'll talk to you if you listen . . . I have learned a lot from trees: sometimes about the weather, sometimes about animals, sometimes about the Great Spirit.[56]

> (VERSE 54)
> Jesus said, "Blessed are the poor, for yours is the kingdom of heaven."[57]

There was a time when the poor were never a concern for Bill Neidjie, the term does not exist in the *Dreaming*, nor in his youth. It is a cultural import, unfortunately many who have massive amounts of personal wealth seem less than satisfied with what they have and continually crave for more.

"Fish . . . he listen. He say, 'Oh, somebody there'. Him frightened, too many Toyota. Make me worry too."[58] His angst is understandable, as Bill's reason for existence is predicated upon the sacred act where each person must look after their country, never "Toyota." Other's, with far less noble attitudes, don't want to look after country as they much prefer to look after their bank balance. Bill fears "Toyota" and all of the passengers and luggage they bring, he knows they constantly want more and never give back, and what troubles him is that what "Toyota" really wants has only one master; money. Regardless, he, and the poor continue to fight for the rights of the "kingdom of heaven."

Until the day Bill crossed over, multinational mining companies constantly pressured Bill's tribe for the right to mine uranium on some of their tribal land. They were relentless, kept "on asking, asking, meeting, keep on asking, asking. People sick of it now . . . 'Too much asking'. Well he can make money. E get im from underneath, riches from in the ground. E make million, million might be. But trouble is . . . dying quick! People . . . big mob they might die because lot of money."[59]

As the mining companies rip up their earth seeking out more radioactive poisons, Bill, and his people pleaded with the government, the rich and "Toyota" to leave things as they are meant to be. Only then will "fish" and Bill no longer feel "frightened." Until this balance is re-established, only the "poor" will enter "the kingdom of heaven," the rich have a different path to travel.

(VERSE 63)
Jesus said, "There was a rich man who had much money. He said, 'I shall put my money to use so that I may sow, reap, plant, and fill my storehouse with produce, with the result that I shall lack nothing.' Such were his intentions, but that same night he died. Let him who has ears hear."[60]

"People . . . they can't listen for us. They just listen for money . . . money."[61] Bill Neidjie can most assuredly "hear" what Jesus was advising others not to do. He was concerned that many who come up in "Toyota" are unable to ignore the temptation, nor begin to understand the consequences the addiction to money creates. Regardless how successful those investing and purchasing are, the end result is always the same. Jesus would fully agree with Bill who said, "forever and ever him make million dollars . . . him die."[62]

(VERSE 64)
Jesus said, "A person was receiving guests. When he had prepared dinner, he sent his servant to invite the guests.
"The servant went to the first and said to that one, 'My master invites you.'
"That person said, "Some merchants owe me money, they are coming to me tonight. I must go and give them instructions. Please excuse me from dinner.'
"The servant went to another and said to that one, 'My master invites you.'
"That person said to the servant, 'My friend is to be married and I am to arrange the banquet. I shall not be able to come. Please excuse me from dinner.'
"The servant went to another and said to that one, 'My master invites you.'
"That person said to the servant, 'I have bought an estate and I am going to collect rent. I shall not be able to come. Please excuse me.'

"The servant returned and said to his master, 'The people whom you invited to dinner have asked to be excused.'
"The master said to his servant, 'Go out on the streets and bring back whomever you find to have dinner.'
"Buyers and merchants [will] not enter the places of my father."[63]

This is the longest saying in the book, and that must carry extra impact. It would appear the topic of money needs further elaboration.

It would seem the last line could be read literally. When combined with the preceding Verse (63), which speaks of a "rich person" meticulously saving then "that very night he died," Jesus seems to be adopting an openly antagonistic attitude towards any person directly involved in the business of money. The commentaries Jesus offered on the subject of money in the *New Testament* reinforces his dislike of financial matters, and doesn't differ that much from what Jesus says here.

When *Time Magazine* referred to Gnostics as "World Haters,"[64] perhaps verses like these had a marked influence on the formation of such a critique. If all economists are apparently damned, and he advises us elsewhere, "If you have money, do not lend it at interest, but give [it] to one from whom you will not get it back,"[65] surely these sentiments could cause instability and threaten the underlying framework of our capitalist economy.

If Jesus is speaking against the ownership of any capital or cash, many are doomed never to enter "the places of my father." Conversely, if he is speaking about whether this volatile resource is used to benefit others foremost, we only have ourselves to answer to. Money is an inanimate device and is entirely neutral; its worth lies solely in the hands of the provider or accumulator.

Bill Neidjie saw little benefit in the accumulation of masses of money, he was wary of any obsessed by its hypnotic allure. "We want goose, we want fish. Other men want money. Him can make a million dollars, but only last one year. Next year him want another million."[66]

Once "him die,"[67] the larger the bank balance the greater the difficulties navigating the shores of Heaven. In the *New Testament* there are numerous references to the many associated perils of greed, some specify that ascension for the rich being as difficult as passing through the eye of a needle.

Jesus knew, as did Bill, "Dreaming Place . . . you can't change it, no matter who you are. No matter you rich man, no matter you king. You can't change it."[68] The allure of the entrapment money offers entices many; but it carries with it a double-edged sword. "But white man . . . Maybe he be slave himself, maybe slave work for him . . . But no good."[69]

(VERSE 70)
Jesus said, "That which you have will save you if you bring it forth from yourselves. That which you do not have within you [will] kill you if you do not have it within you."[70]

Bill is adamant, there is no option, once the journey of self-realisation begins, "if you got story, heart... then speak yourself, stand for it!"[71] If you do not "stand for" the gnosis ("story") you have been taught or personally discovered, the soul will suffer and become silent. In this vacuum, baser, less altruistic emotions and motivations bubble to the surface and overwhelm the individual. For the soul, what ensues is quite literally the death of a thousand cuts.

In Robert Lawlor's book, *Voices of the First Day,* when concluding a chapter titled "Cycles of Initiation," he selected Verse 70 as the final point to reflect upon when summarising the overall objectives of Aboriginal sacred ceremonies. Of all the ancient literature and countless oral traditions available, he felt this verse was the most eloquent when it came to assessing the esoteric complexities and similarities of the *Dreaming* and Gnosticism. Lawlor noted that the sentiments expressed in this saying succinctly encapsulated the "purpose and meaning of initiation for individuals and society."[72]

The danger being that if this potential for the soul to evolve is repressed, problems fester. Lawlor believes "western society brings forth or externalizes the world Dreaming in wilful, self-centred, environmentally destructive endeavours. The Aborigines externalize the original Dreaming through ritual enactment, marked by remembrance and respect."[73] If all that western society can bring "forth" is a litany of "destructive endeavours,"[74] Jesus is right, this greedy behaviour has the potential to "kill" your soul.

(VERSE 84)
Jesus said, "When you see your likeness, you are happy. But when you see your images that came into being before you and that neither die nor become visible, how much more will you bear!"[75]

Earth... like your father or brother or mother, because you born from earth. You got to come back to earth. When you dead... you'll come back to earth... That's your bone, your blood. It's in the earth, same as for tree.[76]

For many the question of what comes into "being before you" yet, paradoxically, can still be "your image" leaves us floundering. According to Thomas these images exist before the body we recognise as ourself began and can not be made "visible." These "images" are the various guises of "you," yet are invisible and can never die; this must be our past-lives.

A past life is no longer a retrievable, physical entity, yet never dies, and is still an integral part of any individual as they stand today. If you come into being for one solo appearance, the saying is either wrong or a heresy. The selection of the plural "images" suggests life is not a one-off event, and only strengthens the concept of rebirth. This duality is an essential element of the *Dreaming.*

A *Dreaming* story, recorded by Roland Egglestien called "*The Baby Makers,*" has a literal account of what happens after we cross over. The content is self-explanatory and requires no commentary. "These babies were always allowed to be born again and to choose the mother they wanted."[77]

David Gulpilil, a talented Aboriginal actor, author, tracker and Elder, spoke of the same eternal link Bill Neidjie and many *Dreaming* stories constantly allude to in his book *Gulpilil's Stories of the Dreamtime*. "To the Aboriginal, death is not the end of life. Death is the last ceremony in this present life; then the soul is reborn, thus all living people are reincarnations of the dead. The soul lives on and finds a new body to inhabit. This belief in reincarnation provides a direct link back to their Ancestors of the Dreamtime."[78]

To "bear," means to carry something, the Saviour is suggesting we have to carry something with us. It could be this load is our body, or perhaps it is an increase in spiritual wisdom? However, whatever this load is, it most certainly won't be a burden, but a privilege. The realisation we return to a place time after time is a blessing and an opportunity, or, a curse. Its impact is simply a matter of choice and behaviour.

(VERSE: 85)
Jesus said, "Adam came from great power and great wealth, but he was not worthy of you. For had he been worthy, [he would] not [have tasted] death."[79]

According to many versions of early Gnostic lore, Adam is as much a symbol as a person. He came "from great power and great wealth," and was respected as a profound philosopher. However, Jesus suggests if Adam had been "worthy," he would never have tasted death. At first glance this observation seems a touch odd, for surely death is the one commonality that defines all life on the planet.

Reincarnation basically means attending class until we get it all right, then and only then, do we earn the right to stop attending. Only then is one able to "not have tasted death." If Adam is still incarnating on this planet, his compulsory re-attendance means the grades previously awarded were inadequate for divine graduation.

Numerous Gnostic texts assert we are at least equal to the Apostles, Adam and our deluded Creator, *Yaltaboath*, who mistakenly believed he was the ultimate creator. This verse only reinforces the belief of equality and emphasises our innate potential to sit alongside God.

In our Western societies the measure of an individual's worth is assessed in terms of "great wealth" or power. The more an individual possesses, the more control and status is gained. In Bill Neidjie's society these trinkets are given their true worth. "Don't think about money too much. You can get a million dollar . . . but not worth it. Million dollar . . . he just go 'poof'. Couple of weeks . . . you got nothing."[80] Both Bill and Jesus comprehend the worth of this man-made construct, and knew no matter how noble the intentions of the possessor, once money is part of the equation, the upmost caution is essential.

Money is a device, and has no persona, as it is an inanimate object and can be used to garner untold misery or benefit. If used poorly, it, and all that is associated with money will take many casualties. And so it goes on, until one day "poof."

As Aboriginal Elder, Reuben Kelly, warned any with the sense to listen, "centuries ago you white people chose the path of science and technology. That path will destroy the planet. Our role is to protect the planet. We are hoping that you discover this before it's too late."[81]

In many cases when dealing with money, little or no care has been taken. Unfortunately the ills and maladies this dereliction of duty has caused, confront us today. It is not surprising Bill feared for the welfare of their future generations, as he felt their youth, the "cheeky mob"[82] are becoming tainted by this import. He sensed the problems ahead, for he had no choice but to lament, "now all this coming up with Toyota."[83]

(VERSE: 86)
Jesus said, "[Foxes have] their dens and birds have their nests, but the child of humankind has no place to lay his head and rest."[84]

"We walk on earth, we look after . . . like rainbow sitting on top."[85]

The people of the *Dreaming* had no permanent place "to lay his head and rest." Their time on this place lay in the laps of the Gods. If it was to rain, if the mullet ran, if the acacias bloom, these were matters for the Spirit's grace. The clan moved wherever food, ceremonies and their tribal estate would permit. Such a reverent life made it obligatory that, "This Earth . . . I never damage, I look after."[86]

If true to his vow of "never damage," Bill had to continue living within the boundaries of the *Dreaming* and the land choosing a lifestyle were he could feel the trees and hear the voices of the first day. A life in the big-smoke will always cause "damage," and Bill could never consider living in a manner that would create a situation where he would be unable to "look after" his tribal estate. "We like white-man alright. We like im in city But city make you sick of it Better this."[87] Bill is firmly connected to the heartbeat of the land and knows this mystical link spans generations and incarnations.

It could be Jesus and Bill are reminding us that the material collection of chemicals we call a body isn't our permanent abode. There could be an alternative meaning behind "place" and "rest." It may be a metaphor symbolising a time to reflect and meditate in the afterlife, as we believe, or have a more literal meaning, which relates to seeking out a home, some form of bricks and mortar.

Jesus calls us a "child of humankind," referring to our earthly manifestation and the consequence of our choice to remain. Until we reclaim our alternate Spiritual parentage, we are fated to be cast yet again into the prison of the flesh. It may be our real home can only be found outside the flesh.

(VERSE: 95)
[Jesus said], "If you have money, do not lend it at interest. Rather give [it] to someone from whom you will not get it back."[88]

The directive seems to be very simple and uncluttered. There are either a variety of subtle literary devices and deeper underlying meanings at play, or it is an all-inclusive command. If taken literally, no-one is exempt from this proscription.

Verses of this character have added substance to the accusations of heresy the *Gospel of Thomas* has endured. A shallow analysis of this verse could find many a critic alleging this is yet another example of these World Haters exhibiting their disdain for all aspects of materialism.

However, it is a shallow critique; a person can only be charitable if they have already accumulated goods or cash. To state "if you have money"[89] and offer no admonishment for being so fortunate, must mean Jesus has no problem with money or commerce per se. The real issue for Jesus is whether this resource is used selfishly or shared with the needy.

Many other commentators, who are unable or unwilling to read between the lines, would stridently claim such a frivolous proclamation would unsettle the economic fabric of our capitalist system. Equally, the finances of the many religions and denominations have always been more than bountiful, and often, less than generous. Many economists would claim these proclamations would stifle incentive and the motivation to work harder and invest. They would insist that such a charitable climate would remove the incentive to work and harms the economy.

They may be right; in our individualistic capitalistic society communal sharing contradicts the profit motive and greed that underpins much of what we do. According to Big Bill's world, their life holds a better way. He saw no point in even bothering, "million no good for us. We need this earth to live because . . . we'll be dead, we'll become earth."[90] In a society that truly shares everything with all of the clan, money could only ever have one function; to share with others with an expectation to never "get it back."

As Elder Jaqui Katona stressed, "our cultural values cannot be traded for money."[91] This resource is quite literally feared by many Elders. A joint statement compiled by Bill, Yvonne Margarula and Jacob Nayinggul, reinforces the grave fears many Elders hold towards money and all the associated by-products. They believe that their "cultural values cannot be traded for money . . . we have to deal with the massive intrusions that development brings to our country. Our priority is protecting the country and by doing this protecting our people and our future."[92]

What else could be expected? Traditional Aboriginal society regarded all as equals, where all were judged by whether others benefited. The concept of personal ownership and greed is contradictory, particularly if people were living in a time when "my mother, my grandad, my father was hunting there and wasn't in no clothes,"[93] and at a time when there was no money then.

(VERSE 108)
Jesus said, "Whoever drinks from my mouth will become like me; I myself shall become that person, and the hidden things will be revealed to that person."[94]

The "hidden things" Jesus spoke of come from a "dreaming place."[95] Bill Neidjie knew this "Secret place is biggest one, everywhere . . . powerful."[96] Bill's daily life was dedicated towards unifying his soul and his people with the *Dreaming,* where nothing can be hidden. No physical senses are necessary, in fact, they are a hindrance. Bill and Jesus have both drunk from the "mouth" of the Divine, it is for this reason these "hidden things" are "revealed." This mystical unification permeated every pore of Bill's body and soul. He could "feel it with my body, with my blood. Feeling all these trees, all this country. When this wind blow you can feel it. Same for country . . . you can feel it. You can look, but feeling . . . that make you."[97]

(VERSE: 113)
His followers said to him, "When will the kingdom come?"
"It will not come by watching for it. It will not be said, 'Look, here it is,' or 'Look, there it is.' Rather, the father's kingdom is spread out upon the earth, and people do not see it."[98]

Our story is in the land. . . it is written in those sacred places. My children will look after those places, that's the law.[99]

We note once again Jesus answers "when" with where. Jesus replies using a typically traditional Aboriginal approach, questioning the accepted concept of time when speaking about God. As Bill Neidjie revealed, "our story is in the land," or as Jesus explains, our story is "spread out upon the earth."

Jesus is not suggesting that heaven is on this planet; he has no intention of being subtle. He is insisting we accept heaven is on and in "the earth." Since the Saviour gave a specific location of the "kingdom," we must we treat our "earth" as if it is the "father's kingdom." It would appear we are compelled to give more reverence to a tree than any book written or dollar printed.

The Aboriginal people rarely built any structures, and none were meant to be permanent buildings of a religious nature. There was no need to chop down a tree to construct a steeple or church. Such blatant disrespect would not go undetected, as Bill knew that "tree . . . he watching you . . . They grow with your body, with your feeling."[100] This interconnectedness between people and the Ancestral land is total. In Bill's eyes, harming the creations of the Spirits can damage the individual and perhaps others. If one was to blaspheme and intentionally harm a tree "you maybe 40 years, might be 50 years old, you feel pain in your back. Because you cut tree."[101] Everything and everyone is interrelated, not only trees, but even the grass needs to be treated with the utmost respect. "If you feel sore . . . headache, sore body, that means somebody killing tree or grass."[102]

In Bill's world, the tree and God are synonymous. In our world, every tree is a diminishing resource, a facilitator of income and, at best, a piece of shade. If allowed the privilege of remaining upright, in many cases, it is relegated to that of an incidental backdrop and home for exotic feathered pests.

If God's kingdom, including the abode of those who crossed over, is "spread out upon the earth" and "people do not see it," perhaps the emerging science of quantum physics may redefine our collective vision. Our next chapter, *Thomas Revisited*, addresses the connection between this verse and a theory many quantum physicists believe explains the mechanics of the universe.

(VERSE: 114)
Simon Peter said to them, "Mary should leave us, for females are not worthy of life."
Jesus said, "Look, I shall guide her to make her male, so that she too may become a living spirit resembling you males. For every female who makes herself male will enter heaven's kingdom."[103]

Bill Neidjie said, "We all same."[104]
Is Jesus, as some allege, being sexist?
Some critics claim because Jesus never explicitly stated the reverse in his reply I will make the male into female, his lack of response proves he is sexist. It is a superficial criticism, as there was never an opportunity for Jesus to make such a declaration, in those times and locales it is extremely unlikely any male would complain to Jesus about females sexually harassing men. With Peter in the room, females were fortunate just to draw breath.

Jesus was not advocating a sex change, nor is this a savage critique on the unworthiness of females. This statement is only reflecting an ongoing Hellenistic tradition. The esoteric belief was that all material objects are feminine, while anything that involves the spiritual plane and personal gnosis is male. His symbolic reply highlighting Mary's pathway to salvation, has been literally misread by some as an affirmation of gender prejudice.

Accepting this proposition, many scholars could contend this symbolic license should be afforded to Peter, that he too was symbolically commending Mary to adopt a more spiritual "male" centred approach. It is possible, if this critique from Peter stood alone, this observation may have some substance. However, there are numerous other comments attributed to Peter that seem to afford far less room for symbolic interpretation. Many observations Peter offered elsewhere openly denigrate Mary and all women.

Of course when this superficial criticism of Jesus being sexist is presented, Verse (22) is conveniently disregarded, it reads, "and when you make male and female into a single one, so that the male will not be male nor the female be female."[105] This passage, combined with Verse (106) where Jesus said, "when you make the two into one . . ."[106] are just different perspectives of the belief that unity and harmony within either male or female can make a "mountain, move from here."[107]

Some may assert Jesus should admonish Peter for making such an outrageous request. The observation may appear to have some merit, but all were aware this hatred was a fundamental part of his persona. It is possible a more conciliatory stance maintained harmony with Peter and any of the more sexist members of the ensemble.

At first glance it seems Peter is being blatantly sexist. The obvious consideration for a tolerant person relates to ascertaining whether any mitigating factors could explain how he could make such outrageous comments. To assert that all women, including Peter's mother, are not worthy of life is a rather challenging statement, if not something far more sinister and disturbing.

If there is a degree of antagonism within the group creating a religious schism, this may be the base from which everything else seeps. The animosity Peter held towards Mary, according to many Gnostic accounts, was the initial catalyst that led to the splintering of the early Christian movement.

There is no doubt there is some significance in Thomas selecting this saying to appear as the last comment from Jesus. With the exception of Judas, there is no other saying or verse in either type of Scriptures that portrays any of the male Apostles in a more negative light. In many of the Gnostic scriptures it is fairly obvious there is no Apostle who receives poorer press than Peter. It is equally true these same types of criticisms with Jesus berating Peter's ignorance exist in the *New Testament*.

Sexism is the antithesis of the *Dreaming*, Robert Lawlor succinctly summed up the underlying truth that binds and maintains Aboriginal societies.

> Underneath their apparent submission to male pomp and ceremony, women maintain their balance of power *physically* by providing 80 percent of the food consumed by the tribe and *spiritually* through their own tradition of magic and sorcery, which men rarely dare to challenge. Although men apparently control most of the formal relationships in society, such as the bestowal of wives, women's informal control ensures that the entire society adheres to characteristics conducive to women's concerns for procreation, growth, and nourishment of life. The resulting characteristics of Aboriginal society—its stability, continuity, and interrelatedness—are in direct contrast to our modern male-dominated society, which is marked by violent upheaval, rapid change, progressivism, and discontinuity.[108]

Any form of antagonism against the feminine is an action beyond Bill Neidjies' comprehension and the *Dreaming*.

> *Rock stays, earth stays. I die and put my bones in cave or earth.*
> *Soon my bones become earth . . . all the same.*
> *My spirit has gone back to my country. . . my mother.*[109]

Chapter 6
Thomas Revisited

His disciples said to him, "When will the kingdom come?"
Jesus said, "It will not come by waiting for it. It will not be a matter of saying 'here it is' or 'there it is'. Rather, the kingdom of the father is spread out upon the earth, and men do not see it."[1] (Verse 113, Gospel of Thomas)

Is this verse the clue Albert Einstein and Stephen Hawkings needed to resolve their unease? Both were seeking a unified theory of everything, an explanation to account for the existence of everything found in the universe, whether an electron or a galaxy.

Albert Einstein and Stephen Hawkings spent a great deal of time and effort trying to construct a unified theory to explain everything. They were seeking out some type of formula or fact that will unlock God's master-plan. Unfortunately their efforts were in vain, as the final key that reveals this esoteric mystery was never a number, nor even an empirically proven fact. We believe the universal truth they sought is hidden within this ancient verse found in the *Gospel of Thomas*.

The problem being that Einstein's acclaimed theory of $E=MC^2$ works perfectly at a cosmic level, but does not function in the sub-atomic world. Conversely, the intricate equations quantum physicists of the last century calculated that satisfactorily explain the mechanics of electrons, protons and neutrons, have no relevance in Einstein's universe.

String Theory, according to many well-credentialed experts, overcomes these irregularities by tying together two apparently opposing processes. In the simplest terms matter, in all its variations, is no more than a material representation of different strings of matter we refer to as energy. The accompanying mathematical equation can accommodate for all forms of existence, whether examining a constellation or an atom. Even though this recent theory is accepted by many respected academics, it carries with it one somewhat challenging aspect; a universe of eleven dimensions. For the hypothesis to be mathematically consistent, there are supposed to be four dimensions in the here and now and another seven on the other side. The nature of these nebulous off-world dimensions located elsewhere is a protracted exercise in conjecture for these theorists. Some scientists suggest these undetected dimensions are populated with beings almost identical to us but living in alternate realities, or a life where different choices were made, others suspect it to be the abode of aliens, Gods and all points in between. Perhaps the answer to this eternal riddle may be found within the Nag Hammadi texts.

The *Gospel of Thomas* provides the location for all eleven dimensions, earth. As Jesus constantly reminded any with ears, the kingdom of the father is spread upon the earth. All that is left is to examine the kingdom's nature and associated hierarchy.

The *Apocalypse of Paul* is a recount of Paul being taken to heaven (on earth) and provides specific details in relation to the location of all other dimensions. This scripture begins with Paul being transported from earth entering "the fourth heaven"[2] and concludes with him being taken "up to the tenth heaven."[3] Both Paul and the quantum physicists are in accord, either reaching the same conclusion through faith or calculation, believing there are seven levels on the nebulous other side.

Their agreement carries one minor misunderstanding, while Paul acknowledges there are three heavens beneath the ethereal place where his journey begun, the many proponents of String Theory insist a fourth element, time, along with length, width and breadth, must also be factored into their calculations.

The concept of time is merely a convenient human construct used as a reference point, as it doesn't exist in the upper seven levels. Traditional Aboriginal society rejects the notion of time existing in a straight line, holding that it is circular in nature containing neither a starting or finishing point. Other supposedly more educated experts dismiss such beliefs as relics of less informed times and primitive customs.

The nature of Paul's heavens warrants further reflection. The "fourth heaven,"[4] which was the first level Paul encountered, has a familiar ring to it. Here the angels were "whipping"[5] a soul in judgement, punishing it for the errant deeds and words created during its last incarnation. After finally acknowledging the many misdemeanours this individual was responsible for, "the soul that had been cast down, [went] to a body which had been prepared [for it.]"[6] Many commentators could confuse or misinterpret this heavenly layer as being synonymous with hell. In Paul's gospel, this fourth heaven is created "according to class."[7] As it is the least advanced level of the afterlife, this realm is reserved for those with a variety of personal insecurities still unresolved, and many challenging incarnations still to atone for when cast into many more bodies and lifetimes.

The other side, whether given a name we feel comfortable with or not, is eternal. Whatever label is attached, ancient myths throughout the world speak of ageless deities with supernatural powers that contradict all traditional understandings of science and material life. If time doesn't exist in 63% of the 11 dimensions needed to balance the equation of life, yet is claimed to be present in the other 37%, the logic underpinning such a proposition is contradictory.

Chapter 6: Thomas Revisited

Quite simply, once the problematic concept of time is accepted as merely a measuring stick invented by humans and is subtracted from String Theory, the ten levels of heaven Paul was privileged to experience merge into one unified mathematical and spiritual equation. Eliminating a level that was used to measure eternity is logical. Time is a human device that gives us a sense of direction within the three dimensions we are directly aware of; its only function is to measure the rise and fall of the sun.

Stephen Hawkings believes time is a construct that serves three purposes within the dimensions we can perceive; measuring cosmological expansion, entropy (measure of decay) and a psychological device to give "direction in which we feel that time passes."[8] Time has no purpose in the dimensions we are unable to detect; in the after-life (Heaven) there is no death (entropy), no direction for time to pass to or from and is beyond any cosmological process, whether expanding or contracting.

The Aboriginal *Dreaming*, Nietzsche and the Christian Gnostics are also in accord, time is an enigmatic circle. Others with a more conventional expectation approach such matters with narrower vision and commandeer the same circle, cut the chord and lay it out in a straight line. Many on this side claim to recognise time as a predictable concrete commodity with a finite beginning and end. All on the other side recognise this three-dimensional problem-solving approach for what it is; a distraction that impedes any seeker from reaching a timeless beginning and end. If time has no beginning or end, there is no middle or any point in between, and, by inference, is impossible to measure. Under these conditions a clock can record nothing beyond human misunderstanding and personal insecurities.

The similarities between the words of Thomas and Bill are striking and need close scrutiny. We examined in varying depth 21verses in the previous chapter, but this is quite literally the tip of the ice-berg. The biggest hurdle we faced related to which verses were discarded. It is our belief we could have continued in the same manner for some considerable time and increasing length. We omitted 32 verses that had direct links to the *Dreaming*, and by association, Bill Neidjie.

Combined, this adds up to 59 verses with obvious connections to the *Dreaming*, and of the 55 not selected there were many other sayings where the link is tenuous, but still not without similarities. The mathematics that ensue from this equation are worthy of consideration. More than half (51.75%) of the words Jesus uttered resonate to an extremely ancient source; the *Dreaming*. Sayings Thomas recorded that directly accessed the voices of the first day, which we chose not to study in the previous chapter included Verses 2, 5, 7, 10, 11, 15, 17, 22, 24, 29, 38, 47, 48, 49, 56, 58, 59, 62, 67, 68, 75, 77, 78, 80, 81, 82, 83, 94, 100, 104, 106, 110, 111 and 112.

It could all be a huge coincidence, but the numbers don't seem to add up. The only issue remaining is to determine whether this extensive interrelationship is purely a chance occurrence, or strong inferential evidence of a link.

To obtain a definitive answer is impossible, as there can be nothing beyond circumstantial evidence to draw upon. Nowhere does Jesus or Mary implicitly state their teachings come from an ancient Southern Continent, but they do leave some compelling indications.

There are two components in this equation, the source and the messengers.

The source: A society that created a spiritual, technological and artistic heritage 50,000 years ago which was absent throughout the globe for at least another 20,000 years. A place and philosophy where sharing is obligatory, where the first fully modern human being evolved, where women are regarded as equals, and a place where people who transgress the Law face no prison, just a harsh word, a frown, perhaps physical punishment or even worse, banishment for life. There is no equivalent on the planet; these people are alone in their intellectual sophistication, democratic principles and esoteric wisdom.

The message: Mary and Jesus speak openly against the empty rituals of prayer, diet, fasting, sacred buildings and infallible scriptures. With no leaders or authorities to mislead us, we are asked to look within, and do what is right. This must exclude sermons delivered from the pulpit, which can only illustrate one point of view and often much worse.

When the first white farmers and traders came and settled the stolen country, many lamented bitterly about the unreliability of the Aboriginal people. This unlimited source of free labour, and whatever struck their fancy, would often disappear for weeks on end going walkabout.

What some saw as a lazy and indolent act was actually a personal spiritual trek. It was an attempt to fulfil the needs of the soul and establish contact with their Ancestral Spirits. Early European settlers saw such aimless wandering as a waste of time, a loss of income and an erratic unproductive trait which had to be eliminated. Those involved in these pilgrimages regarded this time as an opportunity to look within, seek out their Spirits, past, and birthright.

The Aboriginal people were only obeying the Law and Spirits. When we compare this custom with the lifestyle recommended by Jesus, the links seem obvious and the possibilities astounding. There seems no plausible explanation beyond a shared parentage.

Chapter 7
The Gospel of Mary.

(Gospel of Mary) *"Whence do you come, slayer of men, or where are you going, conqueror of space?"*[1]

[...] (pp. 1-6 missing) will matter then be destroyed or not?" The Saviour said, "All natures, all formations, all creatures exist in and with one another, and they will be resolved again into their own roots. For the nature of matter is resolved into the roots of its nature alone. He who has ears to hear, let him hear."
Peter said to him, "Since you have explained everything to us, tell us this also: What is the sin of the world?" The Saviour said, "There is no sin, but it is you who make sin when you do the things that are like the nature of adultery, which is called 'sin.' That is why the Good came into your midst, to the essence of every nature, in order to restore it to its root." Then he continued and said, "That is why you become sick and die, for [...] of the one who [... He who] understands, let him understand. Matter gave birth to a passion that has no equal, which proceeded from something contrary to nature. Then there arise a disturbance in the whole body. That is why I said to you, 'Be of good courage,' and if you are discouraged be encouraged in the presence of the different forms of nature. He who has ears to hear, let him hear."
When the blessed one had said this, he greeted them all, saying, "Peace be with you. Receive my peace to yourselves. Beware that no one lead you astray, saying, 'Lo here!' or 'Lo there!' For the Son of Man is within you. Follow after him! Those who seek him will find him. Go then and preach the gospel of the kingdom. Do not lay down any rules beyond what I appointed for you, and do not give a law like the lawgiver lest you be constrained by it." When he had said this, he departed.

There are a few scholars who believe the first section of this scripture is different from the rest of this text, and that it was added at a later date.

But they were grieved. They wept greatly, saying, "How shall we go to the gentiles and preach the gospel of the kingdom of the Son of Man? If they did not spare him, how will they spare us?" Then Mary stood up, greeted them all, and said to her brethren, "Do not weep and do not grieve nor be irresolute, for his grace will be entirely with you and will protect you. But rather let us praise his greatness, for he has prepared us and made us into men." When Mary said this, she turned their hearts to the Good, and they began to discuss the words of the Saviour.

Peter said to Mary, "Sister, we know that the Saviour loved you more than the rest of women. Tell us the words of the Saviour which you remember— which you know but we do not, nor have we heard them." Mary answered and said, "What is hidden from you I will proclaim to you." And she began to speak to them these words: "I," she said, "I saw the Lord in a vision and I said to him, 'Lord, I saw you today in a vision.' He answered and said to me, 'Blessed are you, that you did not waver at the sight of me. For where the mind is, there is the treasure.' I said to him, 'Lord, now does he who sees the vision see it through the soul or through the spirit?' The Saviour answered and said. 'He does not see through the soul nor through the spirit, but the mind which is between the two— that is what sees the vision and it is [. . .]." (pp. 11-14 missing).

We are less convinced, destroyed may be a more appropriate term.

"[. . ..] 15 it. And desire that, 'I did not see you descending, but now I see you ascending. Why do you lie, since you belong to me?' The soul answered and said, 'I saw you. You did not see me nor recognize me. I served you as a garment, and you did not know me.' When it had said this, it went away rejoicing greatly.

"Again it came to the third power, which is called ignorance. It (the power) questioned the soul saying, 'Where are you going? In wickedness are you bound. But you are bound; do not judge!' And the soul said, 'why do you judge me although I have not judged? I was bound though I have not bound. I was not recognized. But I have recognized that the All is being dissolved, both the earthly things and the heavenly.'

When the soul had overcome the third power, it went upwards and saw the fourth power, which took seven forms. The first form is darkness, the second desire, the third ignorance, the fourth is the excitement of death, the fifth is the kingdom of the flesh, the sixth is the foolish wisdom of flesh, the seventh is the wrathful wisdom. These are the seven powers of wrath. They ask the soul, 'Whence do you come, slayer of men, or where are you going, conqueror of space?' The soul answered and said, 'What binds me has been slain, and what surrounds me has been overcome, and my desire has been ended, and ignorance has died. In a world I was released from a world, and in a type from a heavenly type, and from the fetter of oblivion which is transient. From this time on will I attain to the rest of the time, of the season, of the aeon, in silence.'"

The varying reactions of the male Apostles to Mary's revelations highlight the beginning of a philosophical divide.

When Mary had said this, she fell silent, since it was to this point that the Saviour had spoken with her. But Andrew answered and said to the brethren, "Say what you wish to say about what she has said. I at least do not believe that the Saviour said this. For certainly these teachings are strange ideas." Peter answered and spoke concerning these same things. He questioned them about the

Saviour: "Did he really speak with a woman without our knowledge and not openly? Are we to turn about and all listen to her? Did he prefer her to us?"
Then Mary wept and said to Peter, "My brother Peter, what do you think? Do you think that I thought this up myself in my heart, or that I am lying about the Saviour?" Levi answered and said to Peter, "Peter, you have always been hot-tempered. Now I see you contending against the woman like the adversaries. But if the Saviour made her worthy, who are you indeed to reject her? Surely the Saviour knows her very well. That is why he loved her more than us. Rather let us be ashamed and put on the perfect man and acquire him for ourselves as he commanded us, and preach the gospel, not laying down any other rule or other law beyond what the Saviour said."
When [. . .] and they began to go forth to proclaim and to preach.[2]

******

Andrew doesn't object about the gender of the messenger, but he is unsettled by the message. He is a parabolic student who was never acknowledged in any Gnostic writings of Jesus as the recipient of any mysteron or secret teaching before the Saviour departed. Thus Andrew's ignorance in these esoteric matters is understandable, as he has neither the facilities nor faculties to read between the lines. Andrew was one of the students of Jesus who was only allowed to see and hear, but never perceive or understand. The deeper esoteric secrets weren't his province. That Andrew identifies Mary's allegory as "strange"[3] and containing notions "he has never heard before,"[4] is reflective of his status and knowledge. This issue seems to crystallise the philosophical divide beginning to emerge between the Apostles.

Just to accentuate the difficulty Jesus' closest disciples had in dealing with these multi-layered teachings, Andrew's Gospel was rejected by the Council of Nicea for being *Hellenistic*. Obviously these teachings became a little less strange over the passing years.

Mary's reply to Peter's promptings is far too eloquent and symbolic in its description of the soul's ascension through these ethereal regions, for the intellectual palate of Andrew or Peter. Andrew's knowledge of these esoteric secrets was meagre, and he was unable to either compare or contrast. With precedence as his companion, he did what many do when lost for a response— he queried the credentials of the messenger.

It is a reaction somewhat similar to the response some offer today when confronted by protesters, and those who demonstrate against some environmental or economic injustice. Many invariably ignore the intricacies of their complaints or the cause they champion and attack the character of the individuals involved. Those offended by these hippies and yuppies will react with shallow indignation; denigrating their appearance, lack or abundance of income, or any other superficial flaw that upsets their sensibilities. Throughout the bitter critiques, the reason these malcontents volunteered their heart and soul to a cause is conveniently forgotten.

However, Andrew is not blameless. Both Andrew and Peter did not have the privileges the wealthy expect. The sophisticated elite within the twelve gained a far more expansive education than these two could ever dream of. Even so, Andrew created his own unforgivable precedent. Granted, he was not the first and he will not be the last to claim Mary a liar. By saying "I at least do not believe that the Saviour said this,"[5] Andrew immediately called the speaker's credentials and truthfulness into question. Quite simply, he claimed Mary was dishonest and untrustworthy!

Peter and Andrew were more than a little unsettled by these secret teachings, but not all present were outraged. Levi (Matthew) was not alone in his admiration of Mary and one wonders whether the other Apostles could now see the irony in one of her observations, especially after Peter's dismissive reaction to her revelation.

Mary asked, "Whence do you come, slayer of men, or where are you going, conqueror of space?"[6] Wrath boasts of the pernicious gift it offers us and its' seven guises, or if we deny this opportunity, the divine choice that is ours to make and take.

Our potentiality has no bounds and is only limited by choice, but only when "what binds me has been slain."[7] Mary is correct, we are a combination of our limitations and our Divinity, but our character flaws can be resolved in an instant or remain for an eternity.

Peter's preoccupation with the perceived inferiority of the female body binds and blinds him, he has willingly chosen to become a slayer of women. Peter does not contend the undeniable wisdom of Mary, pleading with Mary to reveal secrets, which "you know but we do not, nor have we heard them."[8] Peter knows of these secrets, and does not doubt the existence of the message; in fact he earnestly demands to hear it. However, he has substantial concerns over the right of any post-woman carrying such a sacred package.

When Peter declared, "Did he really speak with a woman without our knowledge. . ."[9] his question shows both the weakness of his stance, and that which blinds him the most. But by also saying, "we know the Saviour loved you more . . . Tell us the words of the Saviour which you remember,"[10] Peter contradicts himself and invalidates any pretence of a belief based on logic. Perhaps, something much more unsettling than hypocrisy is at play here?

In reality, Peter is saying, I know he told you special things, because he loved you more than anyone else and unfortunately we must "listen"[11] to a mere woman. Then upon hearing what Peter begged for he calls Mary a liar, claiming Jesus would have no reason to reveal secrets to the one, according to Levi (Matthew), "he loved . . . more than us."[12] Matthew adds to his defence of Mary demanding to know, "who are you indeed to reject her?"[13] Matthew's enquiry suggests Peter's status, in comparison to Mary, is a fair way beneath her station.

Peter is rarely restrained when it comes to speaking his mind, yet he is at a loss to respond at all to Matthew's spirited defence. This vacuum indicates either a begrudging tacit agreement, or Peter being struck mute. Regardless of how compelling reason may be, Peter also believes such a woman is "not worthy of life."[14] The quandary he faces relates to balancing his intuition with his imperfections, as he is unable to fathom why any male would waste such wisdom on a mere "woman."[15] Such a conundrum can only be resolved by letting Peter's sexism run rampant, driven onwards by the third power of wrath, ignorance.

During the soul's ascension, the soul disputes the right of desire to claim ownership and control. Desire is concerned, for it was sure that this soul could only "belong to me."[16] The soul denies desire's legitimacy, countering that; "I served you as a garment."[17] This separation, the detachment between the spirit and the material vehicle that bears it, seems to present a superficial dichotomy. Some critics and advocates of Gnosticism assert Mary is advocating a monastic life of self-depravation and abstinence from earthly desires.

This is an oversimplification. The authoress drunk wine, continually kissed Jesus and had sex with him, wept (normally while Peter was around), was proven to be a person of considerable financial worth, dressed with a sense of style and is universally reputed to have been an extremely beautiful woman. As Mary sat in the Gnostic bridal chamber with Jesus, she was fully aware of the worth of a smile, knowing that everything and event is part of God's creation. Her philosophy is simple, as she tries to either "profit or to forfeit"[18] from every earthly and divine experience. It is better to contentedly wear the garment of the flesh and discern what is the "foolish wisdom of flesh,"[19] knowing that both "heaven or . . . earth"[20] come from the same source and should be treated with the same reverence.

We couldn't be sure that the chaste, unsullied virgin Philip demands will be any more qualified to be a spiritual seeker than a zealous devotee of sex, drugs and rock and roll (we suspect the second type would be a more suitable personality). To know what is right, not to do what you hate implies experience, not abstinence, is the only antidote. To listen to or obey another is, at best, following the thoughts of others. Our predestined role is to find our voice and intuition, never to mindlessly recite the beliefs of acquaintances.

To control desire in a manner Philip would endorse suggests mere repression. All have seen what a dangerous path the Catholic churches have fumbled through, the perils this bizarre practice spawns are a legacy far too many young children have been forced to suffer.

Unlike many reputedly more civilised societies, traditional Aboriginal cultures were characterised by a complete openness when it came to all aspects of sexuality. Nothing was hidden and sexual acts were never condemned. The only offence that could ever occur in relation to sexual relationships, pertained specifically to who were regarded appropriate partners, as determined by rules of kinship. What happened could never be an issue, only who was considered relevant.

Children's games reflected the enlightened approach taken on matters of sexuality. Their games were never competitive and often imitated the most personal aspects of adult-life. Husbands and wives, making camp, secret liaisons and even intimate details of love-making were re-fashioned into play. Owing to the communal style of living, all members of the tribe never wearing clothes and the absolute conviction sex was a normal part of daily life; these children were raised in a society that would have offended many a devout Christian, Jew, Muslim and devotee of nearly all institutionalised religions.

Their nakedness and lack of shame shocked many early settlers in Australia, and almost immediately after contact clothing was no longer a curiosity for the clan, but compulsory. The sight of a naked body was far too confronting for many white settlers to elicit any response beyond biblical outrage, and a reassuring vindication of the superiority of a culture that championed the maxim, "clothes maketh the man." The problem being, in the eyes of many the reverse applied; no clothes maketh no-man, and once the entire race was ordained vastly inferior, there is only suffering and theft ahead for no-man.

When Mary speaks of "what binds"[21] and "surrounds me"[22] being overcome, she is suggesting an interaction with the entity performing the binding. Until an individual soul perceives the inner nature of any experience, it can not understand its essence and purpose then ultimately evaluate its worth. Once analysing its intrinsic merit, the soul is then able, if deemed necessary, to profit or forfeit from this experience.

Hiding behind four walls, pious vows of abstinence, celibacy, rote intoning of scriptural certainties and a multiplicity of other righteous acts of faith are championed as proofs of spiritual worth, but they are no more than a denial of reality. Once closeted in a remote place, a recluse can silently observe, but the lack of involvement in the world surrenders their right to do anything but expose their inability to cope with life's complexities.

After the Saviour "had said this, he departed."[23] The canonical four stop at his departure; none are prepared to venture past this vanishing point. The question that should immediately flow from this absence is why stop now. It would appear whatever took place after his death was unimportant and of no consequence. However, there is the potential that the motivation behind this omission was inspired by embarrassment and shame. Just before the group broke up Levi (Matthew) did say, let us be ashamed.

There is a distinct atmosphere of déjà vu, reminiscent of Jesus' final moments. "But they were grieved . . . wept greatly . . . how will they spare us."[24] As it was when Jesus was crucified, no male Apostle appears to have handled the situation particularly well. Instead of an expected traditional macho response of laughing off danger and travelling on high moral ground, we see tears, gnashing of teeth, and an overriding concern for personal welfare.

Amidst the sea of despair and fear one Apostle stood and called the others to account. Only one had the skills or courage to lead and encourage during this dire crisis; Mary. She was the only one who showed none of the despair many of the males were unable to conceal and unwilling to record.

"Do not weep and do not grieve nor be irresolute, for his grace will be entirely with you and will protect you."[25] When Mary "turned their hearts to the

Good"[26] in their moment of greatest peril, she was taking on the role of de-facto stewardship. Her attempts to embolden their wavering resolve, reminding all have the capacity to turn "into men,"[27] may appear to present a dilemma. However, Mary's recommendation is not a decree to change sex or a denigration of women, but rather a matter of Greek semantics. The term male symbolises anything spiritual or esoteric, and is a reflection of Gnosis. The opposite, female, represents the material or earthly existence. Later editions of the *Gospel of Mary* interpret the term male as being fully human or a true human being, rather than confuse the term with a specific gender.

Regardless of Mary's intentions, this presumptuous act of taking control was what troubled Peter so greatly. Simply because all knew she was the only rightful claimant. Furthermore, in every accepted account, after the Saviour fell and was resurrected the only person universally accepted as staying behind was Mary. There is nothing inconsistent in her adopting the role of leader during these volatile times. On every level bar one, Mary is Peter's superior; but that counted for very little in a patriarchal society where woman were treated as goods and chattels.

Mary's impassioned response to Peter's rejection left him speechless. When Levi (Matthew) stood up and defended Mary, Peter remained mute. She wept, not out of personal fear or concern, but in utter despair at the thought of being accused of misrepresenting or lying about the "Saviour"[28] and her consort. She directly challenges Peter in front of his compatriots, sobbing as she asks whether he really believes she "thought this up"[29] or was "lying."[30]

All, including Peter, knew Mary was incapable of such an outrage, and from that point, not one syllable passes his lips in protest. Peter's protracted silence leads one to believe he had nothing left to dispute, bar his own personal insecurities. Levi's (Matthew's) defence of Mary began by attacking Peter's predisposition for being "hot-tempered,"[31] yet still nothing by way of self-justification was forthcoming; his silence seems to imply a speechless admission of guilt.

An alternate ending to this supposed heretical account can be found on a fragmentary Greek copy of the *Gospel of Mary*. In this account Matthew (Levi), unable to tolerate the lack of respect shown to Mary, storms off in disgust and vows to make no further contact with any of the male Apostles. In some respects this conclusion is more in keeping with the general tone of the Gospel.

There is some substance in the assertion that while the gospel remaining in the jar doesn't directly support this version, there are some indications and deletions that leave behind some interesting possibilities. After Matthew stridently defends Mary's honour, the line that follows his speech begins with "when"[32] and is followed by a gap. Past this omission are ten concluding words stating that the Apostles left then began to preach in various un-stated locations. What did Matthew do immediately after berating Peter?

Matthew had the podium up to that point, and it would seem logical to assume "when" referred to what Matthew did immediately after he finished berating Peter. There appear to be three variations available; perhaps it may have been a non-descript reply reading something like, when he finished speaking he meekly sat down, or it is possible Matthew could have reconsidered his stance and repeatedly apologised for his impertinence realising Peter was correct and all women are indeed "not worthy."[33] Equally, there is the potential that "when" Matthew finished speaking, as it was in the Greek version, he was deeply offended by Peter's continuous disrespect. It is possible the distress Mary experienced, Peter's insinuations and the absence of any other male colleague springing to Mary's defence may have been too much to bear; leaving him with no alternative bar storming off and vowing never to speak to these men again.

After Jesus' departure, upheaval and grief overwhelmed the panicky ensemble. It was an unsettled time marked by weeping out of utter frustration, new esoteric revelations, Matthew vigorously defending Mary's honour, Andrew's ignorance and Peter's sexism. Yet within a climate of accusation, dread and tears the whole event appears to peter out into a benign exaltation to preach. If this conflict was, as many allege, a defining moment in the evolving splintering between esoteric and exoteric teachings, Levi's spirited defence may have continued past accusing some of his comrades of being unworthy.

Instead of the reputed feeble common response of agreeing to begin preaching everywhere, thereby leaving this argument unresolved, it would seem far more likely Matthew's indignation was not so easily soothed and he voted with his feet. Such a reaction is more consistent with the emotionally charged atmosphere, than the claimed indifference to the outcomes of Peter's accusation.

Mary speaks of Jesus first appearing before her in a vision, three of the four Gospels indirectly agree. In each of their accounts, Mary was either alone, or claimed to be with others when Jesus reappeared. It is the semantics of the word "vision" that needs deeper thought and reflection.

Within the *Gospel of Mary* no-one disputed Mary's character as she revealed her vision. None called into question the concept of Mary's style of revealing, being in any way, without precedent or of dubious merit. What she said two of the Apostles contended, but the esoteric way it was gathered left none of her critics prepared to voice any concerns before, during or after her revelations.

The vision occurred before Jesus "departed"[34] (or his ascension) and most definitely after his crucifixion, placing the appearance of the resurrected Messiah to Mary at an interesting approximate position on the time line. Its impact is emphasised when considering Peter's uncharacteristic back flip, as he implores Mary to reveal all those "hidden"[35] words. On no other occasion does Peter address Mary in such a respectful manner. She is the same "sister"[36] who was also "not worthy of life."[37] Mary's uncontested vision is of such monumental significance Peter is prepared to momentarily discard the phobias he holds dearest, just to listen to a mere woman. "The woman,"[38] who he openly acknowledges received a privilege he was never privy to and, equally, secret knowledge rightly deemed too deep for such an undeveloped soul as his.

When Mary asks the Saviour about the nature of her vision, she is praised as one who "did not waver"[39] in his presence. It seems a puzzling commendation, as it is unusual to fear the familiar sight of her closest companion, fear invariably relates to the unknown. If the resurrected physical body of Jesus stood before Mary, she may be startled for a second or two, but she should not waver or flee. The connotation behind wavering implies a degree of fear, perhaps a willingness to escape, from something misunderstood. A spirit or ghost would surely elicit such a response. It is possible this could be the same appearance or resurrection the *New Testament* refers to. An ethereal manifestation could easily explain this well documented lack of recognition Mary and others offered when first sighting the resurrected Jesus.

The same spirit, which first revealed itself to Jesus' partner and consort, then en-masse to his disciples, could be the same spiritual manifestation of light that appeared to the nineteen Apostles in *The Sophia of Jesus Christ.*

When Jesus finished speaking, "he departed."[40] No description of a fanfare is provided, just an anti-climatic economy class departure. There is no angelic manifestation or choral trumpeting, as the rejuvenated corpse slowly ascends up towards the celestial abode of the ethereal yonder.

"He departed," carries no regal majesty, in fact, it is neutral. The description is benign. Narratives of individuals normally have destinations and means of getting there. Apparently, Jesus came from somewhere, and returned to . . . nothing. Any Spirit that appears is an unknown event and unexplainable in this materialistic world. Where the apparition goes to, is only a bigger mystery. The spirit comes then departs, everything past that is a mysteron.

Many would object, insisting a body rose from the crypt and a body ascended upwards into the heavens. They insist the four Gospels have the answers, and they are correct. In a rare concordance all four do agree, Mary was definitely there. Yet when her account is finally unearthed, she speaks of a bland departure and symbolic journeys of the soul. There is nothing to support the notion of a material entity ascending upwards escorted by a multitude of angelic beings.

A fair proportion of the *Gospel of Mary* is damaged, and thus incomplete. Perhaps the most vexing omission are the words that would have followed "that is what sees the vision and it is . . ."[41] The next four pages were destroyed, and the sentences that followed may have explained many mysteries. Regardless, there is enough that survived to make some reasonable observations when assessing the meanings of the remaining sections of the text.

The final, undamaged segment of Mary's vision of the soul's ascension though these earthly temptations seems to parallel Milton's struggle with the seven deadly sins in *Paradise Lost.*

Wrath can be simple resentment and could, when placed in the wrong hand or collective hands, grow into righteous indignation of God. Wrath can be recognised in one of its seven incarnations, "darkness . . . desire . . . ignorance . . . excitement of death . . . flesh . . . foolish . . . wrathful wisdom."[42]

Wrath offers the soul all these blessings and seven gifts, with the potential of a life-long engagement. We need only accept its patronage then comply. Our soul reminds us of the possible future we could acquire, as long as we resist the allure of revenge. The anger, resentment, jealousy, things others do and say that annoy us, can be overcome and we can be unfettered, or, if one chooses, bound to for an eternity.

"Wrathful wisdom" can guide and inspire a righteous war fought on behalf of God. This clarion call has echoed throughout the ages and blighted nearly every continent since civilisation began. Wrath can be global or personal, whether primal motives that gratify the individual are nobler or baser than the wrathful wisdom many righteous nations champion, is more a matter of personal endeavour than impact. Either way it is harmful and the guilt is equally shared, whether others are affected is irrelevant to the personal damage the soul will still suffer. The soul recognises the potential harm and states, "what binds . . . and what surrounds me has been overcome, and my desire . . . and ignorance has died."[43]

The last words Jesus left behind were the most prophetic and tragic.

"Do not lay down any rules beyond what I appointed for you, and do not give a law like the lawgiver lest you be constrained by it."[44] According to the *Gospel of Thomas*, do not "tell lies"[45] or do what you "hate."[46] These two simple words are, in a nutshell, the secret wisdom Jesus bequeathed to the world. He left us rules, for he knew punitive laws constrain mankind and often lead to fanaticism. He sanctioned neither punishment nor inquisition, just personal guidelines.

Is the act of murder, the breaking of a rule or a law? Obviously it is a serious breach of a fundamental tenet of society and one of the major laws that underpins nearly every form of civil behaviour. Rules never deal with such grave issues, and don't apply to our penal system. So, by elimination, a rule and its non-adherence, should elicit a less severe penalty. Sports clubs and community associations set rules. Those who transgress are spoken to privately, occasionally fined and then publicly warned. If all else fails, they are politely asked to vacate the premises. The elected officials are prohibited from torturing, beheading and massacring any recalcitrant golfer. There's no doubt Jesus would not have approved of the many atrocities perpetrated by his church, on his behalf and with his blessing.

What actual rules did he set down? If one goes to the only book that exclusively contains Jesus' words and secret teachings (*The Gospel of Thomas*). There appears to be ten essential covenants he places on personal conduct. Ten seems a somewhat ironic number and, equally, predisposes one to rework these approaches into a familiar fashion. Each is based, and contains, at least one word from *Thomas*.

THOMAS' TEN COMMANDMENTS: (Revisited)

1. Do not "pray"[47] just accept.
2. Do not "fast";[48] sustain your body in comfort, then nurture your soul.

3. Whatever is placed on your table "bear"[49] it willingly unless you "hate"[50] it.
4. Whatever you "hate"[51], whether it be done to you or by you, neither copy or repeat.
5. Do not tell "lies"[52] to yourself or others.
6. Do not betray your integrity or say things "that which will defile you."[53]
7. "Give"[54] anything you really don't need to someone "from whom you will not get it back."[55]
8. "Businessmen and merchants,"[56] those that buy or sell their soul can never enter the "places of my father."[57]
9. Do not continue performing "circumcision,"[58] scar, sacrifice to, or intentionally hurt in the name of any God. (We are aware this request calls into question some Aboriginal rituals. No society or man-made set of rules can be perfect.)
10. Look "within"[59] yourself and every "stone."[60] God and Nature are identical, treat both with utmost reverence and the deepest respect.

All of these ten edicts are in accord with every word and deed of Mary.

Many accounts of Jesus spoke of the delineation between esoteric wisdom and his popular teachings, as well as a (presumably corresponding) disparity in the talents of each Apostle. One thread that remains constant throughout both texts relates to Mary's elevated station, they concur with the recently revised, if muted, acknowledgement of her status in the Vatican— that she was indeed, as Hippolytus claims, the "apostle to the apostles"[61].

Unfortunately this acceptance of Mary's status and dignity was never universal; others looked with different eyes and heard with different ears.

Chapter 8
Dialogue of the Saviour and Associates

(Dialogue of the Saviour): (60) Mary said, *"Tell me, Lord, why have I come to this place to profit or forfeit?"*[1]

(53) Mary said, "Thus with respect to 'the wickedness of each day,' and 'the labourer is worthy of his food,' and 'the disciple resembles his teacher.'" She uttered this as a woman who had understood completely.[2]
(54) The disciples said to him, "What is fullness and what is the deficiency?"[3]
(55) He said to them, "You are from fullness and you dwell in the place where deficiency is. And lo! His light has poured down upon me!"[4]
(56) Matthew said, "Tell me, Lord, how the dead die and how the living live."[5]
(57) The Lord said, "You have asked me about a saying [...] which eye has not seen, nor have I heard it except from you. But I say to you that when what invigorates a man is removed, he will be called 'dead'. And when what is alive leaves what is dead, what is alive will be called upon."[6]
(58) Judas said, "Why else, for the sake of truth, do they die and live?"[7]
(59) The Lord said, "Whatever is born of truth does not die. Whatever is born of woman dies."[8]
(60) Mary said, "Tell me, Lord, why have I come to this place to profit or to forfeit?"[9]
(61) The Lord said, "You make clear the abundance of the revealer!"[10]
(62) Mary said to him, "Lord, is there then a place which is [evil] or lacking truth?"[11]
(63) The Lord said, "The place where I am not!"[12]
(64) Mary said, "Lord, you are fearful and wonderful, and ... [...] ..... and those that do not know you."[13]
(65) Matthew said, "Why do we not rest at once?"[14]
(66) The Lord said, "When you lay down these burdens!"[15]
(67) Matthew said, "How does the small join itself to the big?"[16]
(68) The Lord said, "When you abandon the works which will not be able to follow you, then you will rest."[17]
(69) Mary said, "I want to understand all things just as they are."[18]
(70) The Lord said, "He who will seek out life! For this is their wealth. For the ... [...] ... of this cosmos is [...], and its gold and its silver are misleading."[19]

(71) His disciples said to him, "What should we do to ensure that our work will be perfect?"[20]
(72) The Lord said to them, "Be prepared in the face of everything. Blessed is the man who has found . . . [. . .] . . . the contest . . . his eyes. Neither did he kill, nor was he killed, but he came forth victorious."[21]
(73) Judas said, "Tell me, Lord, what the beginning of the path is."[22]
(74) He said, "Love and goodness. For if one of these existed among the governors, wickedness would never have come into existence."[23]
(75) Matthew said, "Lord you have spoken about the end of everything without concern."[24]
(76) The Lord said, "You have understood all the things I have said to you and you have accepted them on faith. If you have known them, then they are yours. If not, then they are not yours."[25]
(77) They said to him, "What is the place to which we are going?"[26]
(78) The Lord said, "Stand in the place you can reach!"[27]
(79) Mary said, "Everything established thus is seen."[28]
(80) The Lord said, "I have told you that it is the one who can see who reveals."[29]
(81) His disciples, numbering twelve, asked him, "Teacher, [. . . . . . serenity . . .] teach us . . . [. . .].[30]
(82) The Lord said, ". . . [. . .] . . . everything which I have . . . [. . .] you will . . . . . . [. . .] . . . you [. . .] . . . everything."[31]
(83) Mary said, "There is but one saying I will speak to the Lord concerning the mystery of truth: In this have we taken our stand, and to the cosmic we are transparent."[32]
(84) Judas said to Matthew, "We want to understand the sort of garments we are to be clothed with when we depart the decay of the flesh."[33]
(85) The Lord said, "The governors and the administrators possess garments granted only for a time, which do not last. But you, as children of truth, not with these transitory garments are you to clothe yourselves. Rather, I say to you that you will become blessed when you strip yourselves! For it is a great thing [. . .] outside."[34]
(86) [. . . said . . .] . . . speak, I . . . [. . .]. . ."[35]
(87) The Lord said, ". . . [. . .] . . .your Father . . .[. . .] . . ."[36]
(88) Mary said, "Of what sort is that mustard seed? Is it something from heaven or is it something from earth?"[37]

This scripture was penned after Jesus was crucified, and many biblical scholars are comfortable with a date "some time during the 2nd century."[38] For some, the time span is of an appropriate length to distance itself from the time the four accepted gospels were written, when the stories of Jesus' life were still first-hand accounts and the memories of Jesus' preaching was still comparatively fresh. The greater the gap in time, the greater the potential for amendments and revision, and, of course, the increasing span in time calls into question the documents reliability.

However Helmut Koester and Elaine Pagels are far from convinced, and suspect an earlier date is more in keeping with the content and presentation. They noted "parallels to the author's understanding of baptism in deutero—

Chapter 8: Dialogue of the Saviour and Associates

Pauline epistles suggest a date close to the turn of the first century."[39] If one wanted to be a little more adventurous, there is as much evidence to allow any commentator to state the date could be before "the turn of the first century,"[40] as there is after the first century.

All early biblical documents rarely depend upon any verifiable dating technique, Carbon 14 or any other scientific analysis. The manner of presentation and incidental events within the text may give indications of a general timescale, but we believe it is impossible to so specific as to calculate the time of authorship in terms of one or two decades. The particular century is viable and it may be one could be a little more definitive by narrowing down options in terms of half a century. To be any more precise needs a lot more than two highly respected scholars providing a subjective comparative corroboration between different scriptures, and we would argue whether this scripture was compiled just before or just after "the turn of the century"[41] is inconsequential. If the text was written when the four gospels were penned barely ten to twenty years later is irrelevant, as either date suggests it was created at the same time, or very shortly after the four gospels.

Within the thirty-five verses selected from the *Dialogue of the Saviour* are nineteen statements or questions attributed to Thomas, Matthew or Mary. These three Apostles were separated from the other disciples to receive secret teachings, deemed too advanced for the rest of the disciples. Within Gnostic circles, it was generally agreed they were the most favoured and privileged of Jesus' entourage when it came to esoteric matters. United, they seek answers from Jesus on four occasions, Matthew makes three enquiries and offers one elaboration, Thomas questions Jesus three times while Mary asks three questions (two are rhetorical) and supplies five observations or elaborations. There is no doubt Jesus is actively encouraging Mary in her endeavours.

Does Mary "profit"[42] or "forfeit"[43]? Both; she is right to assert the more you learn the less there is to know and the more there is to comprehend. To be a "revealer"[44] and to "understand"[45] means she above all, has done both. Every experience is only of benefit if something is gained or lost, if nothing occurs there is no point becoming involved. From every experience something must either be added or subtracted.

Within the same dialogue, Matthew asks of a saying which Jesus responded by saying "nor have I heard it,"[46] and Matthew is corrected. This response is hardly a resounding endorsement of the quality of Matthew's musings. On other occasions the response Jesus gives Matthew is often personalised, suggesting the need for a correction of personal misunderstandings yet to be fully developed. (e.g. 66. "When you,"[47] 68 "When you"[48]) Matthew's limitations are contrasted against Mary's wisdom.

The saying (83) concerning the "mystery of truth,"[49] is of such gravity and depth that Mary must "speak to the Lord"[50] by herself. This exclusion suggests Thomas and Matthew are not part of whatever preceded her announcement. The secrets spoken of were not for their ears, and more importantly, who is revealing to whom? If I say I wish to speak to someone about anything, whatever follows will be at my instigation. The inference being, I am the possessors of something I decided to share with another, who is unaware of the topic to be raised. Moreover, at no stage beforehand did Jesus indicate a desire to speak on this type of issue. The enquiry is exclusively Mary's idea and her wisdom, and is offered in the plural form as she speaks on behalf of their union.

The absence of any previous reference to such a weighty matter is puzzling. There is no apparent continuity or follow up, in Verse (84) Thomas and Matthew are chatting amongst themselves, deliberating over what they will ask the Saviour next. In fact this interlude is the only time during the entire gospel "Judas said to Matthew,"[51] or any disciple directly addresses anyone other than the Saviour. But that is exactly what they are doing, talking among themselves sharing personal concerns about the decay of the flesh. Neither directly speaks to Jesus or acknowledges his presence as they share their common concerns.

This segment seems erratic, with the distinct hint of later deletions. The inconsistency could be due to a variety of innocent reasons. It may well be due simply to a result of decay. Some may claim this is purely co-incidental, but we suspect any further elaboration on this esoteric topic would only serve to enhance Mary's reputed wisdom of the deepest mysteries. The same pattern is evident in the *Gospel of Mary*, where just as Mary begins to reveal a vision she shared with Jesus, the next four pages are missing. The text resumes with Mary's concluding three paragraphs of her monologue followed by Andrew and Peter accusing Mary of lying. As was most probably the case in *Dialogue of the Saviour*, an orthodox scribe may have felt compelled to edit or delete whatever followed Verse (83), as any extension of this topic would only augment Mary's reputation. Her proclamation announcing the next area she wished to discuss, is an action no male Apostle would consider, as it is beyond their capacities. Mary has no such limitations. If the text is intact and untouched, then the only motivations that appear available to explain Matthew and Thomas' private musings are a distinct lack of courtesy, or a distinct lack of Saviour and Mary.

In Verse (36) Jesus takes the three chosen Apostles to the "edge of heaven."[52] Apparently the other Apostles disappear from that point onwards, yet, Verse (81) begins with "His [disciples], numbering twelve, asked him . . ."[53] He offers them a reply in Verse (82) and then Mary speaks about the nature of truth to Jesus and by Verse (83) the twelve decamp. In Verse (84) the remaining two male disciples seem to be alone or extremely rude. Something has been deliberately hidden or others have revised the text, and since this scripture is primarily a dialogue, we are left groping in the dark. The chronology and sequencing of this section is a real dilemma. It reads as if a censor, or censors, have rearranged or deleted any segment that relates to Mary's more probing enquiries and expositions. If so, the motivation could be because what was said was considered too sacred, as truly secret teachings can't be written down, or perhaps this is another attempt to conceal Mary's proper status.

Chapter 8: Dialogue of the Saviour and Associates

The fact that the twelve momentarily appear as a homogenous group is worthy of reflection. There are questions that immediately arise that relate to Judas, the reputed betrayer of Jesus. The inference being, whenever the appendage twelve is used in biblical matters, it is automatically assumed to include Judas. Regardless whether Judas was a member of the enclave, this anonymous group were identified by its' number and even though no names were given, there can be no room for Mary when discussing the make-up of the elite twelve. We have to assume Mary had temporarily vanished. No explanations or preparatory statements are supplied beforehand. Nor does the nebulous group of twelve speak again; the next twenty verses are conspicuous by the absence and silence of at least ten of the twelve Apostles.

Alone, Thomas discusses with Matthew what he will say next to the Lord, using the plural form in their deliberations. The original conversational format between the three Apostles and Jesus is re-established in Verse (85) and continues uninterrupted until the passage is complete. It was as if the minor interlude never occurred. It reads like there were four, thirteen, two then four, and all of these changes in personnel occur over five verses. It appears the scribe was either being cryptic, creative or clumsy.

Many biblical scholars claim this Gospel closely resembles the *Gospel of John* paralleling many of the brief dialogue units. Other commentators go even further, claiming *John* was actually penned by Mary, her brother Lazarus or perhaps her son John was the author. Considering Mary is either individually or collectively involved in over sixty per cent of all comments offered by the three Apostles in *Dialogue of the Saviour*, some could suggest Mary is the unifying ingredient within both Gospels.

Based on this dialogue, who rightfully earned the appendage beloved Apostle? Mary is the one "he loved . . . more,"[54] knew more and "reveals."[55] The woman Peter turned to because she knew words "we do not."[56] Philip, Thomas, Levi (Matthew) and Bartholomew independently nominate Mary's wisdom and knowledge as unparalleled amongst the Apostles. These affirmations contradict everything any patriarchal society cherished, and surely male referees of this pedigree should be of some consequence. The cultural affront these men enthusiastically chronicled highlights the issue central to all of the mysteries, Mary's role in Jesus' ministry.

When Mary is unaccompanied by her consort, as was the case in the *Gospel of Mary*, she is an object and mirror of the inadequacies of some observers. Whether it is Andrew's ignorance in the face of these unsettling "strange"[57] teachings, or Peter's rampant sexism, she seems to be in a constant state of defence. Without the Saviour's protective presence, Mary's role is reduced to a common liar and of an inferior gender when in the presence of some of her male comrades. When the Saviour is present, her status is far more elevated, as Jesus' public displays of affection and commendation make her worth indisputable. The only question remaining relates to where to redraw the line.

The other two Apostles were chosen by Jesus to reveal some esoteric mysteries because of their talent. Both ask the Saviour about all manner of pragmatic concerns that many today would equally be concerned about. They enquire about death, the place of "rest,"[58] why rest is not guaranteed, matters "eye has not seen,"[59] the "beginning of the path,"[60] the "end"[61] and the "garments"[62] we are to be clothed in after we die.

Mary was silent when it came to enquiring about these practical issues. She acts as a revealer; elaborating and cryptically questioning Matthew and Thomas when expounding upon esoteric matters such as; wickedness, purpose, reality, Heaven, the "place where I am not"[63] and the mystery of truth. The character and depth of the topics chosen suggests there existed delineation in wisdom between the Apostles in respect to the deepest mysterons. These two male Apostles seek answers to a variety of pragmatic issues, yet Jesus never wavers in his response, continually returning to Mary's revelation of "profit and forfeit."

Jesus draws from the notion of profit or forfeiture, as one attempts, lifetime upon lifetime, to live in a manner that "resembles his teacher."[64] When he tells them to "stand in the place you can reach,"[65] the depth and span of their stance is predicated around what individual gains and losses (your personal gnosis) were accepted while cast into these lodgings. Neither Jesus, nor Mary, said "stand in the place we can reach," as it is not we but you that seeks. The best we can offer is an attentive audience, sympathy and occasional assistance. When Mary added "everything established thus is seen,"[66] it was always dependent upon a viewpoint. To see and be "seen" is a task for the individual. It's not we but you; how you look, where you look and what you look with. Once again the recurring theme re-emerges; books, individuals and institutions who claim to be authorities cannot, in themselves, guarantee an achievement of any substance in our personal quest for knowledge and salvation.

Mary's gnosis is amply illustrated in Verse (53). We found the contents far too daunting to even attempt to offer an incomplete statement as to what this verse could possibly mean. Very few are foolhardy or arrogant enough to claim they understand "completely,"[67] and since we have no right to make a claim of perfection, it may be wiser to let discretion prevail. It seems more prudent to leave any commentary on the verse with a question mark next to it.

Does the teacher select the student, or is the reverse true? Would past lives have an impact on these choices? What causes "the wickedness of each day"[68]? Where does one go to seek guidance? Is there a need to go anywhere? What is the "food"[69] and who is always the "laborer"[70]? What task or hurdle does the toiler in physical burdens have to undertake? Is the manner in which the task is undertaken the reward or "food"? Or, can the reward be dependent on the outcome or result? The eventual success or failure: who is responsible, the student or teacher? What or who is a teacher? How does one recognise the student? Is this all a form of karma, a sort of cause and effect?

In Verses (56) & (57) Matthew seems to be asking about mortality, about what happens when the "dead die."[71] It appears a valid concern and legitimate question. The whole enquiry is dismissed out of hand, and the abrupt manner of Jesus' rebuttal must have surprised Matthew. If Jesus hadn't heard of it before "except from you,"[72] it must be manifestly false. Apparently Jesus is denying the fact that we live and die.

It would appear Jesus is refuting the concept of life and death itself. The superficial shell, the flesh we are cast into will fall, but that is not necessarily the essence of the soul. If the soul is immortal, it can never die. If the soul is flesh, Matthew was right to ask and Jesus wrong in his reply. However Jesus was compelled to object, he knows the flesh is a vehicle, a mere carriage in need of a driver and road map with a destination to head towards, or, if the navigator chooses, away from. The route each chooses is unique, but one thing all can be sure of, it is endless and still under construction as we speak, act and think. That is why when "what is alive"[73] (soul) "will be called upon"[74] (judged), it can never die, as it is the soul that "invigorates"[75] a person and makes them "alive."[76] When finally called to account after completing each Earthly manifestation, the soul is asked to bring to their judgement all the words, deeds and thoughts it produced.

Within the damaged segment of this text there appear to be four participants (excluding Verse 81); two are seeking answers, one is offering answers, and then there is Mary. Her position in the equation is open to conjecture, but one fact seems incontestable; whatever station is assigned to her, it can not be any less than above the Apostles. Alongside is insufficient and demeaning, the scope of above is the only aspect open for debate. Never do the male disciples orchestrate Jesus' agenda claiming to speak to or for the Lord regarding, simply because it is beyond their capabilities. They receive from the Saviour at his initiative, as they would never consider selecting topics they feel need to be raised; only Mary could do that.

Just as it was in *Thomas*, the sparse and damaged account of these three Apostles does not call into question our belief in an Aboriginal inspiration behind these esoteric teachings. There is nothing written which would contradict any elemental component of the *Dreaming*. Both philosophies are insistent that each individual's salvation lies solely within their grasp, never another's.

Thomas was corrected by Jesus when he stated that the "governors dwell above us, so it is they who will rule over us!"[77] Jesus was concerned Thomas would rely upon the "governors" of the material realm who would attempt to influence him and others, yet they were patently unworthy. He chastised Thomas, reminding him that it "is you who will rule over them,"[78] but then adds a proviso. Thomas, along with any seeking Jesus and Mary's mystical wisdom, must "rid yourselves of jealousy"[79] before they are fit to rule over anyone.

A task of such complexity needs an awareness of the society Thomas and his associates were trapped in, and an ability to identify the factors that can create an environment full to the brim with "jealousy" and incompetent "governors." Any society that regards the acquisition of power and money as a worthwhile pursuit, and equates poverty and the lack of personal possessions as a sign of weaknesses and an imposition, must be saturated in inequity and "jealousy." Thomas, and others, lived in a place and time where if you did "have money"[80] and gave it to someone "from whom you will not get it back,"[81] most would regard such an act as fiscally irresponsible that will inevitably see the citizen lose wealth and status and finally, lapse into financial insolvency.

Societies that adopted the *Dreaming* as their moral and spiritual base are obliged to share whatever they have. As well as accepting the communal ownership of everything, each person is required to go on long personal sabbaticals referred to as walkabouts. The individual may be gone for weeks on end until he or she makes personal contact with the Creator and prioritises their life so that they can maintain their interaction with the spirits. At no stage during this time of introspection is the individual required or inclined to give any credence to the "governors" Thomas and Jesus were familiar with. These Aboriginal men and women were seeking out their spirits for spiritual wisdom and guidance, never financial advice and strategies to increase the worth of their personal portfolios and investments.

When this person returns from their spiritual pilgrimage to his or her clan, their will be no personal possessions to covet or positions of leadership inherited due to the accumulation of wealth or through some supposed blood-line that distinguishes their superior parentage from others. All are equal in every respect, whether a toolmaker, weaver, artist or storyteller, every skill is valued equally. Living under such conditions where there is no money or private stash of wealth (whether it is money, shells or pigs is irrelevant) creates a society where the potential to harbour jealous thoughts, coveting another's possessions or position of authority contradicts every aspect of their lifestyle and a central tenet of the *Dreaming*. We are not naïve enough to suggest these destructive thoughts didn't occur, after all, all humans share one common trait; imperfection. Accepting our human frailties are a shared attribute, this societal structure was attempting to redress our flaws and create an environment where sharing was obligatory and the personal accumulation of anything material was a vice.

Perhaps, at this juncture, when assessing Mary's standing, there is a need to accept and state the obvious. Philip made it clear that Jesus loved her more, her mind, beauty and wisdom, because it was her reward. Unfortunately the devotion Jesus showered upon Mary was not infectious. If any woman became one of the two primary deliverers of gnosis, amongst an audience which would contain many chauvinistic men, most males would storm out in revulsion before Mary's first sentence was completed. As things stood, the best she gets from some of her associates is smouldering aggression. It was their message and story, but one had his hands nailed to a tree and soon after the other was forced to flee.

There are some undeniable clues as to Mary's significance and the reason she is exalted by some and hated by others. Her deep wisdom is reflected within the comments she offers after announcing her intention to begin a private discussion with Jesus into the deepest mysteries of truth (Verse 83).

Chapter 8: Dialogue of the Saviour and Associates

(88) "[Mary said, "Of what] sort is that [mustard seed]? Is it something from heaven or is it something from earth?"[82]

The verse begins with Mary deciding to discuss what the essence of a mustard seed is and its place of origin. At first glance the statement seems a touch confusing, simply because neither the seed nor any appropriate analogy was raised earlier by Jesus within the discourse.

Elsewhere, Gnostic texts deal with such specific issues. *The Gospel of Thomas* Verse (20) contains Jesus' response to the disciples asking about the "kingdom of heaven."[83] Jesus compared the kingdom to a mustard seed, because of its potential to shelter and protect the "birds of the sky"[84] (our soul). The metaphor relates to the primary function of heaven and the motivation behind Jesus' ministry.

As it was earlier when Mary cryptically told Matthew and Thomas of their duty to both "profit" and "forfeit," so it is here. This revelation was not for Jesus' ears, as Jesus spoke of this same topic on many occasions. The celestial place the Apostles seek is, as Mary states, here. The place of the Father, the kingdom they are unable to locate is, as Mary reveals to the two Apostles, "something from heaven"[85] and "from earth."[86]

The two rhetorical questions Mary supplies (Verses 60 and 88) are solely for the edification of the spiritual novices in the gathering (Matthew and Thomas). Mary's knowledge and gnosis of the deepest mysteries, gives her that right. Jesus endorsed her elevated position and made it clear her knowledge of the esoteric matters was superior to any male Apostle.

Thomas highlights the comparative chasm in esoteric wisdom by following Mary's insight into duality and the place of redemption, seeking to know the manner in which he should pray. This concern appears to be a somewhat a petty issue Jesus had dismissed as being inconsequential many times before (e.g. *Gospel of Thomas*, Verse 6).

We chose the term partner with the greatest care and with some reluctance. We would be satisfied to acknowledge Mary's station as simply above the disciples, and leave the cynics and fundamentalists insulted, rather than outraged. Unfortunately, Verse (98) leaves us with no other plausible alternative.

Jesus' reply to Mary's damaged inquiry is one of the most revealing statements found within the entire set of documents discovered at Nag Hammadi.

(98) "[The Lord said, "Right. For] you know [. . .] . . . if I dissolve [. . .] . . . will go to his [place]."[87]

Mary (Verse 97) asks of "works"[88] and, of that "which] dissolves a [work],"[89] beyond that, too much is missing to assert anything with confidence. However, once again the raising of the next topic of discussion, the act of transforming, is at her behest. It is Jesus' reply, or that which still remains that reveals so much.

"Right": is a simple and elementary affirmation. What was said by Mary was worthy of commendation and lacked the need for any elaboration. Whatever the insightful observation was, it may appear to be another victim to the decay of time. Yet within the rest of his reply there are some powerful indicators of the importance of her observation. "For you know," is no less challenging. Mary is praised for her wisdom and what she revealed in the preceding verse. Mary's revelation was totally in accord with the Lord's grace and knowledge. After this point all that is left behind is to "dissolve" and "go to his [place]." For many, if not nearly all, the act of spiritual ascension and the destination this resurrection leads the soul is the ultimate mystery, not so in Mary's case.

According to Jesus Mary knows of this "place" and the manner of our crossing over once we (dissolve) vacate our bodies. It would appear she understands the great mystery; the essence of mysticism is based around a conviction that one can commune with the divine— with God and heaven— directly without the intercession of a priest or sacred scripture. Jesus is unequivocal; Mary can do this, as she knows of "I" (Jesus) and of "his place" (Heaven). Once "everything established thus is seen,"[90] there are no mysteries and no place or person on this mortal sphere left for Mary to "profit" or "forfeit" from. It is her karma and right to stand alongside Jesus. Perhaps this does reinforce Laurence Gardner's belief that Mary Magdalene knew the secret name of God.

The rest of the male Apostles are repeatedly admonished in the canonical Gospels for their inability to detect the "kingdom is inside of you."[91] All Mary receives is God's blessing, and far less from some of the more prejudiced Apostles. Their words were tainted by a biased perception that distorted original truths into reassuring renditions. Their expectations morphed the message into one far more acceptable to their male sensibilities. Of all the outrages Peter had to endure, none was more insulting than being forced to respect the words and deeds of a mere female.

Much that followed the revision at Nicea could not be further from the truth. The supposedly heretical text, *Sophia of Jesus Christ* begins with "his twelve disciples and seven women continued to be his followers,"[92] that it continued is a surprise, as the great majority of the general public are unaware it began with a mixed ensemble of nineteen Apostles.

As briefly mentioned earlier why were the male Apostles referred to as twelve? This is not an isolated event, as Verse (81) refers to "his disciples numbering twelve"[93] and neither account contains any caveats or remonstrations about the inappropriate presence of Judas at these special meetings occurring after Jesus' death. Surely on every occasion this number appears, as it often does throughout the New Testament, this label automatically includes Judas? As the apparition detailed in the *Sophia of Jesus Christ* took place 550 days after Jesus' crucifixion, it appears Judas' attendance in *Sophia* and *Dialogue* seems to support the alternate interpretation of the events leading up to Judas kissing Jesus on the cheek, as found within the recently rediscovered *Gospel of Judas*.

Whatever did take place; according to this scripture, was never an act of betrayal. Judas was portrayed as one of Jesus' closest companions and merely obeying the Saviour's instructions. Judas had a higher mission to fulfil, and it was for this reason *Matthew* stated that Jesus declared "friend, do what you are here to do ... the prophecies of the Scriptures must be fulfilled."[94]

The text is not a recent creation or a forgery, as Tertullian complained about the allegations made in this Gospel in 180 A.D. It was known of well before Tertullian recorded his unease because of the supposed heretical nature of these writings, and could quite possibly be compiled around the same time, or soon after, the canonical Gospels.

The demarcation in status between Mary and the Apostles we feel is present throughout *Dialogue of the Saviour;* is also the major element within the *Sophia of Jesus Christ (Pistis Sophia)*. The text is primarily a dialogue between Jesus and Mary, with the duties of the male Apostles relegated to that of incidental participants and witnesses. Mary's personality is so dominant and culturally challenging, that Peter was unable to restrain his tongue, remonstrating with Jesus yet again, about Mary's impertinence and monopoly of conversation. Unwilling to accept this offence continuing, Peter complained bitterly to Jesus. In Peter's eyes, Mary had no right to speak, "My Lord, we will not endure this woman, for she taketh the opportunity from us and thath let none of us speak, but she discourseth many times."[95]

Peter was partially correct in his observation, as Mary was responsible for well over half the questions recorded within this scripture. However, as was the case in *The Dialogue of the Saviour*, Mary does much more than adopt the role of questioner. Some commentators claim she takes on the role of an "interlocutor,"[96] raising matters at her instigation, offering "interpretations of Jesus' teachings"[97] as Mary attempts to "illuminate what Jesus is saying."[98]

The concerns Mary feels obliged to discuss are quite expansive, and very similar to those raised in *Dialogue of the Saviour;* the end of the world, the source of truth, the soul's purification, the true meaning of what "way will the souls have delayed themselves here outside, and in what type will they be quickly purified"[99] could mean and many other cryptic topics are expounded upon.

As it was in *Dialogue of the Saviour*, it could be that Jesus and Mary were conducting a rhetorical conversation for the benefit of those privileged to listen. We believe Mary is claiming a status well above her station (which is highly unlikely), or being patronised by Jesus to speak on such esoteric matters. No other Apostle ever adopted the position of explaining Jesus' intentions and prompting him. They were neither encouraged nor motivated to act as translator and guide, highlighting at their whim passages and thoughts, then meticulously explaining the spiritual nuances involved within the answer. Jesus allocated this privileged task to his most talented Apostle, Mary.

Some male contemporaries and critics claim Mary's usurping the rightful male role of Peter as interlocutor and assistant to Jesus, is a reflection of her ego or the biased revisionism by women and their misguided male supporters, attempting to create a false rationale to justify a formal female role within the Church structure. They may believe the blatant overstepping of the limits of what women were allowed to do and say publicly, outraged many, and was due to misguided encouragement or arrogance. While this belief is feasible, we believe they are mistaken. Jesus' intention was to act as a catalyst, constantly commending Mary in *Pistis Sophia* as being blessed, having a heart more spiritual than any mortal and the only person to earn the privilege to inherit the Kingdom of Light.

Mary had no choice but to obey. Jesus was insisting she adopt the role of revealer. Upon crucifixion her station as an apprentice had surely come to an end, as her equality in status is enshrined within his commendations. Only this consideration would explain why Jesus was compelled to exalt and praise Mary (Maria), stating, "Excellent, Maria. Thou art blessed beyond all women upon earth, because thou shalt be the plemora of all Plemoras and the completion of all completions."[100] As far as Jesus was concerned, nothing he knew could be hidden from Mary, as she was complete. To be nominated by Jesus to be the "completion of all completions," infers the task is finished and it is time to move on to the next stage. Jesus was emphatic, her duties were finished, it was for this reason he insisted she "speak openly and do not fear. I will reveal all things which thou seekest."[101]

The general impact of this scripture appears to separate Jesus' Apostles according to talent and esoteric wisdom. Mary's gnosis is complete; she has no mortal equal. Perhaps her unique status is best illustrated by Mary's reaction to one of Jesus' revelations. It wasn't a case of what she did or said, but more the opposite. To break into an extended meditative state for an hour and utter nothing beyond asking leave to speak, and then be praised in extremely complementary terms, demands further deliberation.

There were no questions or incredulous shrugs offered by Mary, as was often the case when Jesus chose to reveal an esoteric secret to some of his male followers. Mary chose to react to Jesus' words by gazing "fixedly into the air for the space of an hour."[102] After she broke her extended silence, she requested permission to speak openly and presumably share her vision.

Her temporary sabbatical, although shorter in duration, has many similarities to the Aboriginal walkabout. This was a time of silence and reflection when the initiate spent time alone walking through their Tribal Estate and devoted every second seeking out introspective spiritual truths. We believe that all that actually differs between Mary and the *Dreaming* when it comes to seeking out the voices of the first day is the timing.

Jesus responded to her request with complete confidence in her abilities, he saw no need in waiting for Mary to speak, confident in assuming whatever she was about to say after an hour of silence and intense meditation was deserving of the highest praise. He spoke in a reverential manner that seems to have echoed across many other banished Gnostic texts. "Mary, thou blessed one, whom I will perfect in all mysteries, of those of the heights, discourse in openness, thou, whose heart is raised to the Kingdom of Heaven more than all my brethren."[103]

The similarities to the *Dreaming* are not restricted to meditative style, but also relates to content. In Chapter 25 of *Pistis Sophia* there is an account resembling *Genesis*, but with an obvious connection to a far more ancient inspiration. "And Melchisedec, the Receiver of the Light, purifieth those powers . . . gather together all matter from them all; and the servitors of all the rulers of the Fate and the servitors of the sphere which is below the aeons, take it and fashion it into the souls of men and cattle and reptiles and wild-beasts and birds, and send them down into the world of mankind . . . and they become souls in this region."[104]

In this version of creation there is no separation between species, "they" is inclusive and involves the same "matter" expressed in different material forms. Whether beast, bird or human, the whole equation occurs simultaneously and is drawn from the same eternal spring. The *Dreaming* accepts no distinction, every Spirit that created a human tribe also created an animal tribe— they are, in every sense of the word, their soul brothers and sisters. All material creations that are given a soul come from the same "matter," there is no edict ordaining the superiority of one species above any other.

A *Dreaming* story about *Woonyoomboo* (the Creation Spirit), shared by the *Jarlmadangah* people of the Kimberley Region, describes how enmeshed the Spirits of humans, animals and even seeds are within the fabric of their culture. It is their belief "in the Dreaming, all the animals were first human beings or Ancestral Spirits before they became animals. The people of today come from the spirits of these animals."[105]

Woonyoomboo travelled across the country and was joined by companions including "children/whistle ducks"[106] and a "man/crocodile called Linykoora."[107] As their journey continued they camped by a billabong where *Woonyoomboo* saw the giant serpent *Yoonygoorookoo* and "speared"[108] the sacred reptile, then "rode away on the back of the serpent."[109] The further the two went the more land formations and rivers were made, they continued until their task was completed. *Woonyoomboo* turned into a "rufous night heron"[110] and all that accompanied him on his walkabout were transformed into "animals, seeds, flowers and fish. These are the Creation People."[111]

Bill Neidjie advised any who have the inclination to accept the precepts of the *Dreaming*, that they must embrace parity between all creations as an elemental truth. According to *Pistis Sophia*, the equality of species means "the souls of men and cattle and reptiles and wild-beasts and birds"[112] are identical, as is Bill's observation. "Listen carefully, careful and this spirit e come in your feeling and you will feel it . . . anyone that. I feel it . . . my body same as you. I telling you this because the land for us never change round. Places for us, earth for us, star, moon, tree, animal, no-matter what sort of a animal, bird or snake . . . all that animal same like us. Our friend that."[113]

In Bill's world, and that of the *Jarlmadangah* people, everything is the "same like us." There is no metaphor here, it is extremely literal. Bill draws his inspiration from the *Dreaming,* from a time where "the rulers gather together all matter"[114] under the "servitors"[115] of "the rulers"[116] (Ancestral Spirits). These Spirits "send them down"[117] (men, cattle, reptiles, beasts, birds) to "the world of mankind."[118] Bill is certain there is unity in all creations; that is why "we came this world, animal and man and woman."[119]

Irrespective of whether the connections to the *Dreaming* can be substantiated in this text, there is one aspect of this text where there is a consensus; Mary receives more praise, time and latitude than any other Apostle. Indications of Mary's endorsed superiority can also be found within the Gospels of *Thomas, Mary* and *Philip*. Her unique role as spiritual guide, esoteric questioner and revealer is a common theme and was also made evident in the lost texts, *The Greater Questions of Mary Magdalene* and *The Lesser Questions of Mary Magdalene*.

All copies of these scriptures have coincidentally disappeared however the historian and theologian, Epiphanius of Syria, did make some references to certain details found within *Greater*. Epiphanius' report (*Against Heresies*) should have some standing, as his account was meant as a critique, not a commendation, and he would have no reason to exaggerate the scope of Mary's wisdom or talents. The reality was, as an ardent devotee of Orthodox Christianity, if revision did occur, he would be more inclined to minimise or conceal any act or word that may substantiate Gnostic claims of her being the beloved Apostle. Regardless, when discussing the contents of *The Greater Questions of Mary Magdalene*, Epiphanius does acknowledge Mary was taken to a mountaintop by Jesus: who then revealed to her a secret teaching that shocked Mary so profoundly it caused her to faint.

This is by no means an isolated account of her Divine powers and knowledge. Stories and rumours of Mary's wisdom and power are prevalent. According to the *Golden Legend,*[120] one of the many miracles performed by Mary Magdalene involved restoring to life a woman who had been dead for two years. In gratitude to Mary, the Prince of Marseilles (his wife was revived) decreed that Lazarus was ordained Bishop of Marseilles, and Maximin the Bishop of the neighbouring city of Aix. He banished all other religions and philosophies within his lands in deference to Mary and her wisdom.

Modestus, the seventh century ruler of Jerusalem, recorded that Mary Magdalene was a Saint and martyr. He described a scene from the travels of Philip, Bartholomew and Marianne (Mary). They apparently attracted the unwanted attention of the authorities after Mary healed the pro-Consol's wife from almost certain death. Outraged by the perceived use of sorcery and magic amulets, Bartholomew and Philip were stripped, searched then tortured. Unable to find a potion or charm to explain the miracle, they turned their attentions on Mary. After stripping her, she became an "ark of glass full of light and fire and everyone ran away."[121] All, including Mary's companions, fled in terror. This account may be fictional, but the source is highly regarded, and we fail to see what motivation could inspire the male ruler of Palestine to exalt a female's miraculous powers, beyond an earnest desire to report the truth or a perverse need to be publicly ridiculed.

In every early account of Mary, although penned by different authors, there is a commonality. No male chronicler made an attempt to question the veracity of the information given, nor did they challenge the notion of this woman receiving special knowledge or possessing supernatural powers, their reports were presented as a factual report of an actual event.

With the notable exception of the mystical and extremely challenging Gnostic text, *Pistis Sophia*, there is a distinct pattern when it comes to every other account recovered (regardless of complexion) when Mary is involved. Even if she is reluctantly permitted to speak and her words are recorded for posterities' sake, her time at the podium seems to be vigorously supervised by many editors and impatient censors. All of the long treatises and extensive elaborations of many esoteric topics that were present in *Greater/ Lesser Questions of Mary Magdalene* are lost.

The exposition of the true nature of Mary's vision in the *Gospel of Mary* begins as abruptly as it ends with, "what sees the vision and it is . . ."[122] and is followed by a vacuum, as Pages 11-14 have co-incidentally vanished. The text resumes at the completion of her discourse on the soul's inner essence, but the scant and disjointed presentation remaining hardly does justice to the secret teaching Peter begged Mary to reveal.

It could be possible to deduce the *Gospel of Mary* may have been revised with one major imperative; any page dealing solely with Mary was destroyed. Mary's lengthy exposition of this vision vanished along with the next four pages, the text concludes with Mary's final three paragraphs before Andrew, then Peter, call Mary a liar. The remains of the *Gospel of Mary* only contain pages that feature other Apostles with Mary, supplemented by five sentences and three paragraphs from Mary. Surely there could be no other Gospel or scripture that has less spoken or written by an Apostle it was named after?

What compounds our suspicions is the deafening silence when dealing with Mary's role within the Synoptic three. Mary is not permitted to utter one syllable throughout these Gospels, while her script is restricted to a brief cameo appearance during the resurrection in *John*. According to many accounts, Mary was a woman of impeccable degree and highly regarded, yet apparently, her words were shunned by many scribes and authorities. People avoid whatever makes them uncomfortable, she either said and did nothing, or said and did far too much.

Even within the Gnostic texts where Mary is featured, she is always restricted in format to question and answer. Ignoring *Pistis Sophia*, nowhere else in either type of scripture is Mary accorded the right to speak in consecutive paragraphs and is rarely permitted the luxury of a sequence of three connected sentences. The reason for this brevity must be due to coincidence or design.

The reasons for the continued presence of *Pistis Sophia,* which was also pronounced heretical, was solely due to the ingenuity of true believers who, over the centuries, managed to keep some copies of the scriptures hidden until the times were more accepting. This lengthy text is in tact and obviously unedited, as more than half of the questions and explanations offered are from Mary.

The esoteric saying Jesus taught Mary was, according to Epiphanius, of such gravity it caused her to faint from shock. Her extreme reaction is out of character; Mary has witnessed her consort's crucifixion, attended to Jesus' corpse and was the first witness of the resurrection, yet collapses when merely spoken to. However, Bartholomew did claim Mary was able to "consume all the world"[123] by uttering one saying. There may be a connection, it could be Mary's final earthly lesson culminated in Jesus revealing this ultimate power, and as such, a dramatic experience of this magnitude could cause her to faint. An esoteric teaching of this omnipotent breadth would surely unsettle any mortal, and if true, it could be asserted Bartholomew was right, as Mary literally held the world in her hands.

There seem to be two categories of secrets existing within these texts, the hidden secrets, the gnosis some need to be reborn, and the contrived mysteries. They are the male-made hindrances and obstacles some mortals have manufactured in an attempt to resurrect their flawed personal interpretations, and insert them into what is purported to be the sanctified teachings of Jesus.

Chapter 9
The Alternate Genesis

(The Sentences of Sextus: 355) "*Speak concerning the word about God as if you were saying it in the presence of God.*"[1]

Up until this juncture, it has been our intention to analyse what Mary and Jesus said and did, supplemented with a variety of second and third hand accounts. However, quite a few Gnostic texts made no mention of Jesus or Mary and were concerned with events that occurred long before they were born.

It is possible every word found within the Nag Hammadi texts is a fabrication, it is undeniable the opportunities to add or delete exist for every Biblical scripture on both sides of the philosophical fence. Accepting this potential for revision and omission creates degrees of uncertainty wherever one looks, we believe a brief overview of some of the more renowned incidents described in the *Old Testament* and the contrasting Gnostic interpretations of these myths would be beneficial. To accentuate the difference between the exoteric and esoteric perspectives, we have inserted six verses, originally penned by the Gnostic philosopher, Sextus, into this chapter.

From Jesus' ministry onwards we have a fairly reasonable base of fact, not hearsay to draw upon, including both sets of biblical texts and some unrelated, yet supporting documentation. Accepting the facts centred around Jesus as a base, some generalities and specifics can be proposed with a fair degree of confidence. When and why will always be open to debate, but when addressing whom; all sit on fairly solid ground.

As we step further back in time, the definitive full stop gives way to an uncertain question mark. As stated earlier, nearly all that occurred before Jesus was born is nowhere close to a historical certainty, a possibility at best, while the real chance of distortion is as much the rule as the exception. All of what sits inside the *Old Testament* and the Gnostic texts that was penned, or exclusively related to the times preceding Jesus, share the same uncertainties the decay of time offers all stories and traditions that relate to the distant past.

Flooding the entire globe meant the sea level would have to be ten thousand metres higher than it is today. It would take forty months of continuous global torrential rainfall to get remotely close to one-tenth that depth, and discounts the fact such a global weather pattern is without precedent. No geologist or climatologist has found one piece of supporting evidence that could validate such a fanciful tale. This deluge would involve increasing the amount of water available on this globe, which has been an eternal scientific constant for the last three billion years, by three hundred per cent.

When Noah and his family re-emerged after their nautical sabbatical, they alone represented the earth's entire human breeding stock. From this parentage, the variety of colours and ethnicity that constitute humanity flourished. History does indeed repeat itself; it seems as if we are to be blighted with a second serving of genetic mutation through inbreeding. According to the accepted version in the *Old Testament*, Adam and Eve were the sole inhabitants on the entire globe and begat three sons and one daughter, or possibly more, but all that follows from such a biological equation are genetic mutations and infertility. Noah's circumstances may differ, but the outcome is identical, a genetic disaster predicated upon a scientific impossibility.

Screaming at the walls of Jericho causing it to crumble and topple, Moses parting the Red Sea, these truths and many more tales of this nature can be found within the pages of the *Old Testament*. By today's standards it leaves the reader stumbling in the dark trying to sieve fact from fiction, from allegory, from other sources, from additions, and from untruth.

As one steps further back in time, utmost care is needed as to where you tread, regardless of which road map the seeker uses. The Gnostic texts that deal with distant matters should be given the same degree of rigour as the *Old Testament* demands. The supporters of Christianity claim the right to use the tried and tested interpretation of symbolism when pressed to defend some pages of the Bible, yet, do not extend the relevant Gnostic texts the same courtesy in their scathing reviews. Both scriptures should be read with discretion, as they were penned during illiterate and uninformed times, where mindless superstition and survival often walked hand in hand. With that proviso established, perhaps some of the Gnostic scriptures could effectively explain how this contrived balance came about.

(373/374) *It is God's business to save whom he wants; on the other hand, it is the business of the pious man to beseech God to save everyone.*[2]

In ancient times (before the birth of Buddha and Jesus), nearly all religions and sects shared stories about vengeful and bickering Gods. Often these deities insisted upon, as a sign of piety, the spilling of blood. On many occasions it was human blood that was spilt, sacrificed to appease their sensibilities and divine cravings.

Whether Abraham offering his son's life in homage to Jehovah, an Aztec priest presenting human blood and entrails in supplication, an animist Shaman healer slaughtering an animal in deference to the Creator or the obligatory inbreeding of Egyptian pharaohs, these ancient Gods seem heartless and uncaring, as we forlornly attempted to satisfy their selfish demands. The character and merit of these celestial entities begs much circumspection. There is no God-given reason to wantonly sacrifice the life of a human, animal or tree in the name of any God. Such a fickle god deserves no respect.

> (338) *Not only do not hold an opinion which does not benefit the needy, but also do not listen to it.*[3]

If anything, these deceitful deities seem to be the source of untold strife and a curse, not a blessing, on the people they demanded pious devotion from. Some dismiss these ancient myths and legends as primitive superstition, a sign of less refined times and a baser clientele we evolved from. Such a patronising attitude says more about the character of the reviewer than what is reviewed.

We feel none of the above applies. There can be found, within many Gnostic texts, a different and more plausible reason for this communal subservience beyond crass stupidity. In all the ancient myths and tales there is a common theme that spans both continents and time. A recurring theme Enoch investigates in some detail, in his eyes all the strife and discord inflicted upon humanity is primarily the outcome of the activities of the "two hundred,"[4] the "fallen"[5] angels who Enoch refers to as "Watchers."[6]

> (174) *The sins of those who are ignorant are the shame of those who have taught them.*[7]

The Watchers were entrusted by God to observe, to watch, but never meddle in the mundane affairs of humans. These divinely anointed beings disobeyed this order and usurped the role of their father. "Enamoured"[8] by women, they broke the sacred covenant with their maker and entered the physical world. Enoch names each of them, then states what gift they brought down to humanity e.g. metallurgy, cosmetics, warfare, economics etc. These fallen Spirits demanded much in return, as their gifts came at a price of their own selfish determining. It seems they asked for nothing less than unquestioning subservience, and many gladly acquiesced. Whether the label be Thor, Zeus, Odin or Apollo; the list is endless and is always associated with erratic and selfish behaviour, culminating in the coerced devotion of the masses. The two hundred have incurred God's eternal wrath and they are aware of their eventual damnation, all that is left for them is to play games with humans.

The paradigm of the *Dreaming* harmonises comfortably with the observations of Enoch. This was a culture where there were no sacrificial offerings to the Gods, no compliant dynastic inbreeding or the enforced labour of thousands to create massive monuments to pay homage to their spirits.

> (171) *When you are with believing persons, desire to listen rather than speak.*[9]

Traditional Aboriginal people also believed in interventionist Gods, and many *Dreaming* stories detail the first acts of these Spirits and the interaction between malevolent and benevolent Spirits. In Cape York some of the *Quinkan Spirits* assist the tribe, while the *Turramulli Spirit's* main purpose is to harm and lead the tribe astray. Knowledge of this capricious Spirit was given to everyone from a young age, each tribal member was fully aware that some celestial deities are driven by evil intent and can never be trusted.

Throughout the planet, during ancient times, every religion chronicles disputes between good and evil spirits. This is consistent, considering Enoch claimed the realm he visited had province over the Earth, and that these disgraced angels (Watchers) intended to influence global affairs and meddle in the development of humanity. Such an endeavour must include all places and races. According to Enoch, these celestial deities were endowed with a variety of supernatural powers. It would seem over the ages many of these manipulative gods sourced from a variety of religions have demanded exorbitant tributes to appease their desires.

The similarities between the *Dreaming* and Enoch are quite striking and seem to repeat a pattern that is evidenced in so many other locations and ancient religions. We believe that these fallen messengers always intended for their influence was to be global. The acceptance or refusal of the authority of the Watchers was an entirely different matter.

Throughout the continent every Aboriginal person was aware of each God's nature and motivation and who these evil Spirits were, irrespective of individual clan-names their motives were known to throughout the land. Such misguided creations were to be avoided and feared from an early age. This intimate knowledge of the varying worth of many celestial deities was never lost; unfortunately many other civilisations were less discriminating. In other continents aberrant deities of this ilk were venerated.

All *Dreaming* stories that refer to the beginning have many entities of varying temperament involved in our origins, as do some interpretations of Adam and Eve. One Gnostic account claims Cain and Abel were not Adam's sons, but sired from one of the "two hundred."[10] Seth is claimed to be Adam's first-born, and the inheritor of his wisdom and bloodline. Eve's two sons are afforded no standing because of their mixed parentage.

It is our belief the *Dreaming* is a matter between *Biamie/Birrahgnooloo*, (Creator/ *Sophia*) and a variety of evil Spirits (the two hundred) and good Spirits (angels).

(160) *May the right time precede your words.*[11]

Between and within each return into rest (heaven) from motion, (earth) our resting place is the direct outcome of our karma. In Enoch's eyes he identifies ten stations or levels of Nirvana. In each ascending position a more advanced spiritual soul bides its time between incarnations, the very lowest level, the fourth (the three lowest stations of existence are located on earth) is reserved for the Watchers and their most committed human devotees, while in the highest levels reside those who have virtually completed their terrestrial examinations.

Enoch was taken to heaven and allowed to return for thirty days to record his rites of passage. Once his tasks were completed, Enoch was transported into the ethereal realm where it is claimed he, not Peter, sits at the Gates of Heaven in judgement of each soul every time it crosses over.

Eve and Adam are religious prophets, the two greatest mortals of an earlier epoch, or the only two human souls inhabiting the entire globe. We can't have it both ways; at least one version has to be wrong. Many Gnostic texts claim they were two out of many, not two out of none. In-breeding is not an issue here, but their roles are.

In the *Old Testament* Eve is an afterthought, a part of Adam's rib. Her role is that of a female appendage created as a compliant object to amuse him during his idle moments. More a pleasant distraction than a divine creation, Eve is often portrayed as a naked temptress trying to seduce the wholesome Adam. Entirely responsible for the original sin, the somewhat dull seductress is led astray by Satan. All the while the decent and chaste Adam fights the valiant fight, struggling against the surging tide of deceit, until he is reluctantly overwhelmed by hormones and finally relents to Eve's beguiling, lustful charms.

Some Gnostic versions involve the same characters but with a different script. Sophia was claimed to have incarnated into a snake and advised Eve of the deceit they were subjected to. The distorted vision and compliant lifestyle was the Demiurge's creation and could only be disposed of by eating from the tree of knowledge, thus freeing humanity from the bondage of ignorance manufactured by *Yaltaboath*. However, such an account of female wisdom and initiative was discarded in preference for a more gender accommodating interpretation.

Who must accept fault and derision for humanities descent, everyone but Adam. And who gets the blame and shame from that point on, the female. Mary is not alone, Eve walked the path many of her sisters have been forced to follow.

The myth of the rib is in stark contrast to a passage from *The Apocalypse of Adam*. "When God had created me out of the earth along with Eve . . . she taught me a word of knowledge of the eternal God. And we resembled the great angels, for we were higher than the God who had created us."[12] "Created" and "along with," is not out of or separate, but the outcome of a shared act of miraculous conception. Eve's appearance has nothing to do with Adam's need for companionship. Moreover the bearer of wisdom and gnosis is not Adam or a God, but Eve. Eve is the teacher and Adam is the student. The salient points are that these words were attributed to Adam and this is the opening passage. It could be feasible to suggest that the "word of eternal knowledge" Eve shared with her consort came from the tree of knowledge.

To momentarily digress, why is it sinful to eat from the tree of knowledge, and what or who is this tree? It would appear that it is evil to want to know more.

Yet Jesus implores us to better ourselves and gain knowledge of what is good and what is evil. If the *Old Testament* interpretation is correct, every time I learn of a truth, it will be an offence to God. If so, this God desperately wishes to conceal knowledge from us.

The concealment of forbidden knowledge found within *Genesis* may be related to earlier Middle Eastern myths like the Epic of Gilgamesh. These accounts could be seen as a parable of the transition from a hunter-gatherer society to a lifestyle based around agriculture and domesticating animals. This sedentary lifestyle that inevitably competes against Nature is presented as a prostitute trying to lead the central nomadic character astray. The knowledge that is forbidden, the activities involved in agriculture, involve a denial of the Traditional ways. This abandonment leads to a loss of spiritual power and weakens contact with the Gods and the land. This myth seems to resonate to the beat of a distant drum; the *Dreaming,* and in particular, the reasons that led up to the banishment of those Aboriginals who chose to farm. The conflict between lifestyles is identical, all that is left to debate is which culture came first.

The Gnostic narrative of the exile from the Garden of Eden explains what secret teaching Eve revealed to Adam actually is, "we were higher than the God that created us." In Gnosticism the trinity still exists, but the cast has been amended. It is made up of The Creator, *Sophia* (the Holy Mother) and *Yaltaboath* (Samuel) who was created by his mother *Sophia*, but supposedly without the knowledge of the Creator.

Samuel becomes blinded by his own power and deluded sense of uniqueness, creating a set of material beings (humanity) fashioned in his image. He seeks to create a carbon copy, a vassal to compliantly follow and obey his every whim. Samuel's mother *Sophia* discovers the deceit, admonishing him, and then places within us a spark of her essence; our soul. Trapped within the imperfect vessel that is Samuel's creation exists our eternal spirit. This wisdom was the gift of secret knowledge Eve bestowed on her consort Adam, and the ensuing curse Samuel bequeathed upon humanity.

(333) *You cannot receive understanding unless you know first that you possess it. In everything there is again this sentence.*[13]

As stated before, both sets of ancient texts, if taken literally, are laden with problems and neither have any direct impact on Jesus' secret teachings. However, one of these versions does offer something dramatically different from the traditional view of pre-Jesus/Buddha religious expressions and influences. Which of the two perspectives is more logical and coherent is open to debate as both writings have merit, but, one rendition does attempt to address the reason why there was so much suffering and injustice during ancient days.

One interpretation of human genesis could provide some clarity as to the motives that underpin a plethora of ancient institutionalised creeds. This account elevates Eve to be the equal, if not the better of, the original male prototype,

Adam. One version of our ancient ancestry requires each soul to be responsible for its own gnosis and finds that within all the legends and myths of vengeful Gods there lay more than a germ of truth.

All speak of a fallen architect and of a faulty design but, a plan is a concept not a construct, it's the builder alone who works in bricks and mortar.

Chapter 10
Mary's Legacy

(The Gospel of Philip: 63-64) *The Saviour loved her more than all the disciples and used to kiss her often on her mouth. The rest of [the disciples. . .]. They said to him, "Why do you love her more than all of us?" The saviour answered and said to them, "Why do I not love you like her?"*[1]

These words are the most revealing given by any of the Apostles. It is not because of some profound hidden truth revealed, nor does it narrate or describe some supernatural miracle; but, it does affirm an unrivalled status, and raises a pivotal issue that Christianity has never satisfactorily addressed.

Who was telling the truth and who was close to him? According to Constantine, the Vatican and many respected authorities, some Apostles were faithfully preaching Jesus' teachings, while the majority were not. Was the official proclamation at Nicea relating to the merit of each Apostle's teachings, inspired by divine inspiration or less enlightened motives?

Granted, Philip along with over half of the Apostles could all be liars; but surely such a flaw only reflects poorly upon the inadequacies of their mentor. If Jesus can't get the majority of the chosen males to tell the truth, then the rest of us have virtually no chance of bettering their flawed attempts. Unless one is prepared to accept Jesus is an inadequate tutor, the allegation is false.

Nor are some of these Apostles alone in expressing their reverence for Mary. Modestus, Epiphanius, William Caxton, Jacobus de Voragne, the Prince of Southern Gaul, Leonardo Da Vinci, the male crew banished with Mary from Judea and many other chroniclers claim she was Divine.

These men were prepared to challenge the conventions of those times boldly stating Mary as the equal, if not better, than the most respected icon of Christianity, Peter. Surely they knew the words they recorded would be viewed as being heretical and their inflammatory statements could only cause them grief, criticism or far worse? Suggesting that a woman, formally pronounced an immoral prostitute by Pope Gregory, was superior to the first male Pope was not a position that would engender popularity or security. If they all lied, human nature demands they, as individuals, gained something of worth. The person or people involved in this flagrant duplicity must obtain something of benefit to motivate such blatant dishonesty. With nothing beyond derision and much worse available as an incentive, it would appear they believed they were reporting truths, or they were all afflicted by a perverse form of masochism.

Perhaps the response Jesus offered that immediately follow this enquiry found in *Philip*, amply depicts the truth these men stood next to and the depth of injustice that is now our daily bread.

When a blind man and one who sees are both together in darkness, they are no different from one another. When the light comes, then he who sees will see the light, and he who is blind will remain in darkness.[2]

The verse is not symbolic, nor is it an obscure metaphor; it has an extremely literal meaning. The male Apostles pleaded with Jesus to supply a reason for his preference for Mary over "us," and got a response affording no shades of grey. Mary is the "one who sees," Jesus is the "light" and she is the only Apostle who is able to "see the light." As for the rest, and this must include every male Apostles assembled, Jesus is steadfast in his explanation, they are "blind." They begged him to offer a reason for the separation and preference, and found Mary received Jesus' grace simply because it was her right, but never theirs. According to Jesus they will "remain in darkness," and should feel privileged to have the opportunity to stand near such an enlightened woman.

Traditional supporters of Christianity see a different, more accommodating, explanation. Diedre Good refers to incidences in both scriptures were Jesus kissed other disciples. She highlights an example of James and Jesus kissing and, also reminds us, the title beloved disciple, had also been accorded to Philip, John, James and Matthew by some Gnostic devotees. Esther De Boer extends the range of this equivocation even further, asserting that we "must not understand this 'kissing' in a sexual sense, but in a spiritual sense."[3]

Diedre Good is correct, as there are examples of Jesus kissing men. This is a typical form of greeting for a male from that region, and is customary to this day. However, these acts between males are literally pecks on the cheek, and offered as a formal greeting or commendation. Never do we hear of two males passionately and continuously embracing and kissing.

Two words seem to be conveniently discarded when assessing the impact of the provocative statement of Philip's, "mouth"[4] and "often."[5] No reason was given to account for the Messiah acting in such a manner when with Mary. According to Philip, Mary had said and done nothing worthy of note leading up to the kiss, this particular display of affection appeared to be a spontaneous action. If we are in error, why kiss her on the mouth and why did Philip (no champion of women's rights) feel it necessary to be so specific, as none of Jesus' other platonic kisses are recorded in emotive detail.

No other disciple is kissed "often" anywhere, let alone continuously on the mouth. Regardless of the intent behind such a kiss, if it was on the mouth of a male whether his brother or anyone else, the rumour mills would have been set into overdrive, and there would be numerous strident commentaries on Jesus' homosexuality.

To claim the passage (55.b) is symbolic seems to be pushing the boundary of literary license into unchartered waters. If Diedre Good is right, after Philip was patently trying to be so literal, then virtually everything within any Gospel must have an alternative symbolic meaning.

However, the symbolism De Boer perceives is illogical. In the *Gospel of Philip*, Philip acknowledges this constant physical contact between Jesus and Mary as the catalyst that triggered their concerns, and in some cases, jealousy. The motivation behind the kisses was never implicitly stated because all knew of their relationship. It was the continuous physical display of affection that led to Philip acknowledging Jesus loves "her more"[6] than the rest. It is obvious the act of kissing on the "mouth" bestows on Mary a status no other mortal could claim. This continuous display of public affection seems to justify our belief Mary is the chosen Apostle, and it was for this reason the concerns of some males are juxtaposed around the act. There is nothing symbolic here, and it is only seen as such because of the critics' tunnel vision.

To this very day many steadfastly refuse to permit Mary the right to claim her anointed role as custodian of Jesus' secret teachings. They are adamant the Good Book is sanctified by God and contains all we need to know.

The disputes over what Mary actually said, what was revised and deliberately omitted will continue for quite some time to come, perhaps our only achievement is to add another dimension to the evolving debate. However before concluding our investigation, we feel it would be remiss if we didn't provide a brief coverage of not so much her words, but her deeds. Our interest is centred upon what occurred after Jesus was killed. As it was with Mary's words, the same rules seem to apply when trying to resolve the mysteries involved around the rest of her life; unfortunately many of the details are missing, obscure or cryptic.

After the crucifixion, it did not take long for the male followers of Jesus to spread the word about their Messiah. To begin with, the immediate surrounding region was fertile ground to spread the news of Jesus' revelations. Having established a solid base of local devotees, some male Apostles looked to distant horizons. Within barely one generation Jesus' words had spread from India to Britain. Peter went to Rome, Thomas and Bartholomew to India and Philip was in France, but what of Mary?

If any student restricted themselves to the New Testament, they could be forgiven for thinking she either died soon after, or mysteriously disappeared. Without doubt she is most definitely missing in inaction.

Fortunately there are alternative avenues to investigate that certainly do add much more detail to Mary's life after Jesus died. One of the sources of information, which has been a primary source for many authorities in this field, is the *Golden Legend*. This highly regarded and extremely popular book was written in

1275 by the Archbishop of Genoa, Jacobus de Voragine. As it was with the *Gospel of Thomas*, so too with the *Golden Legend*, both were first amongst equals.

William Caxton was the first to invent the printing press. The pertinent factor is this was the first text he chose to publish. Most may have assumed this devout Christian would have automatically selected the Bible. As impressive as the Bible was, he felt another text was more deserving of such honour, the *Golden Legend*. Such a publication, unique in the annals of publishing, was a portrayal of the 60 greatest Saints, prophets and seers that had walked upon the globe. Within these biographies, the life of Mary Magdalene is one of the longest accounts supplied.

The claims made are quite startling and, if the New Testament is to be used as a comparison, raises many concerns. It could be suggested both the author and publisher must have been aware of the breadth and impact of what was being recorded. The biographer is adamant that Mary and her crew's safety and ultimate survival was due to a variety of miracles. Considering they were exiled, set adrift in a marginally seaworthy vessel without provisions, sail, rudder or oar, rational explanations are scant. Banished in Judea, arriving in Gaul with the same crew, all fit and well, would mean they were exceptionally lucky or extremely blessed.

This outcome, when combined with an impressive list of volunteers who stepped aboard, only strengthens the notion of *Divine Intervention*. The illustrious cast who chose to embark on a journey of peril, and almost certain death were both male and female, yet when Jesus was sentenced then crucified, those who stood by him were of the reputed weaker sex. Even though none of the twelve male Apostles were officially sentenced or in immediate danger, all of them were conspicuously absent when Jesus was nailed to a wooden cross.

The claim, in the *Gospel of John*, that on male Apostle (John) appeared at Jesus' crucifixion and was asked to care for Jesus' mother, is highly dubious. A closer scrutiny of the text give strong indications the few words that supposedly account for John's brief appearance, followed by a rapid departure, were added at a later date.

We have supplied a brief resume of the major members of this crew. The question that demands to be addressed before presenting the credentials of this ensemble, is why were such a distinguished congregation prepared to follow Mary into danger and probable oblivion? Mary's deeds and words, according to the synoptic Gospels, were irrelevant and provide no compelling explanation to account for this selfless devotion that borders on martyrdom. It needs to be emphasised, these people were not following Mary on an evangelical crusade, but willingly chose to virtually lay down their lives in devotion to a woman who was unable to utter one syllable worth recording in the Gospels of Matthew, Luke and Mark.

Mary did state that "the disciple resembles his(/her) teacher,"[7] if she is correct; Mary's pupils showed more loyalty and bravery than any male Apostle of

Jesus. Surely such devotion should give some credence to our belief that once Jesus fell, she was the rightful spiritual heir to his mystical throne.

Rather than offer any commentary on the character of Mary's companions, we believe it is sufficient to let the facts speak for themselves. As a first port of call, we felt it prudent to begin with a passage found within the *Golden Legend*.

> ... *St. Maximin, Mary Magdalene, and Lazarus her brother, Martha her sister, Marcelle, chamberer of Martha, and St. Cendony which had been born blind, and after enlumined of our Lord; all these together, and many other Christian men were taken of the miscreants and put in a ship in the sea, without tackle or rudder, for to be drowned. But by the purveyance of Almighty God they all came to Marseilles ...* [8]

As a starting point Mary's arrival in France is not in dispute, even her critics will accept her presence in Marseille and the surrounding regions as a fact. Beyond that agreed truth there opinions and potential, nothing can be asserted as truth. Many legends maintain she spent the rest of her life in a cave, fed only by two angels with manna from heaven. Some of these accounts are quite explicit in one shared description; she was naked, sometimes depicted as having long red hair flowing judiciously over her shoulders.

If these records are based on fact, Mary was living her life as Jesus commended in Verses (21) and (37) of the *Gospel of Thomas*. In Verse (37), when asked by the male Apostles about how to find salvation, Jesus recommends all to "disrobe without being ashamed and take your garments and place them under your feet like little children and tread on them."[9] He is insistent that once proudly disrobed "you will see the son of the living one, and you will not be afraid."[10] It appears every traditional Aboriginal person within the continent also obeyed Jesus' edict and the teachings of the *Dreaming*; all were naked and cooperated with the daily rhythm of nature. Mary despaired of all the trappings of her society, even to the extent of refusing all offerings of clothing, food and lodgings, living as did traditional Aboriginal people; naked and entirely at the disposal of their Creator.

Many pilgrims are reputed to have sought out Mary for wisdom and advice on mystical matters. It is claimed she never married again and was a fully evolved spiritual being whose knowledge in esoteric matters was faultless and without mortal equal. There are reports Mary kept contact with Thomas, Philip, Bartholomew and Matthew. Matthew's presence would certainly be in keeping with his indignant reaction to Peter's insults as recorded in both conclusions of the Gospel of Mary. Perhaps all of the Apostles interested in the secret teachings of Jesus kept contact with Jesus' heir apparent in all mystical matters? Unfortunately there are too many gaps and distortions chiselled into the historical and religious accounts of nearly every great woman of the past, to make any definitive statements regarding Mary's life once exiled from Judea.

However, the lack of a reliable autobiographical account and presence of a multitude of male censors cannot remove all traces of her life after Jesus was killed. There still remain many fragmentary accounts, myths, legends and reputable records that seem to pry open many fields of conjecture. Rather than organise our research into Mary's life after Jesus left his Apostles (which could be up to 11 years after his crucifixion) and offer personal interpretations and opinions, we feel it would be better for the reader to make their own judgements.

We have arranged our research into two sections; a compendium of general points followed by specific information that relates to one member of the possible crew. Alongside each point a source or reference is provided.

General Points:

- Jewish authorities may have been involved in the exile of Mary and her crew. Almost every legend, myth and tale has her arriving in France in a boat, with no oars, sail or rudder.[11]
- Of all the Christian missions, this was the most peaceful and prolific, converting virtually all of southern France within one generation.[12]
- Many on the boat were empowered to create miracles.[13]
- Many of those who were exiled had spent extensive time in Alexandria.[14]
- Nearly every story states the act of being set adrift was an attempt to murder the exiles by proxy.[15]
- Some legends state that Mary and her followers were escaping the persecutions of the Jewish authorities and Paul.[16]
- Many legends mention a terrible and unnatural storm, (near the coast of France) which nearly kills the boat's occupants.[17]
- All of these accounts stipulate that Mary and the other's safety, during the ocean journey to France, is maintained through the divine intervention of God.[18]

The Crew.

Joseph of Arimathea:

- After spending some considerable time in Gaul, Joseph of Arimathea finally arrives at Avalon (Glastonbury), South-West England in 63 A.D. He built the first above-ground church in England. It was dedicated to his mentor, Mary, who died earlier that year.[19]
- Joseph, in one account, was also known as James the Just (the brother of Jesus).[20] In another narrative, he was the uncle of Jesus and took Jesus, while still in his youth, to Britain for Druidic training.[21]
- Joseph was of aristocratic background (*Noble Decurio*) and a member of the Sanhedrin. He was a highly respected man of affluence and influence.[22]

- Joseph was purported to carry the Holy Grail, or two cruets containing Jesus' blood and sweat. He was also rumoured to have buried the cruets/cup into the ground. The water in the Chalice Well at Glastonbury is tinted red. The myth suggests the waters are red because the cups were buried near the well. Some claim the water that runs through the grail is stained red with the blood of Jesus.[23]
- Another legend maintains that when Joseph and his followers arrived in Britain, he placed his staff into the ground, and announced they were 'weary all' (Wirral hill in Glastonbury). His staff was fashioned from the crown of thorns Jesus wore at his crucifixion. The staff instantaneously took root and grew into a bush. The shrub is a hawthorn bush which is native to the Middle East (Syria) and flowers, not once as is the norm for other plants of that species, but twice a year. The bush blinded the soldiers who were commanded to chop it down during the English Civil War.[24]
- In some narratives of the boat journey to Gaul, it was reported a mystical cloud appeared to assist Joseph in their struggles.[25]

Saint Maximin:

- St. Maximin became the first Bishop of Provence.[26]
- He was one of the seventy-two disciples of Jesus.[27]
- Maximin performed the last rites for Mary Magdalene in his church.[28]
- Maximin was later beatified as a Saint.
- He may have baptised Mary, Martha and Lazarus.[29]

Saint Lazarus:

- Lazarus became the first Bishop of Marsailles.[30]
- He is the brother of Mary Magdalene and Martha.[31]
- Lazarus is believed by some to be Jesus' beloved disciple.[32]
- Other reports suggest he was also known as Simon Zelotes.[33]
- According to the Gospel of John (12:10), when a death edict was passed on Jesus it also included Lazarus, no other disciple or Apostle was indicted for any offence.
- Before he died, many say he requested to be buried next to Mary Magdalene.[34]
- Lazarus travelled extensively and may have spread the word in Egypt, Tunisia, Libya, Morocco, Turkey, Syria, Judea, Jordan and Britain, etc.[35]
- His death is a mystery; some say Lazarus was crucified in Britain, while others claim he died peacefully in Southern France.[36]

Sarah the Egyptian /Saint Sara/ Sara La Kali:

- Sarah later becomes the patron Saint of the Gypsies (Roma). A Romani festival is held for Sarah every 24 - 25th of May, where thousands of Romani elect their Queen in front of Sarah's statue. The statue is paraded through the streets to the sea and dipped into the water.[37]
- Another legend claims Sarah saved her friends during a violent storm off the coast of France, by spreading her cloak upon the sea to form a bridge between the sinking boat and to the land.[38]
- Sarah was also known for her dark skin, therefore appeared to be of Egyptian origin. Some call her the Black Queen; it is possible the Black Madonna cult venerates her and not the Virgin Mary.[39]
- Many accounts insist Sarah was the offspring of Mary and Jesus, and the *Sangreal* or *Holy Bloodline* was passed on through her to the Visigoths and Merovingians etc. Further evidence to validate this possibility relates to the fact that the word Sarah can be interpreted as meaning princess in Hebrew.[40]
- Sarah could be symbolically identified with the Lost Princess of many popular fairy tales, folk stories and myths.[41]
- Sarah stayed at Saintes-Maries-de-la-Mer (Camargue), near the refugee's point of landing in Provence.[42]
- One legend claims Sarah was the servant of Mary Jacobi and Mary Salome.[43]
- She stayed with Mary Jacobi and Mary Salome and helped sustain them while they converted the local population.[44]
- Her burial place most probably is in the local church Notre-Dame de la Mer (Our Lady of the Sea).[45]

Sidonious/Saint Cedonius/Saint Cedony:

- Sidonious was born blind and healed by Jesus then became a devout follower of Mary. He was beatified as a Saint.
- He may have accompanied Maximin to Aix and stayed there with him.
- It is highly likely he was the blind man Jesus healed in Mark (8:22-26).

Saint Mary Jacobe (Jacobi) - Cleophas/Saint Mary the Gypsy/ Mary the Egyptian:

- Mary Jacobe stayed with Mary Salome and Sarah at Ratis / Saintes-Maries-de-la-Mer and preached to the local populace.[46]
- She could have been the sister of the Virgin Mary, thus the aunt of Jesus.[47]

- The Romani venerate Mary Jacobi during the same 24 - 25th May ceremony held for Sarah. Her burial place is in the Church Notre-Dame de la Mer (Our Lady of the Sea).[48]
- It is probable she was married to the disciple James Cleophas (John 19:20). It is rumoured he too, may have been aboard the boat and journeyed with them to Gaul (France).[49]
- Mary Jacobi was a High Priestess.[50]
- A popular cult celebrating Mary Jacobi or Mary the Gypsy has continued throughout the ages. It was popular enough for Emperor Constantine to try to ban it, but the cult persisted into the Middle-Ages in Britain.[51]
- It is possible Mary Jacobi is symbolically represented in popular folk legends e.g. Maid Marian in *Robin Hood*[52] and Aphrodite in Botticelli's *The Birth of Venus*.[53]

Saint Mary Salome-Helena:

- Mary Salome, reputed to be the mother of the disciple John and James the greater, is on board.[54]
- She may have been the consort of Simon Zelotes.[55]
- The Apostle Simon Peter called Mary Salome "a witch."[56]
- Mary Salome, according to one account, was a High Priestess and owned property/land.[57]
- Another legend states she was a midwife present at Jesus' birth.[58]
- Mary Salome was present at the crucifixion, and a close friend of the Virgin Mary.[59]
- According to Gnostic scriptures Jesus often talked to Mary Salome privately.[60]

Saint Philip the Apostle:

- Philip almost definitely travelled to France with Mary,[61] the chances of him arriving independently are remote, but it is a possibility. An avowed Gnostic, his writings were banned and he did much to inspire the Magdalene followers, particularly the Cathars (Albigensians) in southern France.[62]
- He was a founding father of Christianity in France.[63]
- He may have charged Joseph of Arimathea with the mission of travelling to Britain.[64]

Marcella/Martilla/Marcelle:

- Stayed with Martha in Tarascon.[65]

- She was blessed by Jesus.[66]
- Marcella was the faithful servant of Martha.[67]
- She was the biographer of Martha's life.[68] After Martha's death, she went to Sclavonia (Slovenia) and preached for another ten years until she died.[69]

Saint Martha:

- She was from a noble aristocratic background and owned land in Bethany, Magdala, and parts of Jerusalem.[70]
- Martha was present at the Last Supper of Jesus.[71]
- Martha was renowned as a speaker, highly organised, courteous and warm. Martha is often remembered as the Hostess for Jesus.[72]
- According to one legend she defeated a Dragon.[73]
- She built a convent at Tarascon (Vienne province) and led a devout life (e.g. prayed one hundred times a day and one hundred times a night, was vegan, and did not drink wine).[74]
- In one account of Martha's life she did not have a husband or consort.[75]
- Performed many miracles like resurrecting a drowned man and healing the sick. After her death, miracles occurred near her tomb, including the healing of King Clovis I (a ruler of the Franks from the Merovingian House).[76]
- The narrative of her life also maintains Martha foresaw her death.[77]
- She saw and heard Mary's soul being taken into heaven by Angels.[78]
- When Martha was near to death she received visions of Jesus and Mary, which helped comfort her and drove away several evil spirits.[79]
- Martha's remains are most likely at Tarascon.[80]

The Possible Others:

- There are accounts claiming Mary's three children are on board the boat.
- In some versions Mary, the mother of Jesus, is on the boat with Jesus' aunts.
- It is possible some, if not all, of the other seven women mentioned in *Pistis Sophia*[81] who followed Jesus were also present.
- It is quite likely other people were on board e.g. other followers, servants etc. Numerous narratives/legends mention many others, denoting other lesser-known followers who may have joined this group.
- James Cleophas, as previously mentioned, may have been present.[82]
- Other versions of this voyage claim Nicodemus, Joanna and her son Saint Zaccheus were on board, and so the potential crew members continue.

Chapter 10: Mary's Legacy

When Mary was exiled from Judea, those in control were aware of the repercussions of this proclamation. Once set adrift on the Great Ocean, there was only ever one expected outcome; a lingering death.

The immediate question that arises out of this banishment relates to the reasons that led to this punishment. What had Mary done or said to cause so much distress and offence? Surely such a punitive proclamation, which led to the banishment and almost certain death of a considerable number of people, could only be issued by authorities under the pretext of a perceived threat of some magnitude. Some of the people aboard were not common folk, but highly regarded members of the rich and educated upper class. Under these conditions, it would appear whatever Mary was alleged to have done that was deemed to be so seditious to incur this judgement, accorded her a degree of power and influence that seem at odds with other supposedly more reputable accounts of these times. The Synoptic Gospels claim the most impressive role allocated to Mary was that of a passive witness.

Or so the rumour goes, the facts, however, present the same cast but with an entirely different script. The same pattern is repeated, yet another conflict has arisen between the official teachings and the hidden secrets. What we are left with is a half-truth in perpetuity, any institution or philosophy that predicates its existence upon the separation of the sexes, or to put it in simpler terms, the denigration of women, is based on a monumental lie.

Whatever follows this deception can only be measured in terms of men behaving badly, selfish behaviour and warfare; unfortunately this morbid setting is a more than appropriate description of today, and as things stand, the days that follow.

Epilogue
"Gates of Delirium"[1]

Why of course the people don't want war ... that is understood. But after all it is the leaders of the country who determine the policy, and it is always a simple matter to drag the people along, whether it is a democracy, or a fascist dictatorship, or a parliament, or a communist dictatorship ... Voice or no voice, the people can always be brought to the bidding of the leaders. That is easy. All you have to do is to tell them they are being attacked, and denounce the pacifists for lack of patriotism and exposing the country to danger.
  Hermann Goering[2]

We have assembled a diverse assortment of information of genes and bones, thrown in some sticks and stones, then added the contents of a 1600-year-old jar into this archaeological potpourri. These apparently divergent clues have been contrasted against the claims of an anonymous Aboriginal Elder lacking in academic pedigree. Our investigation into the heritage and parallel wisdom of the *Dreaming* and Gnosticism has convinced us of a truth that has two implications, one relates to yesterday, and the other, tomorrow.

All cultures and religions are equal; each serves the same purpose. The variations are irrelevant and stand above mortal judgement. What suits the past or the sensibilities of another is a personal matter between the individual and their Creator. Considering all of us have a variety of different sized beams firmly lodged in both eyes every time we return, no one is in the position to pass judgement on the imperfections of another.

Once accepting this parity and inherent worth within all cultures as a first step, when determining how culture and religion first evolved, and from where, seeking out new possibilities should be relatively easy. We have presented the findings of many respectable authorities from a variety of fields and formed a somewhat unusual conclusion. Perhaps we are in error in our interpretation of the facts, but the conventional explanations accounting for Aboriginal migration from Asia may be convenient, as a theory it is riddled with inconsistencies.

If we have failed to persuade, then the original question still remains, where did the urge to create culture, religion and art originate? This cultural evolution occurred in a variety of places independently of each other, or began at one specific place then spread outwards from that initial point and time. We obviously support the second belief, as we feel no other ancient culture was more advanced and spiritually aware than the Australian Aboriginal people of ancient times.

Even if we are in error, and a group of Homo Sapien sapiens also evolved in Africa and began to settle in new locales, we would suggest they are the second wave of Sapien immigrants who then made contact with the Sapiens from Australia somewhere in Asia. Whether that contact soured into conflict is debatable. There may have been clashes from first sighting, or perhaps the Aboriginal settlers decided discretion was preferable and decided to move camp and sail north along the Asian coast, across the Bering Strait and into an unpopulated land: America.

However, proof and expectation are not identical, and Aboriginal presence in America, Europe, Egypt and even Judea, does not guarantee the *Dreaming* was the esoteric inspiration behind the Gnostic thoughts of Jesus as expressed in *Thomas*. No archaeological technique, bone or gene can establish any definitive association. There is no empirical proof to validate or disprove this proposal; all that we can rely upon is circumstantial evidence. The very best that could be claimed for any theory in this area are varying degrees of potential.

With all these caveats, we should have maintained a modicum of scepticism and balance, but the feat of impartiality is beyond our inclination and intuition. Every meeting we have been privileged to have with keepers of Traditional Aboriginal knowledge reaffirms our belief that they were the first mariners and philosophers. Their unanimous endorsement of this fact leaves no other option but to allow this truth inspire our investigation.

We are convinced there is every possibility Robert Lawlor is correct in suggesting Isiac mythology and Gnosticism are pale reflections of an ancient parent, the *Dreaming*. The *Dreaming's* ancestry and esoteric knowledge set taxing demands no other culture was able to emulate. These failures (with two notable exceptions) were understandable; simply because once sexism and greed become an entrenched part of daily life, the Spirits retreat from the clamour and rush. Over thousands of years much of our esoteric heritage was lost or hidden.

The reactive way we exist today has everything to do with the evolving chaos in which we are forced to exist. What has been either forgotten or concealed is that our existence has always been dependent upon a sacred covenant with the flora and fauna we are obliged to respect and nurture. The apathy we have displayed and the exploitation we have meted out upon a multitude of God's creations augers very poorly for the immediate future. The prime agent lurking behind all the poisons and selfishness simmering everywhere must be confronted now, not tomorrow.

"During times of universal deceit, telling the truth is revolutionary." George Orwell[3]

Until our global addiction to capitalism and the wonders of technology are remedied, nothing will be changed or gained that will benefit the environment and our soul beyond ineffectual conventions and treaties, often amended or rescinded before the ink begins to dry.

The simple solution to all of the Earth's sicknesses resides within a tired old saying; money doesn't grow on trees. Tomorrow, money will have to adapt to a new reality, it must learn to embrace the wisdom of the sacred tree Bill Neidjie nurtures constantly. The money of Verse (95) in *Thomas*, must be given the opportunity to bloom on Bill Neidjie's brother, the tree, otherwise we are all doomed. Money must no longer hold mortgage over the tree Bill reveres. It must assist the tree's growth and become subservient to its needs. Unless the reversal of roles occurs quickly, the fruit we are encouraged to consume will make "headache, sore body"[4] and soon after much, much worse.

We need a new tree and a new gardener, a sacred tree of knowledge tended with feminine sensibilities. This reverent gardening is an essential pre-requisite if humanity is to continue to exist.

Many have coped under the onslaught by becoming jaded and desensitised, where it is far easier to look the other way or apportion blame on everyone else. Anything that disturbs our cultured apathy is subversive and must be ignored or eradicated. Either way those who fail are responsible for their own inadequacies, simply because our leaders assure us there must always be losers. The concept of justice has morphed into vilifying the victim for their plight, who then becomes entirely responsible for the suffering they must endure. Melvin Lerner's theory that we get what we deserve and deserve what we get expressed in his *The Belief in a Just World*,[5] has now become the catch cry that appeases any vestiges of guilt some may harbour, dividing each day into winners and losers.

In Traditional Aboriginal society, after all mechanisms to reconcile and pacify had failed, if two clansmen were still unable to resolve their differences and insisted on pointless physical confrontation, it could only occur if in the presence of women. The logic was indisputable. Fearing the tide of passion and bloodlust might overwhelm the male combatants; the women stood by to step in when they decided to end the conflict. The clan's concern was without the calming influence of women the victor would be blinded by his success, overstep the boundary of commonsense and badly injure his fellow clansman. The permanent or grievous damage that followed any bloodlust would almost invariably see the conflict embrace more combatants and create greater carnage.

This historic pattern of males in combat is a perverse, yet regular event, and tempts many to foolishly assert this aggressive tendency is the natural order of things and the only way we can exist. The gender peddling these insidious myths, in almost every case, is male. Today those in control plead with all to be patient just a little longer, yet remain perpetually prepared during these turbulent times. Our leaders offer duplicity as a solution to brandish when battling any potential terrorist, threat or environmental catastrophe.

However, more of the same, no matter how it is refashioned, is not an answer but an indictment and motivation. It is time for the feminine values espoused by Mary and the *Dreaming* to be summoned; the exploitation of Nature and our perverse notions of infallibility must come to an end.

A society steeped in feminine values with sharing and respect for all of creation is either a mandatory leap of faith, if acknowledged; or a forlorn dream of what should have been, if ignored.

The original plan for humanity began in the *Dreaming*. While humans preferred to live within a culture where their imprint on the land was negligible (hunter-gatherer lifestyle), most societies exhibited variations of a general theme (*Dreaming*). Once some people chose to compete with Nature (intensive forms of agriculture) and each other (money), the Spirits of the land looked away.

This is not to say every person should abandon all agricultural practises and industries then wander off into the bush and adopt the lifestyle of nomadic hermits. A global population of over six billion makes such a proposition pure nonsense. However, to share all with all and treat the earth as a sacred garden inhabited by God or the Spirits, is the vital element of the *Dreaming* and an absolute necessity for our global survival. We believe it is imperative that action be taken immediately to rearrange the iniquitous division of wealth throughout the planet and delegate money to its intended use. It is a tool meant to serve humanity, never a privileged few, yet it has done everything except that. It would appear that for this subservience to occur, those in control of the purse-strings must possess a purse, for many their wallets are far too fat and wilful to control.

The days to come demand new priorities; our collective future can not afford the folly of cloning the errors of the past, or the number of tomorrows left for humanity to squander will be severely curtailed. Our suggestions are basically no different than the observations of many others who also believe more of the same will see humanity and many innocent species rapidly expire.

Our global choice is simple, it is no longer an option but the only truth remaining; we either immediately stop misbehaving so selfishly and make new choices, or perish soon after.

"*The only thing worth globalising is dissent.*" Arundhati Roy.[6]

In our next book, *Far from Grace,* we intend to examine in more detail the master-plan and place from which humanity was originally intended to evolve: the first Garden of Eden. Once embracing the philosophy and obligations, an acceptance of the *Dreaming* entails, all that is needed is some creative tinkering to adapt to the urgent demands of this planet and the immediate future of nearly all forms of life.

We believe Reverend Martin Luther King succinctly encapsulated the major problem the planet faces today; men behaving badly. "Our scientific power has outrun our spiritual power. We have guided missiles and misguided men."[7]

Over the thousands of years civilisation has evolved, we have been guided by thousands of "misguided men" promising their subjects all manner of bounties, and delivering much less. They have convinced the masses to meekly accept all the wars, pollution, economic injustice and unbridled greed as the natural order.

The *Dreaming* and Mary see the folly of this lifestyle and offer one last opportunity to obtain redemption. All they ask is to share everything with everyone and never place personal interests above the needs of any person, tree, rock or animal.

If you tell a lie big enough and keep repeating it, people will eventually come to believe it. The lie can be maintained only for such a time as the State can shield the people from the political, economic and/or military consequences of the lie. It thus becomes vitally important for the State to use all of its powers to repress dissent, for the truth is the mortal enemy of the lie, and thus by extension, the truth is the greatest enemy of the State.
Joseph Goebels, German Minister of Propaganda, 1933-1945.[8]

Notes

Foreword.

1. Big Bill Neidjie, Stephen Davis and Allan Fox, *Australia's Kakadu Man* (Darwin, Australia: Resource Managers Pty Ltd, 1986), 39.
2. G.R.S. Mead, *Pistis Sophia: The Gnostic Tradition of Mary Magdalene, Jesus, and His Disciples* (Mineola, New York: Dover publications, 2005), Chapter 34
3. Mead, *Pistis Sophia*, 45.

Chapter 1: The First Apostle: Mary.

1. J. R. Porter, *The Lost Bible* (London, UK: Duncan Baird Publishers, 2001), 154.
2. Stephen Emmel, trans. "The Dialogue of the Saviour (III,5)", (53), in *Nag Hammadi Library in English*, ed. James M. Robinson (New York: Harper San Francisco, 1990), 252.
3. Lynn Picknett and Clive Prince, *The Templar Revelation* (London, UK: Corgi Books, 1998), 345.
4. Picknett and Prince, *Templar Revelation*, 342.
5. Picknett and Prince, *Templar Revelation*, 342.
6. Laurence Gardner, *Bloodline of the Holy Grail* (Camberwell, Australia: Penguin Books, 2001), 104.
7. Thomas O. Lambdin, trans. "The Gospel of Thomas (II,2)", (21), in *Nag Hammadi Library in English*, ed. James M. Robinson (New York: Harper San Francisco, 1990), 129.
8. Lambdin, "The Gospel of Thomas", (21), in *Nag Hammadi*, 129.
9. George W. MacRae and R. McL. Wilson, trans. "The Gospel of Mary (BG 8502,*1*)", (18), in *Nag Hammadi Library in English*, ed. James M. Robinson (New York: Harper San Francisco, 1990), 526.
10. G.R.S. Mead, *Pistis Sophia: The Gnostic Tradition of Mary Magdalene, Jesus, and His Disciples* (Mineola, New York: Dover publications, 2005) 135.
11. Elaine Pagels, *The Gnostic Gospels* (New York: Vintage Books, 1989), 65.
12. Marvin Meyer, *The Gospel of Thomas* (New York: Harper San Erancisco, 1992), (114), 65.
13. MacRae, "The Gospel of Mary", (10), in *Nag Hammadi*, 525.
14. MacRae, "The Gospel of Mary", (18), in *Nag Hammadi*, 527.

15. Wesley W. Isenberg, trans. "The Gospel of Philip, (II,3)", (64), in *Nag Hammadi Library in English*, ed. James M. Robinson (New York: Harper San Francisco, 1990), 148.

16. Meyer, *The Gospel of Thomas*, (13), 29.

17. M. R., James, trans., "The Gospel of Bartholomew", (II:5), *The Apocryphal New Testament*, (Oxford, UK: Clarendon Press, 1924). In "Gospel of Bartholomew", *The Gnostic Society Library*, Joshua Williams ed., 1995, http://www.gnosis.org/library/gosbart.htm (1 Nov. 2004).

18. Graham Hancock, *Fingerprints of the Gods* (London, UK: Mandarin Paperbacks, 1996), 414.

19. Hancock, *Fingerprints of the Gods*, 414.

20. Hancock, *Fingerprints of the Gods*, 414.

21. Laurence Gardner, *The Magdalene Legacy* (London, U.K.: Element, 2005), 153.

22. John 12:7

23. Matthew 26:13

24. Hyllus Maris and Sonia Borg, story/script writers and James Ricketson, director (Episode 1), "Alinta the Flame", *Women of the Sun*, Bob Weiss prod., David Leonard and John Martin ex. prod. (Canberra, Australia: Ronin Films, 1981).

25. Sharron Rose, "Mary Magdalene, Apostle of Apostles", *New Dawn* 2, (Autumn/Winter 2006), 18.

26. Rose, "Mary Magdalene," *New Dawn*, 18.

27. James, "The Gospel of Bartholomew", (II:5), *Apocryphal New Testament*.

28. Pagels, *The Gnostic Gospels*, 5.

29. Emmel, "The Dialogue of the Saviour", (53), in *Nag Hammadi*, 252.

30. Emmel, "The Dialogue of the Saviour", (60), in *Nag Hammadi*, 252.

31. Emmel, "The Dialogue of the Saviour", (61), in *Nag Hammadi*, 252.

32. Emmel, "The Dialogue of the Saviour", (69), in *Nag Hammadi*, 253.

33. Emmel, "The Dialogue of the Saviour", (77), in *Nag Hammadi*, 253.

34. Emmel, "The Dialogue of the Saviour", (78), in *Nag Hammadi*, 253.

35. Emmel, "The Dialogue of the Saviour", (79), in *Nag Hammadi*, 253.

36. Emmel, "The Dialogue of the Saviour", (80), in *Nag Hammadi*, 253.

37. Emmel, "The Dialogue of the Saviour", (83), in *Nag Hammadi*, 253.

38. Bertrand Russell, "Quotations That Make Us Think", *Third World Traveler*, http://thirdworldtraveler.com/Authors/QuotationsToMakeUSThink.html, (21 Sept. 2005).

Chapter 2: The Gospel Truths.

1. Matthew 16:18

2. Matthew 16:23

3. Laurence Gardner, *Bloodline of the Holy Grail* (Camberwell, Australia: Penguin Books, 2001), 81.

4. Wesley W. Isenberg, trans. "The Gospel of Phillip (II,3)", (55), in *Nag Hammadi Library in English*, ed. James M. Robinson (New York: Harper San Francisco, 1990), 143.

5. Luke 2:49

6. Luke 2:50

7. Matthew 1:1

8. Gardner, *Bloodline of the Holy Grail*, 33.

9. Gardner, *Bloodline of the Holy Grail*, 32.
10. Gardner, *Bloodline of the Holy Grail*, 30.
11. Gardner, *Bloodline of the Holy Grail*, 30.
12. John 20:17
13. George W. MacRae and R. McL. Wilson, trans. "The Gospel of Mary", (BG 8502,*1*), (18), in *Nag Hammadi Library in English*, ed. James M. Robinson (New York: Harper San Francisco, 1990), 527.
14. John 11:11
15. John 11:16
16. John 11: 20, 28-29
17. Mark 16:19
18. Matthew 28:20
19. Luke 24:51
20. John 21:25
21. Gardner, *Bloodline of the Holy Grail*, 36.
22. Gardner, *Bloodline of the Holy Grail*, 36.
23. Gardner, *Bloodline of the Holy Grail*, 36.

Chapter 3: This Recurring Sentence.

1. Big Bill Neidjie, Stephen Davis and Allan Fox, *Australia's Kakadu Man* (Darwin, Australia: Resource Managers Pty Ltd, 1986), 57-58.
2. Matthew 17:12-13
3. Bill Neidjie, *Story About Feeling*, ed. Keith Taylor (Broome, Australia: Magabala Books, 1989), 4.
4. George W. MacRae and William R. Murdock, trans., and Douglas M. Parrott ed., "Apocalypse of Paul (V,*2*)" (20), in *Nag Hammadi Library in English*, ed. James M. Robinson (New York: Harper San Francisco, 1990), 258.
5. Stephen Emmel, trans., "The Dialogue of the Saviour (III,*5*)", (65-66 and 68), in *Nag Hammadi Library in English*, ed. James M. Robinson (New York: Harper San Francisco, 1990), 252-253.
6. William C. Robinson, Jr., trans., "The Exegesis of the Soul (II,*6*)", (136), in *Nag Hammadi Library in English*, ed. James M. Robinson (New York: Harper San Francisco, 1990), 197.
7. John D. Turner, trans., "The Book of Thomas the Contender (II,*7*)", (145), in *Nag Hammadi Library in English*, ed. James M. Robinson (New York: Harper San Francisco, 1990), 207.
8. Fredrick Wisse, trans., "Apocrophyon of John (II,*1*, III,*1*, IV,*1*, and BG 8502,*2*)", (27), in *Nag Hammadi Library in English*, ed. James M. Robinson (New York: Harper San Francisco, 1990), 120.
9. Turner, "The Book of Thomas the Contender (II,*7*)", (139), in *Nag Hammadi*, 202.
10. John N. Sieber, trans., "Zostrionios (VIII,*1*)", (131), in *Nag Hammadi Library in English*, ed. James M. Robinson (New York: Harper San Francisco, 1990), 430.
11. John D. Turner, trans., "The Interpretation of Knowledge (X1,*1*)", (112), in *Nag Hammadi Library in English*, ed. James M. Robinson (New York: Harper San Francisco, 1990), 477.
12. George W. MacRae, trans., "Authorative Teaching (V11,*3*)", (33), in *Nag Hammadi Library in English*, ed. James M. Robinson (New York: Harper San Francisco, 1990), 309.

13. Harold W. Attridge and Dieter Mueller, trans., "The Tripartate Tractate (I,5)", (120), in *Nag Hammadi Library in English*, ed. James M. Robinson (New York: Harper San Francisco, 1990), 95.
14. Yes: Jon Anderson, Steve Howe, Chris Squire and Alan White, "Give Love Each Day", *Magnification* (Beverly Hills, Cal.: Beyond Music/Yes LLC, 2001).
15. Bernard Simon, *The Essence of the Gnostics* (Royston, UK: Eagle Editions, 2004), 220.
16. Peter Gabriel, "Darkness", *Up* (U.K.: Real World Ltd/Peter Gabriel Ltd, 2002).

Chapter 4: The Gnostic Scriptures of Jesus.

1. Marvin Meyer, *The Gospel of Thomas* (New York: Harper San Fransico, 1992), (62), 47.
2. Jean Doresse, *The Secret Books of the Egyptian Gnostics*, (New York: MJF Books, 1986), 93.
3. Helmut Koester intro., "The Gospel of Thomas (II,2)", in *Nag Hammadi Library in English*, ed. James M. Robinson (New York: Harper San Francisco, 1990), 125.
4. J. R. Porter, *The Lost Bible* (London, UK: Duncan Baird Publishers, 2001), 169.
5. Porter, *The Lost Bible*, 168.
6. Porter, *The Lost Bible*, 166.
7. Porter, *The Lost Bible*, 166.
8. Sar Mikhail Melchizedek, "The Lost Teachings of Jesus: Did Jesus teach a secret doctrine?", *New Dawn*. Special Issue, no. 1 (Autumn/Winter, 2004): 57.
9. Thomas O. Lambdin, trans. "The Gospel of Thomas (II,2)", (106), in *Nag Hammadi Library in English*, ed. James M. Robinson (New York: Harper San Francisco, 1990), 137.
10. Lambdin, "The Gospel of Thomas", (42), in *Nag Hammadi*, 131.

Chapter 5: The Gospel of Thomas.

1. Thomas O. Lambdin, trans. *The Gospel of Thomas* (II,2), (114), in *Nag Hammadi Library in English*, ed. James M. Robinson (New York: Harper San Francisco, 1990), 138.
2. Marvin Meyer, *The Gospel of Thomas* (New York: Harper San Fransico, 1992), (3), 23.
3. Lambdin, "The Gospel of Thomas", (77), in *Nag Hammadi*, 135.
4. Big Bill Neidjie, Stephen Davis and Allan Fox, *Australia's Kakadu Man* (Darwin, Australia: Resource Managers Pty Ltd, 1986), 51.
5. Neidjie, *Australia's Kakadu Man*, 51.
6. Neidjie, *Australia's Kakadu Man*, 52.
7. Meyer, *The Gospel of Thomas*, (6), 25.
8. Neidjie, *Australia's Kakadu Man*, 41.
9. Neidjie, *Australia's Kakadu Man*, 61.
10. Meyer, *The Gospel of Thomas*, (13), 29.
11. Neidjie, *Australia's Kakadu Man*, 48.
12. Neidjie, *Australia's Kakadu Man*, 29.
13. Meyer, *The Gospel of Thomas*, (14), 29.
14. Neidjie, *Australia's Kakadu Man*, 49.

15. Meyer, *The Gospel of Thomas*, (16), 31.
16. Neidjie, *Australia's Kakadu Man*, 34.
17. Neidjie, *Australia's Kakadu Man*, 43.
18. Neidjie, *Australia's Kakadu Man*, 43.
19. Neidjie, *Australia's Kakadu Man*, 88.
20. Meyer, *The Gospel of Thomas*, (18), 31.
21. Robert Lawlor, *Voices of the First Day* (Rochester, Vermont: Inner Traditions International Ltd, 1991), 239.
22. Bernard Simon, *The Essence of the Gnostics* (Royston, Britain: Eagle Editions, 2004), 123.
23. Neidjie, *Australia's Kakadu Man*, 58-59.
24. Neidjie, *Australia's Kakadu Man*, 39.
25. Neidjie, *Australia's Kakadu Man*, 30.
26. Meyer, *The Gospel of Thomas*, (21), 33.
27. Lambdin, "The Gospel of Thomas", (25), in *Nag Hammadi*, 129.
28. Bill Neidjie, *Story About Feeling*, ed. Keith Taylor (Broome, Australia: Magabala Books, 1989), 22.
29. Neidjie, *Story About Feeling*, 30.
30. Bill Neidjie, *Story About Feeling*, 96.
31. Meyer, *The Gospel of Thomas*, (26), 35.
32. Neidjie, *Australia's Kakadu Man*, 37-38.
33. Neidjie, *Australia's Kakadu Man*, 38.
34. Dr Karl Kruszelnicki, commentator, (Weekly Science Talkback Show), "Science on Mornings", *Triple J* (Sydney, Australia: A.B.C. [Australia Broadcasting Commission], 11:00-12:00pm 9 Jun. 2005).
35. Kruszelnicki, "Science on Mornings" *Triple J*.
36. Lambdin, "The Gospel of Thomas", (36), in *Nag Hammadi*, 130.
37. Neidjie, *Story About Feeling*, 2-3.
38. Neidjie, *Story About Feeling*, 16.
39. Meyer, *The Gospel of Thomas*, (37), 39.
40. Neidjie, *Australia's Kakadu Man*, 34.
41. Neidjie, *Australia's Kakadu Man*, 34.
42. Neidjie, *Australia's Kakadu Man*, 34.
43. Lambdin, "The Gospel of Thomas", (39), in *Nag Hammadi*, 130-131.
44. Neidjie, *Australia's Kakadu Man*, 46.
45. Lambdin, "The Gospel of Thomas", (39), in *Nag Hammadi*, 130-131.
46. Lambdin, "The Gospel of Thomas", (42), in *Nag Hammadi*, 131.
47. Neidjie, *Australia's Kakadu Man*, 48.
48. Jamake, Highwater, *The Primal Mind* (New York: Meridian Books, 1981), 62.
49. Neidjie, *Australia's Kakadu Man*, 37.
50. Meyer, *The Gospel of Thomas*, (50), 43.
51. Neidjie, *Australia's Kakadu Man*, 57.
52. Neidjie, *Australia's Kakadu Man*, 59.
53. Meyer, *The Gospel of Thomas*, (51), 43.
54. Neidjie, *Australia's Kakadu Man*, 51.
55. Neidjie, *Australia's Kakadu Man*, 53.
56. Schaef, Anne Wilson, *Native Wisdom For White Minds* (Sydney, Australia: Random House, 1995), August 11.
57. Lambdin, "The Gospel of Thomas", (54), in *Nag Hammadi*, 132.

58. Neidjie, *Australia's Kakadu Man*, 42.
59. Neidjie, *Story About Feeling*, 148-149.
60. Lambdin, "The Gospel of Thomas", (60), in *Nag Hammadi*, 133.
61. Neidjie, *Australia's Kakadu Man*, 45.
62. Neidjie, *Australia's Kakadu Man*, 46.
63. Meyer, *The Gospel of Thomas*, (64), 51.
64. "The World Haters", *Time Magazine*, 9 June 1975, http://www.time.com/time/magazine/article/0,917,1005391,00.html (6 Oct. 2007).
65. Lambdin, "The Gospel of Thomas", (95), in *Nag Hammadi*, 136.
66. Neidjie, *Australia's Kakadu Man*, 46.
67. Neidjie, *Australia's Kakadu Man*, 46.
68. Neidjie, *Australia's Kakadu Man*, 48.
69. Neidjie, *Australia's Kakadu Man*, 28.
70. Lambdin, "The Gospel of Thomas", (70), in *Nag Hammadi*, 134.
71. Neidjie, *Story About Feeling*, vi.
72. Lawlor, *Voices of the First Day*, 208.
73. Lawlor, *Voices of the First Day*, 208.
74. Lawlor, *Voices of the First Day*, 208.
75. Meyer, *The Gospel of Thomas*, (84), 57.
76. Neidjie, *Australia's Kakadu Man*, 51.
77. Roland Eggleston, *When Yondi pushed up the Sky* (Sydney: Australasian Publishing Company Pty Ltd, 1964), 107.
78. Hugh Rule and Stuart Goodman, compiler, *Gulpilil's stories of The Dreamtime*, (Sydney, Australia: William Collins Publishers Pty Ltd, 1987), 11
79. Meyer, *The Gospel of Thomas*, (85), 57.
80. Neidjie, *Australia's Kakadu Man*, 58.
81. Schaef, *Native Wisdom For White Minds*, September 24.
82. Neidjie, *Australia's Kakadu Man*, 34.
83. Neidjie, *Australia's Kakadu Man*, 36.
84. Meyer, *The Gospel of Thomas*, (86), 57.
85. Neidjie, *Australia's Kakadu Man*, 48.
86. Neidjie, *Australia's Kakadu Man*, 35.
87. Neidjie, *Story About Feeling*, 163.
88. Meyer, *The Gospel of Thomas*, (95), 59.
89. Meyer, *The Gospel of Thomas*, (95), 59.
90. Neidjie, *Australia's Kakadu Man*, 46.
91. Jacqui Katona, "Speech-MAPW Conference, April 1997", in *Traditional Owners Statement*, 1997,
http://www.sea-us.org.au/trad-owners.html (4 Aug. 2007).
92. Katona, "Speech-MAPW Conference, April 1997", *Traditional Owners Statement*.
93. Neidjie, *Story About Feeling*, 66.
94. Meyer, *The Gospel of Thomas*, (108), 63.
95. Neidjie, *Story About Feeling*, 80.
96. Neidjie, *Australia's Kakadu Man*, 48.
97. Neidjie, *Australia's Kakadu Man*, 51.
98. Meyer, *The Gospel of Thomas*, (113), 65.
99. Neidjie, *Australia's Kakadu Man*, 47.
100. Neidjie, *Australia's Kakadu Man*, 52.

101. Neidjie, *Australia's Kakadu Man*, 60.
102. Neidjie, *Australia's Kakadu Man*, 52.
103. Meyer, *The Gospel of Thomas*, (114), 65.
104. Neidjie, *Australia's Kakadu Man*, 40
105. Meyer, *The Gospel of Thomas*, (22), 35.
106. Meyer, *The Gospel of Thomas*, (106), 63.
107. Meyer, *The Gospel of Thomas*, (106), 63.
108. Lawlor, *Voices of the First Day*, 201-202.
109. Neidjie, *Australia's Kakadu Man*, 62.

Chapter 6: Thomas Revisited.

1. Thomas O. Lambdin, trans. "The Gospel of Thomas (II,2)", (113), in *Nag Hammadi Library in English*, ed. James M. Robinson (New York: Harper San Francisco, 1990), 138.

2. George W. MacRae and William R. Murdock, trans. "The Apocalypse of Paul (V,2)", (20), in *NagHammadi Library in English*, ed. James M. Robinson (New York: Harper San Francisco, 1990) *258*

3. MacRae, "The Apocalypse of Paul", (24), in *Nag Hammadi*, 259.
4. MacRae, "The Apocalypse of Paul", (20), in *Nag Hammadi*, 258.
5. MacRae, "The Apocalypse of Paul", (20), in *Nag Hammadi*, 258.
6. MacRae, "The Apocalypse of Paul", (21), in *Nag Hammadi*, 258.
7. MacRae, "The Apocalypse of Paul", (20), in *Nag Hammadi*, 258.
8. Douglas MacLean, Paul Gannon and Susan J. Gould, *Change and Human Development* (New York: McGraw-Hill Companies Inc., 1997), 12.

Chapter 7: The Gospel of Mary.

1. George W. MacRae and R. McL, Wilson, trans. "The Gospel of Mary" (BG 8502,*1,*), (16), in *Nag Hammadi Library in English*, ed. James M. Robinson (New York: Harper San Francisco, 1990), 256.

2. MacRae, "The Gospel of Mary", (6-10, 15-19), in *Nag Hammadi*, 524-527.
3. MacRae, "The Gospel of Mary", (17), in *Nag Hammadi*, 526.
4. MacRae, "The Gospel of Mary", (17), in *Nag Hammadi*, 526.
5. MacRae, "The Gospel of Mary", (17), in *Nag Hammadi*, 526.
6. MacRae, "The Gospel of Mary", (16), in *Nag Hammadi*, 526.
7. MacRae, "The Gospel of Mary", (16), in *Nag Hammadi*, 526.
8. MacRae, "The Gospel of Mary", (10), in *Nag Hammadi*, 525.
9. MacRae, "The Gospel of Mary", (17), in *Nag Hammadi*, 526.
10. MacRae, "The Gospel of Mary", (10), in *Nag Hammadi*, 525.
11. MacRae, "The Gospel of Mary", (17), in *Nag Hammadi*, 525.
12. MacRae, "The Gospel of Mary", (18), in *Nag Hammadi*, 527.
13. MacRae, "The Gospel of Mary", (18), in *Nag Hammadi*, 527.
14. Thomas O. Lambdin, Trans. "The Gospel of Thomas" (II,2), (114), in *Nag Hammadi Library in English*, ed. James M. Robinson (New York: Harper San Francisco, 1990), 138.
15. MacRae, "The Gospel of Mary", (18), in *Nag Hammadi*, 527.
16. MacRae, "The Gospel of Mary", (15), in *Nag Hammadi*, 526.

17. MacRae, "The Gospel of Mary", (16), in *Nag Hammadi*, 526.
18. Stephen Emmel, trans. "The Dialogue of the Saviour (III,5)", (60), in *Nag Hammadi Library in English*, ed. James M. Robinson (New York: Harper San Francisco, 1990), 252.
19. MacRae, "The Gospel of Mary", (16), in *Nag Hammadi*, 526.
20. Emmel, "The Dialogue of the Saviour", (88), in *Nag Hammadi*, 254.
21. MacRae, "The Gospel of Mary", (16), in *Nag Hammadi*, 526.
22. MacRae, "The Gospel of Mary", (16), in *Nag Hammadi*, 526.
23. MacRae, "The Gospel of Mary", (9), in *Nag Hammadi*, 525.
24. MacRae, "The Gospel of Mary", (9), in *Nag Hammadi*, 525.
25. MacRae, "The Gospel of Mary", (9), in *Nag Hammadi*, 525.
26. MacRae, "The Gospel of Mary", (9), in *Nag Hammadi*, 525.
27. MacRae, "The Gospel of Mary", (9), in *Nag Hammadi*, 525.
28. MacRae, "The Gospel of Mary", (18), in *Nag Hammadi*, 527.
29. MacRae, "The Gospel of Mary", (18), in *Nag Hammadi*, 526.
30. MacRae, "The Gospel of Mary", (18), in *Nag Hammadi*, 526.
31. MacRae, "The Gospel of Mary", (18), in *Nag Hammadi*, 526.
32. MacRae, "The Gospel of Mary", (18), in *Nag Hammadi*, 527.
33. Lambdin, "The Gospel of Thomas", (114), in *Nag Hammadi*, 138.
34. MacRae, "The Gospel of Mary", (9), in *Nag Hammadi*, 525.
35. MacRae, "The Gospel of Mary", (10), in *Nag Hammadi*, 525.
36. MacRae, "The Gospel of Mary", (10), in *Nag Hammadi*, 525.
37. Lambdin, "The Gospel of Thomas", (114), in *Nag Hammadi*, 138.
38. MacRae, "The Gospel of Mary", (18), in *Nag Hammadi*, 527.
39. MacRae, "The Gospel of Mary", (10), in *Nag Hammadi*, 525.
40. MacRae, "The Gospel of Mary", (9), in *Nag Hammadi*, 525.
41. MacRae, "The Gospel of Mary", (10), in *Nag Hammadi*, 526.
42. MacRae, "The Gospel of Mary", (16), in *Nag Hammadi*, 526.
43. MacRae, "The Gospel of Mary", (16), in *Nag Hammadi*, 526.
44. MacRae, "The Gospel of Mary", (9), in *Nag hammadi*, 525.
45. Lambdin, "The Gospel of Thomas", (6), in *Nag Hammadi*, 126,127.
46. Lambdin, "The Gospel of Thomas", (6), in *Nag Hammadi*, 126,127.
47. Lambdin, "The Gospel of Thomas", (6), in *Nag Hammadi*, 126,127.
48. Lambdin, "The Gospel of Thomas", (14), in *Nag Hammadi*, 128.
49. Lambdin, "The Gospel of Thomas", (84), in *Nag Hammadi*, 135.
50. Lambdin, "The Gospel of Thomas", (6), in *Nag Hammadi*, 126,127.
51. Lambdin, "The Gospel of Thomas", (6), in *Nag Hammadi*, 126,127.
52. Lambdin, "The Gospel of Thomas", (6), in *Nag Hammadi*, 126,127.
53. Lambdin, " The Gospel of Thomas", (14), in *Nag Hammadi*, 128.
54. Lambdin, "The Gospel of Thomas", (95), in *Nag Hammadi*, 136.
55. Lambdin, "The Gospel of Thomas", (95), in *Nag Hammadi*, 136.
56. Lambdin, "The Gospel of Thomas", (64), in *Nag Hammadi*, 133,134.
57. Lambdin, "The Gospel of Thomas", (64), in *Nag Hammadi*, 133,134.
58. Lambdin, "The Gospel of Thomas", (53), in *Nag Hammadi*, 132.
59. Lambdin, "The Gospel of Thomas", (70), in *Nag Hammadi*, 134.
60. Lambdin, "The Gospel of Thomas", (77), in *Nag Hammadi*, 135.
61. Lesa Bellevie, *The Complete Idiot's Guide to Mary Magdalene* (New York: Alpha Books, 2005), 14.

Chapter 8: Dialogue of the Saviour and Associates.

1. Stephen Emmel, trans. "The Dialogue of the Saviour (III,5)", (60), in *Nag Hammadi Library in English,* ed. James M. Robinson (New York: Harper San Francisco, 1990), 252.
2. Emmel, "The Dialogue of the Saviour", (53), in *Nag Hammadi,* 252.
3. Emmel, "The Dialogue of the Saviour", (54), in *Nag Hammadi,* 252.
4. Emmel, "The Dialogue of the Saviour", (55), in *Nag Hammadi,* 252.
5. Emmel, "The Dialogue of the Saviour", (56), in *Nag Hammadi,* 252.
6. Emmel, "The Dialogue of the Saviour", (57), in *Nag Hammadi,* 252.
7. Emmel, "The Dialogue of the Saviour", (58), in *Nag Hammadi,* 252.
8. Emmel, "The Dialogue of the Saviour", (59), in *Nag Hammadi,* 252.
9. Emmel, "The Dialogue of the Saviour", (60), in *Nag Hammadi,* 252.
10. Emmel, "The Dialogue of the Saviour", (61), in *Nag Hammadi,* 252.
11. Emmel, "The Dialogue of the Saviour", (62), in *Nag Hammadi,* 252.
12. Emmel, "The Dialogue of the Saviour", (63), in *Nag Hammadi,* 252.
13. Emmel, "The Dialogue of the Saviour", (64), in *Nag Hammadi,* 252.
14. Emmel, "The Dialogue of the Saviour", (65), in *Nag Hammadi,* 252.
15. Emmel, "The Dialogue of the Saviour", (66), in *Nag Hammadi,* 252.
16. Emmel, "The Dialogue of the Saviour", (67), in *Nag Hammadi,* 253.
17. Emmel, "The Dialogue of the Saviour", (68), in *Nag Hammadi,* 253.
18. Emmel, "The Dialogue of the Saviour", (69), in *Nag Hammadi,* 253.
19. Emmel, "The Dialogue of the Saviour", (70), in *Nag Hammadi,* 253.
20. Emmel, "The Dialogue of the Saviour", (71), in *Nag Hammadi,* 253.
21. Emmel, "The Dialogue of the Saviour", (72), in *Nag Hammadi,* 253.
22. Emmel, "The Dialogue of the Saviour", (73), in *Nag Hammadi,* 253.
23. Emmel, "The Dialogue of the Saviour", (74), in *Nag Hammadi,* 253.
24. Emmel, "The Dialogue of the Saviour", (75), in *Nag Hammadi,* 253.
25. Emmel, "The Dialogue of the Saviour", (76), in *Nag Hammadi,* 253.
26. Emmel, "The Dialogue of the Saviour", (77), in *Nag Hammadi,* 253.
27. Emmel, "The Dialogue of the Saviour", (78), in *Nag Hammadi,* 253.
28. Emmel, "The Dialogue of the Saviour", (79), in *Nag Hammadi,* 253.
29. Emmel, "The Dialogue of the Saviour", (80), in *Nag Hammadi,* 253.
30. Emmel, "The Dialogue of the Saviour", (81), in *Nag Hammadi,* 253.
31. Emmel, "The Dialogue of the Saviour", (82), in *Nag Hammadi,* 253.
32. Emmel, "The Dialogue of the Saviour", (83), in *Nag Hammadi,* 253.
33. Emmel, "The Dialogue of the Saviour", (84), in *Nag Hammadi,* 253.
34. Emmel, "The Dialogue of the Saviour", (85), in *Nag Hammadi,* 253,254.
35. Emmel, "The Dialogue of the Saviour", (86), in *Nag Hammadi,* 254.
36. Emmel, "The Dialogue of the Saviour", (87), in *Nag Hammadi,* 254.
37. Emmel, "The Dialogue of the Saviour", (88), in *Nag Hammadi,* 254.
38. Helmut Koester and Elaine H. Pagels, intro. "The Dialogue of the Saviour (III,5)", in *Nag Hammadi Library in English,* ed. James M. Robinson (New York: Harper San Francisco, 1990) 244.
39. Koester and Pagel, "The Dialogue of the Saviour", 244.
40. Koester and Pagel, "The Dialogue of the Saviour", 244.
41. Koester and Pagel, "The Dialogue of the Saviour", 244.
42. Emmel, "The Dialogue of the Saviour", (60), in *Nag Hammadi,* 252.
43. Emmel, "The Dialogue of the Saviour", (60), in *Nag Hammadi,* 252.

44. Emmel, "The Dialogue of the Saviour", (61), in *Nag Hammadi*, 252.
45. Emmel, "The Dialogue of the Saviour", (69), in *Nag Hammadi*, 253.
46. Emmel, "The Dialogue of the Saviour", (57), in *Nag Hammadi*, 252.
47. Emmel, "The Dialogue of the Saviour", (66), in *Nag Hammadi*, 252.
48. Emmel, "The Dialogue of the Saviour", (68), in *Nag Hammadi*, 253.
49. Emmel, "The Dialogue of the Saviour", (83), in *Nag Hammadi*, 253.
50. Emmel, "The Dialogue of the Saviour", (83), in *Nag Hammadi*, 253.
51. Emmel, "The Dialogue of the Saviour", (84), in *Nag Hammadi*, 253.
52. Emmel, "The Dialogue of the Saviour", (36), in *Nag Hammadi*, 250.
53. Emmel, "The Dialogue of the Saviour", (81), in *Nag Hammadi*, 253.
54. George W. MacRae and R.Mcl, Wilson, trans. "The Gospel of Mary (BG 8502, *1*)", (18), in *Nag Hammadi Library in English*, ed. James M. Robinson (New York: Harper San Francisco, 1990), 527.
55. Emmel, "The Dialogue of the Saviour", (80), in *Nag Hammadi*, 253.
56. MacRae, "The Gospel of Mary", (10), in *Nag Hammadi*, 525.
57. MacRae, "The Gospel of Mary", (17), in *Nag Hammadi*, 526.
58. Emmel, "The Dialogue of the Saviour", (68), in *Nag Hammadi*, 253.
59. Emmel, "The Dialogue of the Saviour", (57), in *Nag Hammadi*, 252.
60. Emmel, "The Dialogue of the Saviour", (73), in *Nag Hammadi*, 253.
61. Emmel, "The Dialogue of the Saviour", (75), in *Nag Hammadi*, 253.
62. Emmel, "The Dialogue of the Saviour", (84), in *Nag Hammadi*, 253.
63. Emmel, "The Dialogue of the Saviour", (63), in *Nag Hammadi*, 252.
64. Emmel, "The Dialogue of the Saviour", (53), in *Nag Hammadi*, 252.
65. Emmel, "The Dialogue of the Saviour", (78), in *Nag Hammadi*, 253.
66. Emmel, "The Dialogue of the Saviour", (79), in *Nag Hammadi*, 253.
67. Emmel, "The Dialogue of the Saviour", (53), in *Nag Hammadi*, 252.
68. Emmel, "The Dialogue of the Saviour", (53), in *Nag Hammadi*, 252.
69. Emmel, "The Dialogue of the Saviour", (53), in *Nag Hammadi*, 252.
70. Emmel, "The Dialogue of the Saviour", (53), in *Nag Hammadi*, 252.
71. Emmel, "The Dialogue of the Saviour", (56), in *Nag Hammadi*, 252.
72. Emmel, "The Dialogue of the Saviour", (57), in *Nag Hammadi*, 252.
73. Emmel, "The Dialogue of the Saviour", (57), in *Nag Hammadi*, 252.
74. Emmel, "The Dialogue of the Saviour", (57), in *Nag Hammadi*, 252.
75. Emmel, "The Dialogue of the Saviour", (57), in *Nag Hammadi*, 252.
76. Emmel, "The Dialogue of the Saviour", (57), in *Nag Hammadi*, 252.
77. Emmel, "The Dialogue of the Saviour", (49), in *Nag Hammadi*, 251.
78. Emmel, "The Dialogue of the Saviour", (50), in *Nag Hammadi*, 251, 252.
79. Emmel, "The Dialogue of the Saviour", (50), in *Nag Hammadi*, 251, 252.
80. Thomas O. Lambdin, Trans. "The Gospel of Thomas (II,2)", (95), in *Nag Hammadi Library in English*, ed. James M. Robinson (New York: Harper San Francisco, 1990), 136.
81. Lambdin, "The Gospel of Thomas", (95), in *Nag Hammadi*, 136.
82. Emmel, "The Dialogue of the Saviour", (88), in *Nag Hammadi*, 254.
83. Lambdin, "The Gospel of Thomas", (20), in *Nag Hammadi*, 128.
84. Lambdin, "The Gospel of Thomas", (20), in *Nag Hammadi*, 128.
85. Emmel, "The Dialogue of the Saviour", (88), in *Nag Hammadi*, 254.
86. Emmel, "The Dialogue of the Saviour", (88), in *Nag Hammadi*, 254.
87. Emmel, "The Dialogue of the Saviour", (90), in *Nag Hammadi*, 254.
88. Emmel, "The Dialogue of the Saviour", (97), in *Nag Hammadi*, 254.

Notes

89. Emmel, "The Dialogue of the Saviour", (97), in *Nag Hammadi*, 254.
90. Emmel, "The Dialogue of the Saviour", (79), in *Nag Hammadi*, 253.
91. Lambdin, "The Gospel of Thomas", (3), in *Nag Hammadi*, 126.
92. Douglas M. Parrott, trans. "The Sophia of Jesus Christ (III,*4* and BG 8502,*3*)", (90), in *Nag Hammadi Library in English*, ed. James M. Robinson (New York: Harper San Francisco, 1990), 222.
93. Emmel, "The Dialogue of the Saviour", (81), in *Nag Hammadi*, 253.
94. Richard Owens, "Judas the Misunderstood Vatican moves to clear reviled disciple's name", *Times Online*, 12 January, 2006, http://www.timesonline.co.uk/tol/sport/football/european_football/article787629.ece (22 Jun. 2006).
95. G.R.S. Mead, *Pistis Sophia: The Gnostic Tradition of Mary Magdalene, Jesus, and His Disciples* (Mineola, New York: Dover publications, 2005), 47.
96. Lesa Bellevie, *The Complete Idiot's Guide to Mary Magdalene* (New York: Alpha Books, 2005), 206.
97. Bellevie, *The Complete Idiot's Guide to Mary Magdalene*, 207.
98. Bellevie, *The Complete Idiot's Guide to Mary Magdalene*, 207.
99. Mead, *Pistis Sophia*, 27.
100. Bernard Simon, *The Essence of the Gnostics* (Royston, UK: Eagle Editions, 2004), 129.
101. Sharon Rose, "Mary Magdalene, Apostle of Apostles", *New* Dawn, Special Issue no. 2 (Autumn/Winter 2006): 19.
102. Rose, "Mary Magdalene, Apostle of Apostles", *New Dawn*, 19.
103. Rose, "Mary Magdalene, Apostle of Apostles", *New Dawn*, 19.
104. Mead, *Pistis Sophia* , 27-28.
105. Liz Thompson, *Woonyoomboo* (Melbourne, Australia: Rigby publications, 2008), 5.
106. Thompson, *Woonyoomboo*, 7.
107. Thompson, *Woonyoomboo*, 8.
108. Thompson, *Woonyoomboo*, 12.
109. Thompson, *Woonyoomboo*, 13.
110. Thompson, *Woonyoomboo*, 14.
111. Thompson, *Woonyoomboo*, 14.
112. Mead, *Pistis Sophia* , 27.
113. Neidjie, Bill, *Story About Feeling* (Broome, Ausralia: Magabala Books, 1989), back cover.
114. Mead, *Pistis Sophia* , 27.
115. Mead, *Pistis Sophia* , 27.
116. Mead, *Pistis Sophia* , 27.
117. Mead, *Pistis Sophia* , 28.
118. Mead, *Pistis Sophia* , 28.
119. Neidjie, *Story About Feeling*, 121.
120. Jacobus de Voragine, compiler, and William Caxton trans. "Here Followeth the Life of St. Mary Magdalene",Vol. 4, *Legenda Aurea (The Golden Legend or Lives of the Saints)*, ed F.S. Ellis (Temple Classics edition 1900). From Medieval Sourcebook 2001, http://www.fordham.edu/halsall/basis/goldenlegend/GoldenLegend-Volume4.htm (2 Mar. 2008).

121. M. R., James, trans., "Acts of Philip", (IX:126), *The Apocryphal New Testament*, (Oxford, UK: Clarendon Press, 1924). In *The Gnostic Society Library*, 2005, http://www.gnosis.org/library/actphil.htm (2 Mar. 2008).

122. MacRae, "The Gospel of Mary", (10), in *Nag Hammadi*, 526.

123. M. R., James, trans., "The Gospel of Bartholomew", (II:5), *The Apocryphal New Testament*, (Oxford, UK: Clarendon Press, 1924). In "Gospel of Bartholomew", *The Gnostic Society Library*, Joshua Williams ed., 1995, http://www.gnosis.org/library/gosbart.htm, (1 Nov. 2004).

Chapter 9: The Alternate Genesis

1. Frederik Wisse, trans. "The Sentences of Sextus (XII,*1*)", (355), in *Nag Hammadi Library in English*, ed. James M. Robinson (New York: Harper San Francisco, 1990), 506.

2. Wisse, "The Sentences of Sextus", (373/374), in *Nag Hammadi*, 507.

3. Wisse, "The Sentences of Sextus", (338), in *Nag Hammadi*, 506.

4. Richard Laurence, trans. *The Book of Enoch the Prophet* (San Diego, Cal.: Wizards Bookshelf, 1995), (CHAP. VII, 7), 6.

5. Lyman Abott, "Introduction", *The Book of Enoch the Prophet*, trans. Richard Laurence (San Diego, Cal.: Wizards Bookshelf, 1995), xviii.

6. Laurence, *The Book of Enoch the Prophet*, (CHAP. X, 11), 11.

7. Wisse, "The Sentences of Sextus", (174), in *Nag Hammadi*, 504.

8. Laurence, *The Book of Enoch the Prophet*, (CHAP. VII, 2), 6.

9. Wisse, "The Sentences of Sextus", (171), in *Nag Hammadi*, 504.

10. Laurence, *The Book of Enoch the Prophet*, (CHAP. VII, 7), 6.

11. Wisse, "The Sentences of Sextus", (160), in *Nag Hammadi*, 503.

12. George W. MacRae, trans. "The Apocalypse of Adam (V,*5*)", (64), in *Nag Hammadi Library in English*, ed. James M. Robinson (New York: Harper San Francisco, 1990), 279.

13. Wisse, "The Sentences of Sextus", (333), in *Nag Hammadi*, 505.

Chapter 10: Mary's Legacy

1. Wesley W. Isenberg, trans. "The Gospel of Philip (II.,3)", (63-64), in *Nag Hammadi Library in English*, ed. James M. Robinson (New York: Harper San Francisco, 1990), 148.

2. Isenberg, "The Gospel of Philip", (64) in *Nag Hammadi*, 148.

3. Esther De Boer, "Mary Magdalene: Beyond The Myth", *Secrets of the Code*, ed. Dan Burstein (London, UK: Weidenfeld and Nicolson, 2004), 43

4. Isenberg, "The Gospel of Philip", (63), in *Nag Hammadi*, 148.

5. Isenberg, "The Gospel of Philip", (63), in *Nag Hammadi*, 148.

6. Isenberg, "The Gospel of Philip", (64), in *Nag Hammadi*, 148.

7. Stephen Emmel, trans. "The Dialogue of the Saviour (III,5)", (53), in *Nag Hammadi Library in English*, ed. James M. Robinson (New York: Harper San Francisco, 1990) 252.

8. Jacobus de Voragine, compiler, and William Caxton trans. "Here Followeth the Life of St. Mary Magdalene",Vol. 4, *Legenda Aurea (The Golden Legend or Lives of the Saints)*, ed F.S. Ellis (Temple Classics edition 1900). From Medieval Sourcebook 2001,

http://www.fordham.edu/halsall/basis/goldenlegend/GoldenLegend-Volume4.htm (2 Mar. 2008).

9. Thomas O. Lambdin, trans. "The Gospel of Thomas (II,2)", (37), in *Nag Hammadi Library in English*, ed. James M. Robinson (New York: Harper San Francisco, 1990), 130.

10. Lambdin, "The Gospel of Thomas", (37), in *Nag Hammadi*, 130.

11. Voragine, "Life of St. Mary Magdalene", *The Golden Legend*.
Lynn Picknett and Clive Prince, *The Templar Revelation* (London, U.K.: Corgi Books, 1998), 86.
Micheal Baigent, Richard Leigh and Henry Lincoln, *The Holy Blood and the Holy Grail* (London, UK: Arrow Books, 1996), 299.
Ian Jones, *Joshua The Man They Called Jesus* (Port Melbourne, Australia: Thomas C. Lothian Pty Ltd, 2000), 142.

12. Voragine, "Life of St. Mary Magdalene", *The Golden Legend*.

13. The many able to make miracles could include: Joseph of Arimathea, St. Philip the apostle, Mary Magdalene, Sarah, Martha etc.

14. Margaret Starbird, *Mary Magdalene: The Grail Bearer*, 2001, http://www.magdalene.org/grailbearer.php (15 Nov. 2005).

15. Voragine, "Life of St. Mary Magdalene", *The Golden Legend*.
Picknett and Prince, *Templar Revelation*, 86.

16. Starbird, *Mary Magdalene: The Grail Bearer*.

17. Starbird, *Mary Magdalene: The Grail Bearer*.

18. Voragine, "Life of St. Mary Magdalene", *The Golden Legend*.

19. Laurence Gardner, *Bloodline of the Holy Grail* (Camberwell, Victoria Australia: Penguin Books, 2001), 120.

20. Gardner, *Bloodline of the Holy Grail*, 72.

21. Picknett and Prince, *The Templar Revelation*, 88.

22. Gardner, *Bloodline of the Holy Grail*, 115 and 71.
Mark 15:43.

23. Gardner, *Bloodline of the Holy Grail*, 204.

24. Gardner, *Bloodline of the Holy Grail*, 203.

25. Gardner, *Bloodline of the Holy Grail*, 108.

26. Picknett and Prince, *Templar Revelation*, 86-7

27. Voragine, "Life of St. Mary Magdalene", *The Golden Legend*.

28. Voragine, "Life of St. Mary Magdalene", *The Golden Legend*.
Picknett and Prince, *Templar Revelation*, 87.

29. Voragine, "Life of St. Mary Magdalene", *The Golden Legend*.

30. Baigent, Leigh and Lincoln, *Holy Blood Holy Grail*, 362.

31. Voragine, "Life of St. Mary Magdalene", *The Golden Legend*.

32. Baigent, Leigh and Lincoln, *Holy Blood Holy Grail*, 362.

33. Gardner, *Bloodline of the Holy Grail*, 54.

34. Gardner, *Bloodline of the Holy Grail*, 123.

35. Gardner, *Bloodline of the Holy Grail*, 123.

36. Gardner, *Bloodline of the Holy Grail*, 123.

37. Picknett and Prince, *Templar Revelation*, 90.

38. Ronald Lee, "The Romani Goddess Kali Sara", *The World Tree Volume 1*, 2002, http://home.cogeco.ca/~kopachi/articles/romanigoddess.html (23 Nov. 2003).

39. Starbird, *Mary Magdalene: The Grail Bearer*.

40. Starbird, *Mary Magdalene: The Grail Bearer*.

41. Starbird, *Mary Magdalene: The Grail Bearer*.
42. Lee, "The Romani Goddess Kali Sara", *The World Tree*.
43. Picknett and Prince, *Templar Revelation*, 90.
44. Lee, "The Romani Goddess Kali Sara", *The World Tree*.
45. It is probable as an altar within the church is dedicated to Sarah.
46. Lee, "The Romani Goddess Kali Sara", *The World Tree*.
47. Picknett and Prince, *Templar Revelation*, 86.
48. Picknett and Prince, *Templar Revelation*, 89-90.
49. Gardner, *Bloodline of the Holy Grail*, 109 and 178.
50. Gardner, *Bloodline of the Holy Grail*, 241.
51. Gardner, *Bloodline of the Holy Grail*, 241.
52. Gardner, *Bloodline of the Holy Grail*, 242.
53. Gardner, *Bloodline of the Holy Grail*, 241.
54. "Patrin Saintes-Maries de la Mer", *Patrin Web Journal Romani*, 2002, http://www.geocities.com/paris/5121/stsm_01.htm (2 Oct. 2004).
55. Gardner, *Bloodline of the Holy Grail*, 102.
56. Gardner, *Bloodline of the Holy Grail*, 102.
57. Gardner, *Bloodline of the Holy Grail*, 102.
58. *Salome: Matron Saint of Midwives*, Feb. 2008, http://www.grailchurch.org/salome.htm (7 Mar. 2004).
59. Gardner, *Bloodline of the Holy Grail*, 102.
60. Lambdin, "The Gospel of Thomas", (61), in *Hag Hammadi* 133.
61. Gardner, *Bloodline of the Holy Grail*, 99.
62. Cathar Legend
63. Gardner, *Bloodline of the Holy Grail*, 113.
64. Baigent, Leigh and Lincoln, *Holy Blood Holy Grail*, 362.
65. Jacobus de Voragine, compiler, and William Caxton trans. "Here Followeth the Life of St. Martha",Vol. 4, *Legenda Aurea (The Golden Legend or Lives of the Saints)*, ed F.S. Ellis (Temple Classics edition 1900). From Medieval Sourcebook 2001, http://www.fordham.edu/halsall/basis/goldenlegend/GoldenLegend-Volume4.htm (2 Mar. 2008).
66. Voragine, "Life of St. Martha", *The Golden Legend*.
67. Voragine, "Life of St. Martha", *The Golden Legend*.
68. Voragine, "Life of St. Martha", *The Golden Legend*.
69. Voragine, "Life of St. Martha", *The Golden Legend*.
70. Voragine, "Life of St. Martha", *The Golden Legend*. Gardner, *Bloodline of the Holy Grail*, 100.
71. Gardner, *Bloodline of the Holy Grail*, 106.
72. Voragine, "Life of St. Martha", *The Golden Legend*.
73. Voragine, "Life of St. Martha", *The Golden Legend*.
74. Voragine, "Life of St. Martha", *The Golden Legend*.
75. Voragine, "Life of St. Martha", *The Golden Legend*.
76. Voragine, "Life of St. Martha", *The Golden Legend*.
77. Voragine, "Life of St. Martha", *The Golden Legend*.
78. Voragine, "Life of St. Martha", *The Golden Legend*.
79. Voragine, "Life of St. Martha", *The Golden Legend*.
80. Voragine, "Life of St. Martha", *The Golden Legend*.
81. G.R.S. Mead, *Pistis Sophia: The Gnostic Tradition of Mary Magdalene, Jesus, and His Disciples* (Mineola, New York: Dover publications, 2005)

82. Gardner, *Bloodline of the Holy Grail*, 109 and 241.

Epilogue: "Gates of Delirium"

1. Yes: Jon Anderson, Steve Howe, Chris Squire and Alan White, "Gates of Delirium ", *Relayer* (UK: Topographic Music Ltd, 1974).

2. Hermann Goering, "Quotations That Make Us Think", *Third World Traveler*, http://thirdworldtraveler.com/index.html (21 Sept. 2005).

3. George Orwell, "Quotations That Make Us Think", *Third World Traveler*, http://thirdworldtraveler.com/Authors/QuotationsToMakeUSThink.html (21 Sept. 2005).

4. Big Bill Neidjie, Stephen Davis and Allan Fox, *Australia's Kakadu Man* (Darwin, Australia: Resource Managers Pty Ltd, 1986), 52.

5. Sharon S. Brehm and Saul M. Kassin, *Social Psychology* (Boston, MA: Houghton Mifflin Company, 1996), 101-102.

6. Arundhati Roy, "Quotations That Make Us Think", *Third World Traveler*, http://thirdworldtraveler.com/Authors/QuotationsToMakeUSThink.html (21 Sept. 2005).

7. Martin Luther King Jr., "Martin Luther King Jr. Quotations", *Third World Traveler*, http://thirdworldtraveler.com/Author/MLK_quotes.html (21 Sept. 2005).

8. Joseph Goebels, "Quotations That Make Us Think", *Third World Traveler*, http://thirdworldtraveler.com/Authors/QuotationsToMakeUSThink.html (21 Sept. 2005).

Glossary

Aboriginal: This generic term refers to the original people of Australia. It includes those termed 'indigenous' and those from the Torres Strait Islands. When describing ancient events and times it also includes the population of Papua New Guinea.

Adam: According to the book of Genesis and the Torah, Adam was the first man created by God. There are some parallels with his story in Sumerian Mythology—which is considered by many to be the main source of much Biblical mythology. According to Islamic theology Adam is seen as a prophet, while in Judaic theology Adam's life outside the Garden of Eden is elaborated upon. Concepts such as Original Sin and Satan being the serpent are part of Christianity doctrine, added to the Biblical account. Adam is viewed differently amongst the spectrum of Gnostic sects and Manicheans. Some generalisations can be drawn; Adam was *Protanthropos* (original man), Adam and Eve were an androgynous being with perfect knowledge and power greater than Samuel/the Demiurge, when they were separated into two beings they fell into material existence and there was a struggle between lightness and darkness. Jesus is seen as a reincarnation of Adam and Eve was reborn in Mary's body. Historical authenticity of Adam and Eve is debatable, with some seeing them as literal figures and others as metaphors.

Alfonso X (King): (1221-1284). Alfonso X was the King of Galicia, Castile and Leon [Spain] from 1252 to 1284. Also called "El Sabio", the wise or learned. King Alfonso was a writer of science, particularly astronomy.

Ashera: (Or Asherah) A goddess and originally Yahweh's female consort (worshipped by Hebrews from 940 to 586 BCE). She was the Queen of Heaven until Josiah decided her presence was a hindrance.

Aunty: An earned title or respect, awarded by the local community, the equivalent term from the past would be Elder.

Bell, Dianne: Author of *Daughters of the Dreaming*. This is the first book that intensively detailed some women's ceremonies and practises that had been hidden from non-Aboriginal society.

Biamie: The Aboriginal creation Spirit. It is a common term used throughout the South-East Australia (Kamilaroi/Gumilaroi). He is the god of death, life, rain, shamans and the sky. His regional equivalent is *Nooralee* around the Murray River, *Mungan Ngour* in parts of Queensland and *Peeri-mehial* in the Western Desert Region. In all cases all other Ancestral Spirits are creations of *Biamie* (or his parallel).

Birrahgnooloo: The Gnostic equivalent is Sophia. She is *Biamie's* consort, with equally powerful feminine totems for every part of her body. She symbolises the feminine aspect of creation and is the Goddess of fertility with the power to cause floods. *Biamie* and *Birrahgnooloo* had a son *Daramulum* (or 'one-legged' is a God of the weather, sky, shamans and the moon). Other legends insist *Birrahgnooloo* and *Biamie* never had any offspring, as he did not sleep with her.

Boomerang: A throwing stick. Some return, many do not. This implement could be used to hunt with, as a tool, a musical instrument, an object to paint on, a weapon in warfare, a recreational toy or a sacred object.

Buddhism: A major world religion/philosophy (700 million+ followers) founded by Buddha (Siddhartha Guatama). Major precepts of Buddhism include, the noble eightfold path (the path end of suffering in life), achieving enlightenment, moderation, morality and to obtaining liberation (Nirvanna). Buddhist practices include mediation (dhyana), vegetarian diet and their beliefs embrace the concepts of karma and rebirth. Although Buddhism's teachings originated in Asia, it has become quite popular in the West.

Bundjalung: This tribal area spans from north of the Clarence River (Grafton, N.S.W.) to somewhere near South Stradbroke Island (Queensland). It was estimated the tribal population was at least 5,000. Every three years the entire tribe congregated near the Border Ranges, meeting for months of ceremonies and associated activities at the same time the Bunya Pines bore enormous quantities of fruit.

Canonical Gospels: Traditionally accepted New Testament Gospels: Luke, Matthew, Mark and John.

Cathars: (Or Albigensians). The Cathars were located in Southern France (Languedoc), they originated in the 10th century A.D. and were believed by some to have originated from the Bogomils sect of Bulgaria. These devout disciples of the Gnostic tradition of Mary Magdalene were the catalysts that inspired the Inquisition. The Catholic Church declared them to be heretics and non-Christian. In 1229 they were pronounced to be in mortal sin and in need of being immediately massacred *en masse*, so the Lord could pass judgement upon these fallen sinners. During this 40 year war over 500,000 people were killed. Their beliefs included; sexual abstinence, a vegetarian diet, Jesus existing as a pure spirit, the rejection of Old Testament, veneration of The Gospel of John, the material world being corrupt and a prison and that this material world created by a lesser God (The Demiurge/Satan). They believed this demiurge was an impostor and was also worshipped by the Catholic Church. Their ultimate goal was the liberation from this material realm, as they believed reincarnation was a result of the failure to attain this liberation. Cathar society was subdivided into two groups-the *Perfecti* (Prefects [Clergy]) and the *Credentes* (believers [followers]). The *Perfecti* led chaste lives of charity, preaching etc. while the *Credentes* were exempt from these expectations.

Glossary

Clement of Alexandria: (Titus Flavius Clemens) Clement was one of the founding fathers of Christianity. He was the first traditional scholar to acknowledge the existence of the *Secret Gospel of Mark*.

Constantine I (Emperor): (Or Constantine the Great / Gaius Flavius Valerius Aurelius Constantinus): The first Roman Emperor to allow Christianity to flourish. The Byzantine Empire considered Constantine its founder and he experienced significant military successes, supposedly with the Christian God's assistance. Constantine convened the Council of Nicea.

Corinthians 1 (1 cor.): (Or First Epistle to the Corinthians) A Pauline letter written in the mid-to-late AD 50's and included in the New Testament.

Council of Nicea (First): (A.D. 325) The council consisted of a group of Bishops who were personally selected by the Emperor Constantine. Their brief was to formalise Christianity and decide which accounts were deemed appropriate. Those scriptures deemed to be in error were supposed to be destroyed. Several points of disagreements were discussed i.e. the nature of Jesus in relation to God, the date of Easter and Arianism (founded by Arius who believed God created Jesus and that he was not divine in opposition to the mainstream Church's belief that he was of the same stuff; a God and part of the Holy Trinity). The gathering of this council was the first attempt to unify Christianity (Nicene Creed). It was a significant event for the early Church and history.

de Robin, Bob: A powerful *Bundjalung* Elder and Clever-Fella who was custodian of many sacred sites in the Nightcap Range.

Diranhgaan: Female equivalent of a Clever-Fella/Kadaitcha man; her magic is very powerful and rarely challenged by any Aboriginal male. In one *Bundjalung Dreaming* story the *Diaranhgaan's* task was to examine and initiate any males who wished to become Clever-Fellas.

Enoch: Enoch is the grandfather of Noah. He was an extremely prominent figure in early Judaic mythology then somewhat mysteriously vanished, or was marginalised. In the *Book of Enoch*, Enoch was taken to heaven then returned to earth for thirty days to record his journey. Enoch then ascended to heaven to judge all mortals. Some say he became an Angel and acted as the voice of God, which is why the language of the Angels is sometimes referred to as Enochian. Enoch recorded the existence of fallen angels he called Watchers, who he claims have meddled in the affairs of humankind.

Epiphanius of Syria: (Or Bishop Epiphanius of Salamis) AD 310-403: He was a devout adherent of early orthodox Christianity who wrote some books specifically attacking Gnosticism i.e. Panarion (written AD 373-4).

Essenes: A Jewish religious sect existing from 2nd century BC to AD 70. The Essenes are believed to be the writers of the Dead Sea Scrolls. Quram was their main settlement (located in the Judean desert near the Dead Sea). They are believed to have led a communal and ascetic lifestyle i.e. did not trade, maintained a vegetarian diet, did not sacrifice animals and believed communal ownership of property was essential. They believed in the conflict between darkness and light, were healers/physicians and there are rumours Jesus may have had connections to this group.

Feminine: This term should not be equated to a sex, it is more a state of mind. Some confuse baser emotions, such as aggression and violence urged on by a copious supply of testosterone, as being male. Being foolish and threatening has nothing to do with gender and everything to do with poor personal choices.

Gagadu: Traditional tribal name for an area of land and wetland found in Northern Territory that has been misrepresented as Kakadu.

Gardner, Laurence: He is the author of the bestseller *Bloodline of the Holy Grail*, *Genesis of the Grail Kings*, *Realm of the Ring Lords*, *Lost Secrets of the Sacred Ark*, *The Magdalene Legacy* and *The Shadow of Solomon*. Gardner provides extensive genealogical records and claims the Holy Grail in fact is not the fabled cup/chalice but a hidden Holy Bloodline. Gardner's book details this messianic bloodline, which involves various Old Testament patriarchs and kings such as David and Solomon. It then passes on to Jesus, Mary Magdalene, Joseph of Arimathea, and their offspring. Their descendants included the Merovingian Frankish dynasty and rulers of Southern France, while in Britain notable names include King Arthur and the Grail Knights, various Scottish royal houses including the Stuarts and finally the present Counts of Albany.

Genesis: The first book of the Old Testament and the Bible. It details the creation of the world, Adam and Eve in the Garden of Eden, the tree of knowledge, the serpent and humanities' collective fall. Its legacy is still felt today with the oppression of women and conceptual notion of original sin

God: The original creative force that brought all forms of material life into existence, known in the Bible as Yahweh and in the Koran as Allah and by various other designations in the many cultures where the concept exists. God is described in a great many ways although it is maintained by many that *he* is ultimately unknowable.

Golden Legend (The): (Latin: Legenda Aurea): A collection of the lives of the Saints by Jacobus de Voragine (1280). The text is the first book to be mass-produced by William Caxton and contains an extensive and controversial account of Mary Magdalene's life.

Gospel of Bartholomew: Commonly referred to as a "Passion Gospel" which was written soon after the resurrection.

Gospel of Judas: A Gnostic text recently presented to the public by National Geographic. It is dated early in the 2nd century and portrays Judas as Jesus' closest male Apostle who obeyed his instructions when reputedly betraying the Saviour. This Gospel is Gnostic in nature and can be classified as a dialogue gospel. The gospel of Judas has recently been rediscovered and there is some contention amongst academia relating to its significance.

Greater and *Lesser Questions of Mary Magdalene*: A pair of texts based on Mary's life and words, both texts are lost or destroyed.

Gulpilil, David: An Aboriginal tracker, Elder, writer and actor.

Gumilaroi: (Kamilaroi) The name of the Australian Aboriginal tribe and nation which is found in the North Western Slopes and Plains region of New South Wales.

Hancock, Graham: A leading writer, journalist and pseudo-archaeologist. A prolific author of several bestselling books including, *Lords of Poverty, The Sign and the Seal, Fingerprints of the Gods, Keeper of Genesis, The Mars Mystery, Heaven's Mirror* (co-author Santha Faiia), *Underworld: The Mysterious Origins of Civilization, Talisman: Sacred Cities, Secret Faith* (co-author Robert Bauval) and *Supernatural: Meetings With the Ancient Teachers of Mankind*. Major themes of these books include ancient myths, a lost mother civilisation and archaeo-astronomy.

Hellenistic: Pertaining to or influenced by Greek culture and philosophy.

Hippolytus: (Saint Hippolytus of Rome). Hippolytus was an early Biblical commentator/writer, who praised Mary Magdalene as the "Apostle of the Apostles." Hippolytus was the first anti-pope, who then became a martyr and later a Saint.

Interpretation of Knowledge: A scripture recovered at Nag Hammadi, in which New Testament writings are given a Gnostic perspective.

Isis: (Means Queen of the throne). Isis is the chief Goddess of Egyptian Mythology, and the Isiac mystery school, which flourished in Greco-Roman times. She is the sister-wife to Osiris, mother to Horus, who became a funerary deity, goddess of magic and was eventually amalgamated with Hathor and Mut. Isis held many titles (Queen of Heaven) and was identified by numerous icons e.g. the throne. The legend of Osiris and Isis was a significant part of Egyptian mythology, particularly where Isis resurrects Osiris from death. Isis has some parallels to Christianity through the Virgin Mary and Mary Magdalene.

Jehovah: (Or Tetragrammaton [never pronounced, *HaShem* {the name} used instead for conversation and Adonai {lord} used for prayer], YHWH and Yahweh) The Judaic name for God.

Johnson, Samuel: (Dr Johnson) (1709-1784) An English philosopher, writer, literary critic and poet.

Josiah (King): (Yoshiyahu) King of Judah from 640-609 BCE.

Judaism: The religion of the Jewish people (presently 14 million adherents). The belief in one omnipotent creator God and his commandments/laws expressed in the Torah (Hebrew Bible) are paramount aspects of this faith. Another important text is the Talmud (rabbinic discourse on law, customs etc). To be a Jew one must have converted or be born to a Jewish mother. There are several different denominations of Judaism including, Orthodox, Conservative, Humanist and Progressive Judaism (within these sects are further subdivisions). There are also ethnic divisions and groups within Judaism i.e. the Samaritans. There also exist several cross-religious alternative forms of Judaism that include Buddhism, Paganism-Wiccan, New Age-Kabbalah and Christianity. Characteristics of Judaism include, prayer, the Sabbath and other Holy days, Holy festivals (i.e. Passover), life cycle events (i.e. Bar mitzvah, circumcision rites), a Kosher Diet, Synagogues (prayer house) and the Rabbi (prayer leader).

Kaidaitcha Man: He is often referred to the *feather-foot man*, one of his roles was to keep the Law and deal with those who have transgressed any important Ancestral Law. Punishment may involve death after *singing* the victim, sometimes a secret object is used to amplify and relay his powers into the body of the lawbreaker e.g. bone, quartz stone.

King, Dr Rev. Martin Luther: Peace activist heavily influenced by Mahatma Ghandi's concept of non-violent civil disobedience.

Koester, Professor Helmut: A leading Biblical scholar and Professor of New Testament studies, Ecclesiastical History (Harvard University) and ordained Lutheran minister, who believe the Gospel of Thomas could have been written as early as 50 A.D.

Kruszelnicki, Dr Karl: Respected scientist, author, radio and television personality who has done a lot to popularise science in Australia. His media exposure began through a weekly science segment he conducted on JJJ (Australia's national youth radio station) and presenting *Quantum* (weekly science TV programme on A.B.C.).

Lake Mungo: Part of a series of inland lakes that were once linked together to form the Willandra Lakes System, which created something close to the reputed inland sea early explorers vainly sought. The entire system dried up around 15,000 years ago, and since then has remained in that state. Lake Mungo is the most prolific archaeological site yet discovered in Australia with extensive evidence of human remains and by-products.

Lawlor, Robert: Author of the thoroughly researched study companion to Aboriginal prehistory: *Voices of the First Day*. This book contains many previously unpublished photographs taken by Baldwin-Spencer. Establishes many incidental links between *Isiac* religion and the *Dreaming*.

Lazarus: He was the brother of Mary Magdalene. Jesus raised Lazarus from death, more information about this event and Lazarus' role is provided in the Secret Gospel of Mark. Lazarus, according to Baigent, Lincoln and Leigh, is the Beloved Disciple who is mysteriously alluded to on several occasions in the gospels. While Gardner maintains Lazarus had several names including Simon Magus or Simon Zealots.

Lennon, John: An influential songwriter/singer/musician and public figure who felt peace and love were more fruitful paths to follow.

Lerner, Dr Melvin: A psychologist from Florida Atlantic University who is responsible for the belief in the just world theory.

Leviticus: The third book of the Old Testament and Torah. Leviticus can be divided into two parts, the Holiness Code and the Priestly Code. The Priestly Code refers to rituals, rules of worship, sacrifices and purity. The Holiness Code is concerned with legal matters such as, Sabbath rules, sexual conduct etc. The Jewish view is that Leviticus is the word of God, while the Christians consider this text as a prophecy concerning the Messiah.

Mc Crae, G.W.: A Biblical scholar who also supports the belief that the *Gospel of Thomas* was written before any other Gospel.

Mc Bride, Professor Isabel: An archaeologist from Australian National University who originally investigated some *Bundjalung* sites in the Nightcap National Park.

Milgram, Dr Stanley: (1933-1984). Milgram was a psychologist from Yale, Harvard and New York City Universities. He became famous for The Obedience Study and The Small World Phenomenon.

Mithraism: A mystery cult/religion based around the god Mithras that originated in Persia (Iran) 7th century BC. It became popular in the Roman Empire especially amongst the military. Characteristics of this religion include initiation, rankings, the mithraeum (cavern/cave/crypt), the tauroctony (the icon of Mithras killing a bull) and connections to astrology. Mithraism became banned by the Christian church in AD 391.

Nag Hammadi Texts: These ancient texts were deposited in a jar sometime between 325-400 A.D. They were discovered in a cave by Mohammad Ali and taken home. Many pages from a variety of precious documents were used to stoke the oven when short of kindling. After slowly realising these documents may have some monetary value, these writings rapidly spread. After many assorted adventures, with the exception of a section of *Authoritative Teachings,* (purchased as a seventy-fifth birthday present for Carl Jung) every other text is now stored within the Cairo Museum.

Nazarene: A contentious term which is unclear in how it should be interpreted. Nazarene could have several different meanings. It could mean one who is from the town of Nazareth (traditional view); however, there is a good chance this is incorrect. Nazarene (or Nazarite) could more possibly be a reference to a sect of Essene Jews (or *B'nai-Amen*) (possibly from Galilee). These Nazarene Essenes were ascetics, who could not cut their hair, drink alcohol but took part in baptism and took strict vows (i.e. marriage, betrothal). It is also possibly Nazarene may have Gnostic connotations in a titular sense in referring to Jesus as of the truth.

Neidjie, Big Bill: A Gagadu Elder with extensive traditional wisdom. He was instrumental in the signing of a 99-year lease with the Australian Government, to act as co-custodians of Kakadu National Park. Author of the classic book: *Kakadu Man.*

New Age: A term often used derisively and delivered with raised eyebrows and a condescending grin. This label is used to dismiss a plethora of dreamers; hippies, greenies, latte-sipping North Shore do-gooders, Greenpeace and a variety of other pariahs and daydreamers. Their differences are a testimonial to those who refuse to obey the pulp that is being spoon-fed to the masses as Gospel truth. Until this label becomes an affirmation and unifying clarion call, nothing will change, it can only get worse.

Nimbin: Found slightly inland on the far north coast of N.S.W. Site of the first alternative-lifestyle gathering referred to as the Aquarius Festival which took place in 1972. Since then, Nimbin has adopted the reputation of being the uncrowned *New Age* capital of Australia.

Old Testament: (Or Hebrew Scriptures, *Tanakh* [Jewish]). The Old Testament is the first portion of the Christian Bible. It is divided into topic divisions i.e. law, prophecy and so forth. There are some differences in the exact composition of the Old Testament between Jewish authorities and the various Christian denominations. There is some debate over the historical authenticity of the Old Testament, a chasm in interpretation exists between the minimalists (little truth in Old Testament position) and maximalists (conservative position believing the Old Testament is true), while most scholars sit somewhere in the middle.

Osiris: (Or Asar, Asare, Sepa). The Egyptian God of the underworld and death. Osiris was a deity of primary importance, the god of fertility and husband of Isis. Osiris' symbols and icons include the centipede, royalty, mummification and green skin. An initiatory mystery religion evolved around Osiris, which involved public passion dramas, private wheat and clay rituals and the Osirian sacrament (i.e. bread [body] and beer [blood]). Osiris merged with Greek mythology to become Osiris-Dionysus and later Serapis. The worship of Osiris continued until the AD 6th century.

Papunya Tula Art: Often referred to by the general population as dot paintings, this symbolic style of art originated in the Central Desert region and often began as a sand painting/engraving.

Philip: A Gnostic Apostle who had much to do with the spread of Christianity throughout France. A Gnostic Gospel written in his name is a part of the Nag Hammadi Library.

Pistis Sophia: An introspective text (faith wisdom) that survived outside the scriptures hidden at Nag Hammadi. It contains passages that have strong links to the *Dreaming*. It is based upon interactions with the resurrected spirit of Jesus, and throughout the text, it becomes clear that Mary's status is well above that of the Apostles and is openly objected to by Peter.

Porter, Professor Emeritus, J.R.: Porter is a Theologian and the author of *The Lost Bible* and *The New Illustrated Companion to the Bible*.

Quinkan Spirits: Supernatural beings, both good and bad, found between the top end of Queensland and slightly south of Cairns.

Robinson, Professor James M.: He is a Professor Emeritus of Religion at Claremont Graduate University and the general editor of "The Nag Hammadi Library." He concedes there is a possibility that the *Gospel of Thomas* was created before the canonical Gospels.

Roy, Arundhati: An Indian novelist, socio-political essayist, literary award winner and activist, born in 1961. She is a leader in the anti-globalisation movement.

Samuel: The Gnostic term for the Demiurge who tried to create people as slaves and obedient servants to do his bidding.

Spong, Bishop Dr John Shelby: (1931—) A liberal/radical church academic, Bishop of the Episcopal Church and prolific author. Spong is a prominent leader of what has been dubbed the New Reformation, which demands a rethink and rejection of many Christian ideals and the modernisation of the church. The notion of a bodily resurrection of Jesus and the Virgin birth are rejected, equality is championed and the definition of God needs to be reformulated.

Stradbroke Island: An island located off the coast of southern Queensland, near Brisbane.

Synoptic Gospels: Generally refers to Luke, Mark and Matthew, as they are considered to see eye to eye on many points.

The Book of Thomas the Contender: A Gnostic scripture seen as a revelation dialogue, which was pronounced heretical then apparently disappeared until it was found in the jar at Nag Hammadi. It was composed after the Gospel of Thomas at around 125 A.D.

The Apocalypse of Adam: A set of revelations given to his son Seth by his father, Adam. This account asserts Eve taught Adam mystical truths and Cain and Abel were not referred to as Adam's sons. Three heavenly angels reveal to Adam matters such as the nature of and story of the fall, the actions of the demiurge and the final coming of the third Saviour.

The Apocalypse of Paul: This scripture details Paul's ascension into heaven and his observations. Particularly relevant is an extremely literal description of the process and rationale behind reincarnation and the parallels to String Theory.

The Apocryphon of John: This revelation is an important mythological Gnostic scripture. A resurrected Saviour gave this wisdom to John. The Apocryphon describes the creation and fall of humanity and advises that any who attempt to free themselves from the bondage of the flesh will eventually ascend and escape the cycle of reincarnation.

The Exegesis of the Soul: A short account of the Gnostic myth of the soul's fall into this world and her return to Heaven.

The Sayings of Sextus: These Pythagorean Gnostic sayings were popular among Gnostics and Christians. This text is a collection of sayings dating from the second or third century.

The Sophia of Jesus Christ: (Pistis Sophia) A mystical scripture, which involves revelations given by the resurrected Saviour to three of his Apostles. The content has strong connections to the *Dreaming*. Its date is contentious; some scholars believe it could have been written during the first century A.D.

The Testimony of Truth: A poorly preserved Gnostic scripture. This austere polemic had many critics within Gnostic circles and reflects the division and dilution that occurred within all esoteric traditions that were originally sourced in the *Dreaming*.

The Tripartite Tractate: An extensive treatise with distinct Valentinian influences. Valentinius was the most prominent Gnostic philosopher and teacher of the second century. The Tractate is primarily an account of life from the beginning, cosmic dramas and the fall of humanity.

Turramulli: A fearful Quinkan Spirit from the Cape York Region.

Uncle: Male equivalent of Aunty. A title awarded by the local Aboriginal community in recognition of selfless actions and deeds. Bloodlines and possessions are irrelevant considerations in relation to the bestowal of the title.

Watchers: Otherwise known as the *Grigori*: a group of fallen Angels, which are 200 in number. According to Enoch the *Grigori* were given the task to watch over humans. However, they soon began to lust after women. The resulting offspring are called the *Nephilim*, a race of giants. These Watchers became corrupt and taught the humans a variety of secret skills/gifts i.e. sciences, metallurgy and enchantments.

"Women of the Sun": Four-part dramatic series directed by Hyllus Marus. The first feature was called "Alinta the Flame" and was written in Yolgnu, using primarily semi-traditional people to act out many parts of traditional daily life.

W.L.H. 1: A gracile female skeleton dated at around 26,000 years found at Lake Mungo.

W.L.H. 3: A gracile male skeleton dated at around 63,000 years found at Lake Mungo.

Yaltaboath: According to all forms of Gnosticism he was the deluded Demiurge. Yaltaboath created humanity to act as compliant vassals to obey his every whim. The existence of the duplicitous god-figure Yaltaboath is a central tenet of Gnostic Cosmology.

Yahweh: A Hebrew name for God.

Voices of the First Day: An outstanding resource book on many Aboriginal matters.

Yolgnu: The Aboriginal Australians who inhabit north-eastern *Arnhem* Land (Northern Territory).

Zostrianos: A Gnostic text from the Nag Hammadi Library. This text is considered to be Sethian and Platonic. The book concerns Ziostrianos' revelations about esoteric cosmology.

Bibliography

Bible references are from Authorised King James Version.

Abbott, Lyman. *The Book of Enoch the Prophet*, translated by Richard Laurence. Cal.: Wizards Bookshelf, 1995.
Attridge, Harold W. and Dieter Mueller, trans. "The Tripartate Tractate (I,5)". Pp 58-103 in *Nag Hammadi Library in English*, edited by James M. Robinson. New York: Harper San Francisco, 1990.
Bellevie, Lesa. *The Complete Idiot's Guide to Mary Magdalene*. New York: Alpha Books, 2005.
Baigent, Michael, Richard Leigh and Hanry Lincoln. *The Holy Blood and Holy Grail*. London, UK: Arrow Books, 1996.
Boer Esther De, "Mary Magdalene: Beyond The Myth", *Secrets of the Code*, edited by Dan Burstein. London, UK: Weidenfeld and Nicolson, 2004.
Brehm, Sharon S. and Saul M. Kassin. *Social Psychology*. Boston, MA: Houghton Mifflin Company, 1996.
Doresse, Jean. *The Secret Books of the Egyptian Gnostics*. New York: MJF Books, 1986.
Eggleston, Roland. *When Yondi pushed up the Sky*. Sydney: The Australasian Publishing Co. Pty Ltd, 1964.
Emmel, Stephen, trans. "The Dialogue of the Saviour (III,5)". Pp 246-255 in *Nag Hammadi Library in English*, edited by James M. Robinson. New York: Harper San Francisco, 1990.
Gabriel, Peter. "Darkness". *Up*. UK: Real World Ltd/Peter Gabriel Ltd, 2002.
Gardner, Laurence. *Bloodline of the Holy Grail The Hidden Lineage of Jesus Revealed*. Camberwell, Australia: Penguin Books, 2001.
Gardner, Laurence. *The Magdalene Legacy: The Jesus and Mary Bloodline Conspiracy Revelations Beyond The Da Vinci Code*. London, UK: Element, 2005.
Goebels, Joseph. "Quotations That Make Us Think". *Third World Traveler*. http://thirdworldtraveler.com/Authors/QuotationsToMakeUSThink.html (21 Sept. 2005).
Goering, Hermann. "Quotations That Make Us Think". *Third World Traveler*. http://thirdworldtraveler.com/index.html (21 Sept. 2005).

Hancock, Graham. *Fingerprints of the Gods*. London, UK: Mandarin Paperbacks, 1996.

Highwater, Jamake. *The Primal Mind*. New York: Meridian Books, 1981.

Isenberg, Wesley W., trans. "The Gospel of Philip (II,*3*)". Pp 141-160 in *Nag Hammadi Library in English,* edited by James M. Robinson. New York: Harper San Francisco, 1990.

James M. R., trans. "Acts of Philip". *The Apocryphal New Testament*. Oxford, UK: Clarendon Press, 1924. In *The Gnostic Society Library*. 2005. http://www.gnosis.org/library/actphil.htm (2 Mar. 2008).

James, M. R., trans. "The Gospel of Bartholomew", *The Apocryphal New Testament*. Oxford, UK: Clarendon Press, 1924. In "Gospel of Bartholomew". *The Gnostic Society Library*. Joshua Williams, ed., 1995. http://www.gnosis.org/library/gosbart.htm (1 Nov. 2004).

Jones, Ian. *Joshua, The Man They Called Jesus*. Port Melbourne, Australia: Thomas C. Lothian Pty Ltd, 2000.

Katona, Jacqui. "Speech-MAPW Conference, April 1997". In *Traditional Owners Statement*, 1997.
http://www.sea-us.org.au/trad-owners.html (4 Aug. 2007).

King Jr., Martin Luther. "Martin Luther King Jr. Quotations". *Third World Traveler*. http://thirdworldtraveler.com/Author/MLK_quotes.html (21 Sept. 2005).

Koester, Helmut and Elaine H. Pagels, intro. "The Dialogue of the Saviour (III,*5*)". Pp 244-246 in *Nag Hammadi Library in English,* edited by James M. Robinson. New York: Harper San Francisco, 1990.

Kruszelnicki, Dr Karl, commentator. "Science on Mornings". *Triple J*. Sydney, Australia: A.B.C. (Australia Broadcasting Commission), 11:00-12:00pm, 9 June 2005.

Lambdin, Thomas O., trans. "The Gospel of Thomas" (II,*2*). Pp 126-138 in *Nag Hammadi Library in English,* edited by James M. Robinson. New York: Harper San Francisco, 1990.

Laurence, Richard, trans. *The Book of Enoch the Prophet*. Cal.: Wizards Bookshelf, 1995.

Lawlor, Robert. *The Voices of the First Day*. Rochester, Vermont: Inner Traditions International Ltd, 1991.

Lee, Ronald. "The Romani Goddess Kali Sara". *The World Tree Volume 1*. 2002. http://home.cogeco.ca/~kopachi/articles/romanigoddess.html (23 Nov. 2003).

MacRae, George W., trans. "Authoritative Teaching (VI,*3*)". Pp 305-310 in *Nag Hammadi Library in English*, edited by James M. Robinson. New York: Harper San Francisco, 1990.

MacLean, Douglas, Paul Gannon and Susan J. Gould, *Change and Human Development*. New York: McGraw-Hill Companies Inc., 1997.

MacRae, George, W., trans. "The Apocalypse of Adam (V,*5*)". Pp 279-286 in *Nag Hammadi Library in English*, edited by James M. Robinson. New York: Harper San Francisco, 1990.

MacRae, George W. and R. McL. Wilson, trans. "The Gospel of Mary" (BG 8502,*1*). Pp 524-527 in *Nag Hammadi Library in English*, edited by James M. Robinson. New York: Harper San Francisco, 1990.

MacRae, George W. and William R. Murdock, trans. and Douglas M. Parrott ed. "Apocalypse of Paul (V,*2*)". Pp 257-259 in *Nag Hammadi Library in English*, edited by James M. Robinson. New York: Harper San Francisco, 1990.

Maris, Hyllus and Sonia Borg, story/script writers and James Ricketson, director (Episode 1). "Alinta the Flame". *Women of the Sun*. Produced by Bob Weiss. David Leonard and John Martin executive producers. Canberra, Australia: Ronin Films, 1981).

Mead, G.R.S. *'Pistis Sophia: The Gnostic Tradition of Mary Magdalene, Jesus and His Disciples*. Mineola, New York: Dover Publications, 2005.

Melchizedek, Sar Mikhail. "The Lost Teachings of Jesus: Did Jesus teach a secret doctrine?". *New Dawn*. Special Issue, no. 1 (Autumn/Winter, 2004): 55-58 and 61-64.

Meyer, Marvin. *The Gospel of Thomas*. New York: Harper San Francisco, 1992.

Neidjie, Big Bill, Stephen Davis and Allan Fox. *Australia's Kakadu Man*. Darwin, Australia: Resource Managers Pty Ltd, Darwin, 1986.

Neidjie, Big Bill. *Story About Feeling*, edited by Keith Taylor. Broome, Australia: Magabala Books, 1989.

Orwell, George. "Quotations That Make Us Think". *Third World Traveler*. http://thirdworldtraveler.com/Authors/QuotationsToMakeUSThink.html (21 Sept. 2005).

Owens, Richard. "Judas the Misunderstood Vatican moves to clear reviled disciple's name". *Times Online*. 12 January, 2006, http://www.timesonline.co.uk/tol/sport/football/european_football/article787 629.ece (22 Jun. 2006).

Pagels, Elaine. *The Gnostic Gospels*. New York: Vintage Books, 1989.

_____ "Patrin Saintes-Maries-de-la-Mer". *Patrin Web Journal Romani*. 2002 http://www.geocities.com/paris/5121/stsm_01.htm (2 Oct. 2004).

Parrott, Douglas, M., trans. "The Sophia of Jesus Christ (III,*4* and BG 8502, *3*)". Pp 222-243 in *Nag Hammadi Library in English*, edited by James M. Robinson. New York: Harper Sans Francisco, 1990.

Picknett, Lynn and Clive Prince. *The Templar Revelation Secret Guardians of the True Identity of Christ*. London, UK: Corgi Books, 1998.

Porter, J.R. *The Lost Bible*. London, UK: Duncan Baird Publishers, 2001.

Robinson, William C. Jr, trans. "The Exegesis of the Soul (II,*6*)". Pp 192-198 in *Nag Hammadi Library in English*, edited by James M. Robinson. New York: Harper San Francisco, 1990.

Roy, Arundhati. "Quotations That Make Us Think". *Third World Traveler.* http://thirdworldtraveler.com/Authors/QuotationsToMakeUSThink.html (21 Sept. 2005).

Rose, Sharron. "Mary Magdalene, Apostle of Apostles". *New Dawn*, no. 2 (Autumn/Winter 2006): 17-20. New Gnosis Communications International Pty Ltd, Melbourne, 2006.

Rule, Hugh and Stuart Goodman compiler. *Gulpilil's stories of the Dreaming.* Sydney, Australia: William Collins Publishers Pty Limited, 1987.

Russell, Bertrand. "Quotations That Make Us Think". *Third World Traveler.* http://thirdworldtraveler.com/Authors/QuotationsToMakeUSThink.html (21 Sept. 2005).

____*Salome: Matron Saint of Midwives.* Feb. 2008. http://www.grailchurch.org/salome.htm (7 March, 2004).

Schaef, Anne Wilson. *Native Wisdom For White Minds.* Sydney, Australia: Random House, 1995.

Sieber, John N., trans. "Zostrionios (VIII,*1*)". Pp 403-430 in *Nag Hammadi Library in English*, edited by James M. Robinson. New York: Harper San Francisco, 1990.

Starbird, Margaret. *Mary Magdalene: The Grail Bearer.* 2001. http://www.magdalene.org/grailbearer.php (15 Nov. 2005).

"The World Haters". *Time Magazine.* 9 June, 1975. http://www.time.com/time/magazine/article/0,917,1005391,00.html, (6 Oct. 2007).

Thompson, Liz. *Woonyoomboo.* Melbourne, Australia: Rigby publications, 2008.

Turner John D., trans., "The Book of Thomas the Contender (II,*7*)". Pp 201-207 in *Nag Hammadi Library in English*, edited by James M. Robinson. New York: Harper San Francisco, 1990.

Turner, John D., trans. "The Interpretation of Knowledge (XI,*1*)". Pp 473-480 in *Nag Hammadi Library in English*, edited by James M. Robinson. New York: Harper San Francisco, 1990.

Voragine, Jacobus de, compiler and William Caxton trans. "Here Followeth the Life of St. Martha",Vol. 4, *Legenda Aurea (The Golden Legend or Lives of the Saints).* Edited by F.S. Ellis (Temple Classics edition 1900). From Medieval Sourcebook 2001. http://www.fordham.edu/halsall/basis/goldenlegend/GoldenLegend-Volume4.htm (2 Mar. 2008).

Voragine, Jacobus de, compiler, and William Caxton trans. "Here Followeth the Life of St. Mary Magdalene",Vol. 4, *Legenda Aurea (The Golden Legend or Lives of the Saints).* Edited by F.S. Ellis (Temple Classics edition 1900). From Medieval Sourcebook 2001. http://www.fordham.edu/halsall/basis/goldenlegend/GoldenLegend-Volume4.htm (2 Mar. 2008).

Wisse, Fredrick trans., "Apocrophyon of John (II,*1*, III,*1*, IV,*1*, and BG 8502,*2*)". Pp 105-123 in *Nag Hammadi Library in English*, edited by James M. Robinson. New York: Harper San Francisco, 1990.

Wisse, Frederik trans. "The Sentences of Sextus (XII,*1*)". Pp 503-508 in *Nag Hammadi Library in English,* edited by James M. Robinson. New York: Harper San Francisco, 1990.

Yes: Anderson, Jon, Steve Howe, Chris Squire and Alan White. "Gates of Delirium ". *Relayer.* UK: Topographic Music Ltd, 1974.

Yes: Anderson, Jon, Steve Howe, Chris Squire and Alan White. "Give Love Each Day". *Magnification*. Beverly Hills, Cal.: Beyond Music / YES LLC, 2001.

INDEX

Abel, 96
Abraham, 94
Against Heresies, 90
Albigensians, 109
Alexandria, 26, 106
Alfonso 44
Alinta the Flame, 6
Ancestral Spirits, 6, 24, 30, 43, 51, 64, 89-90; Biamie, 7, 96; Birrahgnooloo, 7, 96
Apocalypse of Paul, 62
Apollo, 95
Ashera, 7
Australian locations: Cape York, 96; Central Desert, 44; Gagadu, 34, 40; Kakadu National Park, 34; Kimberley, 89; Lake Mungo, 5-6; Western Desert, 47
Avalon, 106

Bell, Dianne, 7
Bering Strait, 114
Bethany, 110
Biamie, 7, 96
Birrahgnooloo, 7, 96
Bloodline of the Holy Grail, 13
Boanerges, 21
Book of Kells, 22
Botticelli, 109
Bystander Effect, 46

Caesarea, 41
Cain, 96
Cana, 19
Cape York, 96
Cathars, 4, 109
Catholic Church, 26, 69
Caxton, William, 101, 104
Cedony, Saint, 108

Central Desert, 44
Clement 8, 26
Cleophas, James, 108-110
Constantine, 8, 101, 109
Constructing a New World Map, v, 42, 49
Cook, James, 44
Corinthians, 5
Council of Nicea, 8, 10, 67, 86, 101
    John, v, 5, 10, 14-21, 24, 41, 81, 91, 102, 104, 109; Luke, 14-15, 19-20, 41, 104; Matthew, 2-3, 5, 8-10, 13-15, 19, 21, 23-26, 36, 41-42, 68, 70-72, 77-83, 85, 87, 102, 104-105; Synoptic Gospels, v, 15, 104, 111

Dafur, 28
David, 14-15
Dialogue of the Saviour, v, 8, 9, 25, 34, 36, 77, 79-81, 87
Disciples, vi, 2, 8, 10, 21-24, 35, 41, 61, 67, 73, 77-80, 83, 85, 86, 101-102, 107; Andrew, 21-22, 66-68, 72, 80-81, 91; Cathars, 4, 109; Cedony, Saint, 108; James the Just, 106; Joseph of Arimathea, 106, 109; Judas Iscariot, 15, 21, 81, 86-87; Magus, Simon, 21; Marcella, 109-110; Martha, 17-18, 105, 107, 109-110; Mary Jacobi, 108-109; Mary Salome, 21, 108-109; Maximin, 90, 105, 107-108; Nicodemus, 110; Paul, 6, 7, 14-15, 21, 62-63, 106; Peter, v, vi, 2, 3, 5-7, 13, 15-16, 18, 21-23, 27, 29, 36, 39, 41-42, 59-60, 65-69, 71-72, 80-81, 86-87, 91, 97, 101, 103, 105, 109
Downward Social Comparison, 46
Dreaming stories, 17, 30, 55, 96; Gulpilil's Stories of the Dreamtime,

55; Jarlmadangah, 89; Moon, 23-24, 89; Native Cat, 23-24; Papunya Tula Art, 44; Quinkan Spirits, 96; The Baby Makers, 54; Turramulli, 96; Woonyoomboo, 89; Yoonygoorookoo, 89

Egglestien, Roland, 54
Egypt, 3, 5, 21, 95, 107-108, 114; Alexandria, 26, 106; Isis, v, 2-4, 7, 17; Osiris, v, 5, 7
Einstein, Albert, 61
Elders, 4, 43, 47, 57; Gulpilil, David, 55; Margarula, Yvonne, 57; Nayinggul, Jacob, 57
Elias, 23-24
Enoch, 95-97
Epic of Gilgamesh, 98
Epiphanius, 90, 92, 101
Essenes, 4, 16

France, 103-109; Gaul, 101, 104, 106-107, 109; Marseilles, 105; Saintes-Maries-de-la Mer, 108; Provence, 107-108; Tarascon, 109-110

Gagadu, 34, 40
Gardener, Laurence, 2, 16
Gaul, 101, 104, 106-107, 109

Genesis, 48, 89, 98
Glastonbury, 106-107
Gnostic texts, v, vi, 7-10, 17, 36, 50, 55, 85, 88, 91, 93-95, 97; Apocalypse of Adam, 97; Apocalypse of Paul, 62; Dialogue of the Saviour, v, 8, 9, 25, 34, 36, 77, 79-81, 87; Gospel of Bartholomew, 1; Gospel of John, 81, 104, 107; Gospel of Judas, 86; Gospel of Mark (Secret), 17-18; Gospel of Mary, v, 21, 34, 36, 65, 71-73, 80-81, 91, 105; Gospel of Thomas, v, vi, 2, 33-35, 39, 57, 61-62, 74, 85, 104-105 Interpretation of Knowledge, 25; Nag Hammadi, vi, 1, 25, 33-34, 62, 85, 93; The Book of Thomas the Contender, 25; The Exegesis of the Soul, 25; Tripartate Tractate, 26

Goebels, Joseph, 117
Goering, Herman, 113
Good, Diedre, 102-103
Gospel of Bartholomew, 1
Gospel of John, 81, 104, 107
Gospel of Judas, 86
Gospel of Mark (Secret) 17-18
Gospel of Mary, v, 21, 34, 36, 65, 71-73, 80-81, 91, 105
Gospel of Thomas, v, vi, 2, 33-35, 39, 57, 61-62, 74, 85, 104-105
Gulpilil, David, 55
Gulpilil's Stories of the Dreamtime, 55
Gumilaroi, 30

Hakmiller, 46
Hancock, Graham, 3
Hawkings, Stephen, 61, 63
Herod, 21
Highwater, Jamake, 50
Hinduism, 29, 31
Hippolytus, 75
Holy Grail, 1, 13, 107
Homo Sapien sapien, 114; W.L.H. 1, 6; W.L.H. 3, 6

India, 16, 35, 103
Interpretation of Knowledge, 25
Isis, v, 2-4, 7, 17

James the Just, 106
Jarlmadangah, 89
Jehovah, 94
Jerusalem, 90, 110
John, v, 5, 10, 14-21, 24, 41, 81, 91, 102, 104, 109
John the Baptist, 5, 25
Jones, Ian, 21
Josaic Reforms, 7
Joseph of Arimathea, 106, 109
Josiah, 7
Judas Iscariot, 15, 21, 81, 86-87
Judea, 101, 104-105, 107, 111, 114
Judea, King of, 7
Judean cities: Bethany, 110; Caesarea, 41; Cana, 19; Jerusalem, 90, 110; Magdala, 110; Philippi, 41

Kakadu National Park, 34

Katona, Jacqui, 57
Kimberley, 89
King Clovis, 110
Koester, Helmut, 34-35, 78
Kruszelnicki, Karl, 47

Lake Mungo, 5-6
Latane, Bibb, 46
Lawlor, Robert, 44, 54, 60, 114
Lennon, John, 38
Levi, 2, 15, 21, 67-68, 70-72, 81
Luke, 14-15, 19-20, 41, 104

Madonna, 108
Magdala, 110
Magus, Simon, 21
Marcella, 109-110
Margarula, Yvonne, 57
Marseilles, 105
Martha, 17-18, 105, 107, 109-110
Mary Jacobi, 108-109
Mary Salome, 21, 108-109
Matthew, 2-3, 5, 8-10, 13-15, 19, 21, 23- 26, 36, 41-42, 68, 70-72, 77-83, 85, 87, 102, 104-105
Maximin, 90, 105, 107-108
McCrae, G.W., 35
Merovingian, 108, 110
Moon, 23-24, 89
Morocco, 107
Mother Mary, 14, 19

Nag Hammadi, vi, 1, 25, 33-34, 62, 85, 93
Native Cat, 23-24
Nayinggul, Jacob, 57
Neidjie, Big Bill, v, vi, 23, 34, 40-42, 44, 47-53, 55, 58-60, 63, 89, 115
New Age, 34
Nicodemus, 110
Nietzsche, 63
Noah, 44, 94
Notre-Dame-de la Mer, 108-109

Odin, 95
Orwell, George, 114
Osiris, v, 5, 7

Pantheist, 36

Papunya Tula Art, 44
Paul, 6, 7, 14-15, 21, 62-63, 106
Pen Yair, 4
Peter, v, vi, 2, 3, 5-7, 13, 15-16, 18, 21-23, 27, 29, 36, 39, 41-42, 59-60, 65-69, 71-72, 80-81, 86-87, 91, 97, 101, 103, 105, 109
Philippi, 41
Pistis Sophia, vi, 37, 87-89, 91, 110
Pope, John Paul, 14
Porter, J.R., 1, 35
Prince of Marseilles, 95
Proselytes, 21
Provence, 107-108

Quinkan Spirits, 96

Robinson, James, 34-35
Romani, 108-109
Rome, 8, 103
Roy, Arundhati, 116

Saintes-Maries-de-la-Mer, 108
Samuel, 98
Sextus, 93
Shellby, Spong, 5
Sidonious, 108
Simon, Bernard, 44
Slovenia, 110
String Theory, 61-63
Synoptic Gospels, v, 15, 104, 111
Syria, 35, 90, 107

Tarascon, 109-110
Tertullian, 8, 87
Thaddaeus, 21
The Baby Makers, 54
The Belief in a Just World, 115
The Book of Thomas the Contender, 25
The Exegesis of the Soul, 25
The Golden Legend, 37, 90, 103-105
Therapeutate, 21
Thor, 95
Time Magazine, 53
Tripartate Tractate, 26
Triple J, 47
Turkey, 107
Turramulli, 96

Vatican, 20, 26, 30, 75, 101
Visigoths, 108
Voices of the First Day, 54
Voragine, Jacobus de, 104

Walking Buffalo, 51
Watchers, 95-97
Western Desert Region, 47
Wills, 46
W.L.H. 1, 6
W.L.H. 3, 6
Women of the Sun, 6
Wood, 46
Woonyoomboo, 89

Yahweh, 7
Yaltaboath, 51, 55, 97-98
Yamauchi, Edwin, 23
Yolgnu, 6
Yoonygoorookoo, 89

Zaccheus, 110
Zebedee, Simon, 21
Zostrionios, 25

About the Authors

Steven Strong is a teacher. He has been a principal of a primary school, head-teacher in secondary school and was involved in compiling and reviewing the senior Aboriginal Studies course for the N.S.W. Higher School Certificate. He has spent many years living with, and learning from, Aboriginal friends and Elders from the *Bundjalung* and *Gumilaroi* tribe.

Evan Strong completed a degree in Social Science at Southern Cross University and is in the process of completing a post-graduate degree in Psychology. Evan was raised in an environment where Aboriginal culture was an integral part of daily life.

Everything they have written in their first book *Constructing a New World Map* and *Mary Magdalene's Dreaming* is inspired by the wisdom of many Aboriginal colleagues and Elders: all they have done is put finger to keypad.

www.ingramcontent.com/pod-product-compliance
Lightning Source LLC
Chambersburg PA
CBHW030114010526
44116CB00005B/243